Logical Using reason and evidence to support an assertion; that which proceeds according to a rational plan.

Nonlogical Unrelated to logic or reason; having to do with the emotions or tastes. (Compare "illogical.")

Objective Expressing opinions based solely on observation; not distorted by personal feelings.

Pejorative Unfavorable, denigrating.

Premise A proposition or statement from which reasoning proceeds and from which a conclusion is drawn.

Rhetoric Written or spoken communication that seeks to persuade.

Rhetorical question A question asked merely for effect with either no answer expected or an obvious answer implied. Rhetorical questions do not constitute evidence.

Semantics The meaning of language. A semantic dispute is one in which there is disagreement about the meanings of words.

Subjective Expressing opinions based on personal feelings rather than on observation.

Valid Following the rules of logic. A valid argument is one in which the conclusion necessarily follows from the premises.

Value judgment An assertion that something is good or bad in a moral or esthetic sense.

Value statement A statement that makes a declaration about the worth or value of something.

A Contemporary Rhetoric

HOUGHTON MIFFLIN COMPANY   BOSTON
Atlanta   Dallas   Geneva, Ill.   Hopewell, N.J.   Palo Alto   London

A
Contemporary
Rhetoric

Maxine Hairston   The University of Texas at Austin

Contents

Acknowledgments

My thanks to
My students, who have taught me to teach;
My colleagues in freshman English—
   mostly teaching assistants—
   who have given me invaluable help;
My husband Jim, who has been patient; and
My typist and friend, Mrs. Janis Mather,
   whose efficiency and alertness
   have helped bring this book into print.

Preface

This text has grown out of a decade of experience teaching freshman composition at a large public university, a decade in which I have become convinced that if we are to succeed with our students, we must offer them a writing course that is geared to both their interests and their capabilities. We must move beyond the professional view that tends to condition us to think of writing as something taught for its own sake toward a practical approach that stresses the solid benefits a student will gain by learning to write competently. Most of our students do not, after all, plan to be writers. They do plan to be accountants, lawyers, engineers, doctors, teachers, and business men or women—and all of them will be citizens, consumers, most of them parents, and spouses. They have a right to expect a freshman English course that will contribute in a concrete way to preparing them for all of these roles. This text lays the foundation for such a course by stressing critical reasoning as well as writing and by attempting to create realistic writing situations.

I have written a rhetorically based text because I think the study of rhetoric provides the best method of teaching writing skills that will be useful in a variety of situations. Developing an acute sense of audience helps a speaker or writer whether he is addressing a community meeting, compiling a report, or applying for a grant. Understanding his own persuasive purpose enhances any petitioner's chances of winning his point, whether personal or professional. Being aware of his own voice and knowing what methods of exposition are available in a particular situation gives even the inexperienced writer confidence in his ability to communicate his ideas on an examination or in a letter to his congressman. Learning these rhetorical techniques is not too difficult for the average student. He already has the basic knowledge; our task is only expansion and clarification. That task does not require that we introduce the schemes or terminology of the classical rhetoricians nor that we bring in the history of rhetoric. Nor do we have to employ Latinate labels and the diagrams of formal logic to alert students to the pitfalls of faulty reasoning and careless writing. This text gives students a working knowledge of rhetoric by putting it in the context of everyday situations and by using plain language to explain it.

The teacher who uses this text will notice that it focuses more on teaching students to write clearly, vigorously, and precisely than on teaching them to write complex, rich, and polished prose. It also stresses the content and support of an argument over the language in which it is phrased. Most of us do not have the time to train all of our students to be fine writers. We do, I think, have the time, ability, and responsibility to help them become lucid thinkers and competent writers. It is my hope that this text because of its practical approach and its plain language will make it easier for teachers to achieve these goals.

M. H.

To the Student

Most students begin their college composition courses with more resignation than enthusiasm. They anticipate spending the next ten to fourteen weeks rehashing grammar, sentence structure, topic sentences and searching for new ways to write catchy introductions and impressive conclusions to surround the traditional 500 words that must be turned in on Friday. They suspect—and with some reason —that those themes are going to be little more than exercises in good spelling and neat penmanship, exercises that will have little connection to anything else they will be doing in college or in later life.

In the past several years, however, many college writing courses have changed. The focus has moved from writing for writing's sake to the study of rhetoric: the art of writing effectively and persuasively. Actually, the change is a reversion rather than an innovation; in past centuries, rhetoric was a part of the traditional curriculum in many colleges, but it was taught through the works of the classical writers such as Aristotle, Quintillian, and Cicero. Although we now work with more modern writers and with contemporary material, the goals of a course in rhetoric today are similar to those of earlier times: learning to understand and use verbal skills.

Actually, you already know a great deal about rhetoric. For most of your life, you have been trying to express yourself clearly and effectively and to persuade others to share your views and values. One goal of this text is to help you to perfect those persuasive and expressive skills. By studying and analyzing the methods of expression and persuasion, you can become a more effective and articulate writer and speaker. The other goal of this text is to help you to understand and evaluate the ways in which other people use language to inform and persuade you. These two abilities are two sides of the same coin; one is as important as the other to the student-citizen. You probably recognize that you will be able to function better as both a student and a person if you use language well. You also need, however, to develop a critical sensitivity to the barrage of language that assaults all of us in these days of mass communication. The person who is not aware of the ways in which language is a tool for control is going to be handicapped both in his thoughts and his actions.

The goals of this text, then, are simultaneously simple and ambitious. They are:

1. To help you to write clear, well-organized and well-supported papers for this and other classes
2. To help you to present your views clearly and persuasively in meetings or in print; for example, letters to editors, letters to people in other responsible positions, or petitions
3. To help you to write lucid and concise proposals, reports, or presentations for employers, committees, or groups that you wish to influence
4. To help you to develop the ability to understand, analyze, and evaluate persuasive speeches, editorials, or advertisements; to help you to read and judge expository prose, and to follow and evaluate an argument.

Attaining these first three objectives requires that you develop proficiency in writing. The term "proficiency" is important here; it really means no more than competence, competence that can be attained through training and practice. Because the ability to handle words gracefully and skillfully is partially a talent, almost no composition teacher expects that the majority of his students are going to learn to write polished, professional prose. Nevertheless, just as students with average mathematical ability can, through work and persistence, master the elements of algebra and geometry, the student with modest verbal abilities can learn to write well-organized, clear, and carefully supported prose. Plain, straightforward writing is precisely the kind of writing you will most often need to do, both in college and in later life. This kind of writing can be learned; it is my hope that this textbook will help you to master it—and to master the habits of straight thinking that must underlie effective writing.

Achieving the fourth goal, understanding and evaluating the ways in which other people use language to persuade, is equally important to your education. In *Brave New World Revisited* Aldous Huxley said, "An education for freedom is, among other things, an education in the proper uses of language." His statement seems to take on new force every year. Only when you become aware of the ways in which people use language to manipulate you, can you develop the defenses to protect your freedom against the insidious methods of the demagogue, the silver-tongued confidence man, and the occasional unscrupulous advertiser. For this reason, many of the discussions and writing assignments in this book focus on the critical analysis of rhetoric and on the fallacies and devious strategies that sometimes creep into it.

Rhetoric, of course, is a tool, and like any other tool, can be used for good or evil purposes. Some critics, ancient as well as modern, have attacked the teaching of rhetoric on the grounds that it gives writers and orators a bag of tricks with which to deceive. Such a view is as narrow as one that would condemn freedom of the press because it allows sensational and irresponsible tabloids to flourish along with respectable and responsible newspapers. The realization that people of little integrity can learn to use rhetoric for their own purposes does not negate the value of studying it as an art. In fact, the more we know of it, the less likely it is that those who use it to deceive will succeed.

The best place to begin this study is your own writing.

A Contemporary Rhetoric

1

Writing:
A
Short
Course

One of the perennial questions that plagues both students and teachers who are beginning composition and rhetoric courses is, "Where should we start?" The topic generates a lot of argument, but for a good reason we are not likely to find an answer that is going to satisfy everyone. The reason is that students who are going to start writing papers in the first week of class need to know everything about writing in that first week. Obviously, no course can really fill that need; therefore, we have to set priorities. But setting priorities in a writing course is like trying to decide what skill an intern who is going on emergency duty needs most: setting fractures, taking out appendices, sewing up cuts, or treating patients in shock? There is no "right" answer; he must have all the basic skills to cope with the situation at hand as best he can.

This chapter will help you meet your emergency situation by giving you a skeleton outline of good writing, an outline that will be fleshed out and expanded in later chapters. If you can grasp these guidelines for becoming a competent writer, you can face that first paper with confidence. At least you will know what you are supposed to be doing even if you don't do it well at first. Actually, you are better equipped for the task than you realize. After all, for a long time you have been communicating effectively with people in conversation and in letters. You have ideas and opinions, and you get them across to people by the use of language. You say what you think as clearly as possible and illustrate your remarks with examples drawn from your experience. You should use exactly the same method when you write college papers. What your college composition teacher wants from you is not complicated and elaborate; rather, it is, as one student remarked years ago, "so simple that we can't believe it." "Simple," however, does not necessarily mean easy. Writing clearly always takes time and thought.

COMPETENT WRITING: CLARITY

Simplicity

Many beginning writers get into trouble with their first papers because they have wildly exaggerated ideas of what the college teacher expects of them. They think the teacher will scorn plain language and will expect them to have an extensive vocabulary and an elegant, complex writing style. They have, as one text puts it, "an unfounded fear of simplicity." So they reach for the thesaurus to find an impressive word to replace the plain one they ordinarily use, and they substitute stiff, awkward phrases for the ones that come naturally to them. Here are some examples, with suggested revisions, of such unnatural writing.

Original   He is successful because his descriptions fail in complying with my envisioning of a truly utopian society.

Suggested revision   He is successful because he shows me that *Brave New World* is not the perfect utopian society.

Original   When the subject of drug abuse is brought under consideration, certain restrictions must be made to ensure the validity of the discussion.

Suggested revision   People who talk about drug abuse should specify which drugs they mean.

Original   The eventual outcome in this matter will be contrary to my persuasion.

Suggested revision   I do not like what is going to happen.

Original   We believe that by cohabiting together, more understanding would enter into each of our lives.

Suggested revision   We thought that if we lived together we would learn to understand each other better.

Original   The sum of the experiences can be the best source in shaping the positive action of the future.

Suggested revision   Experience helps one to make better plans for the future.

Original   The satisfaction of sensuous desires in which there is an absence of frustration is the definition of happiness.

Suggested revision   The author defines the happy man as one who is never frustrated because he can satisfy all his desires.

Probably no student would use the original sentences if he were talking, but the frightening prospect of putting words down on paper for someone else to look at can make him lose faith in his natural ability to express himself. Try not to let that happen to you. When you have written a sentence, go back and read it over. Ask yourself, "Would I talk like that?" and "Could a person reading this easily understand what I mean?" If the answer to either question is "No," you would do well to cross out the sentence and start over, trying to make your sentence structure and diction sound natural.

Use talk as a guide

Another obstacle to clarity in writing is composing sentences that are too long and complicated. Although a skillful and practiced writer can successfully handle several ideas in one sentence, the person who is not used to juggling clauses is better off working with one or at the most two ideas at a time. The sentences below illustrate the confusion that comes from trying to do too much in one sentence. A revised version shows how each one might have been improved.

One idea at a time

Original Voluntary agreements among individuals and groups, which are essential if an anarchy is going to function, are impossible to be arrived at with consistency since because of man's irrationality and self-interest he will always do what benefits himself most.

Suggested revision Anarchy will work only if individuals and groups come to voluntary agreements. It is unlikely, however, that men, who are basically selfish and irrational, will make such agreements.

Original Therefore, understanding the idea that all taxpayers should be allowed to attend a state supported institution and all citizens are taxpayers by the mere fact that they are consumers, it is reasonable to state that all citizens should be allowed to attend the state university.

Suggested revision Since all the citizens of a state are consumers, they are necessarily taxpayers. If we grant that all taxpayers have the right to attend a state-supported institution, then all citizens should be allowed to attend the state university.

Original With our minds open, the author introduces his real purpose that was kept hidden through most of the passage, the thought that accepting artificial or secondary things might cause us to be satisfied with these things thus changing our outlook on life.

Suggested revision Once the author has started us thinking, he reveals his real purpose. He wants us to believe that, if we accept synthetic foods, we will be satisfied with substitutes in other important areas of our life.

As these examples demonstrate, writing long, complicated sentences can not only obscure your meaning but also entangle you in serious grammatical difficulties. Too much distance between subject and verb is apt to produce faulty predication, subject-and-verb disagreement, and dangling modifiers. You may have undertaken so much that you cannot keep track of the relationships between your words. The best rule for avoiding these problems is to think your entire sentence through before you begin to write it. It is a difficult rule to

Think out the whole sentence before writing it

observe; all of us are occasionally tempted just to start writing and to trust that somehow all the syntax will come out right. But don't do it. Force yourself to plan out an entire sentence before you put down the first word. It may take ten minutes, but those will be ten minutes well spent.

Concreteness

Another major aid to clarity in writing is concreteness. Other sections of this book, those on abstract language and jargon, will point out specific ways in which overloading your writing with abstractions can make it weak, dull, and confusing. For now, it is enough to say only that you communicate best with people when you use language that appeals to their senses as well as their intellects. Of course, intelligent readers do not need to have everything illustrated for them by descriptions or anecdotes, but you will always strengthen your writing if you bring in concrete examples to reinforce abstract statements. George Orwell employs this technique in the following two sentences from his essay "Politics and the English Language."

Use concrete examples

> But an effect can become a cause, reinforcing the original cause and producing the same effect in an intensified form, and so on indefinitely. A man may take to drink because he feels himself to be a failure, and then fail all the more completely because he drinks.[1]

Here is an example of concrete reinforcement in a student theme:

> In a small high school, the price of individuality is usually ostracism. In order to gain respect and recognition you must participate in your school's athletic programs. People in the high school and the community look down on those who do otherwise. The coaches and the athletes try to make nonathletes feel inferior by treating them like outsiders.

The writing may not be as smooth as Orwell's, but it is clear and effective because the student has drawn on concrete examples that are familiar to his reader.

Try to remember, then, that the best way to forestall criticism that your writing is vague or too general is to keep that pitfall in mind as you write. Choose the concrete rather than the abstract expression

[1] George Orwell, "Politics and the English Language," in *Shooting an Elephant and Other Essays* (New York: Harcourt, Brace, and World, Inc., 1945), p. 81.

whenever possible. If you have to use abstractions—and frequently you will—clarify and explain them with concrete references. If you do these things, you will cut to a minimum nagging marginal comments like these: "Be more specific"; "You need an example here"; "Please clarify"; and "Illustrate this point."

INTERESTING WRITING: VIGOR

Verbs

If you follow these three guidelines—be direct, be concrete, be specific—you should be on your way to becoming a competent writer, one who can say what he means and have his readers understand him. Achieving that much is a major accomplishment. If, however, you want to make your writing interesting as well as clear, you need to add an extra ingredient: vigor. Vigor is the quality that makes writing move and come alive, that gives to it a little muscle and fiber and strength. Concrete subjects and plain language contribute vigor to writing, but the most important single element is the verb. Whether your writing ambles and drags along or moves briskly toward an objective depends largely on the verbs you choose.

The verb is the key

Passive verbs slow writing down

Sentences using passive verb forms (those in which the subject does not act, but is acted upon) devitalize writing in several ways, but our immediate concern is that they slow it down. For example, "The change in the administration was thought by many to be beneficial" plods along, but "Many people favored the change in administration" moves directly to the point. "The conclusion that pigs are more intelligent than cows was arrived at from laboratory experiments that had been conducted over a period of five years" is a tedious, drab sentence; "Five years of laboratory experiments show that pigs are smarter than cows" says the same thing better and faster.

Occasionally, you must use the passive, and sometimes it is preferable. For example, trying to change sentences like "Clothes were scattered all over the room" or "The car was hit from the rear" would be more trouble than it would be worth. But students who are trying hard to sound mature and judicious often become addicted to the passive form. One three-page student paper contained this list of passives: "is confronted," "can be dealt with," "is based on," "is shown," "is brought," "is based," "could be expressed," "can be described," "can be broadened," "is to be found," "would be supplied," "were legalized," "it is argued," and "is justified." The accumulation drained much of the vitality from a potentially forceful theme. Like most habits, an addiction to the passive voice is hard to overcome, but breaking it will significantly improve your writing.

The habit of constructing too many phrases with the linking verb "to be" plus a noun complement also weakens your writing. For example, "He is a basketball player" is weaker than "He plays basketball"; "Inflation is a threat to our economy" has less force than "Inflation threatens our economy"; and "Stevens was a candidate for Congress" is not quite as good a sentence as "Stevens ran for Congress." In each of the sentences with linking verbs the central meaning comes from the noun rather than the verb, so the reader gets no sense of motion. Of course, you cannot completely eliminate this kind of sentence from your writing, but, on rereading your first **Avoid the neutral** draft, if you find several spots where you could replace linking verbs **verb** *to be* with active ones, make the changes. An active verb, which does things, has a life of its own, is preferable to a static, neutral one that serves only as a helper. Notice the difference between the sentences in these pairs.

He is an avid football fan.
In the fall, football dominates his life.

The local administration is full of graft and corruption.
Graft and corruption permeate the city hall.

There was a long counter along one side of the room.
The counter stretched the length of the room.

Although the sentences in each pair *mean* almost the same thing, the difference between them is the difference between the dull and the vivid.

Other Ways to Add Vigor

Following a few general suggestions will also strengthen your writing.
Avoid clichés First, avoid clichés. The advice is easy to give, but not easy to follow. The only ways to clean them out of your writing are to avoid trite phrases in the first place and to go back over your first draft deleting and replacing hackneyed expressions. Second, bring people into your **Use personal nouns** writing when you can. "Soldiers" is more interesting than "armed forces"; either term is preferable to "personnel." "Lawbreakers" is better than "the criminal elements"; "the city commissioners" is better

Be concise

than "the local administration"; and "writers" is better than "the literary profession." Third, be concise. Don't use six or ten words to say what you could better express in two or three. It sounds better to say "If war comes" than "In the event that a war breaks out." "Students who attended this college in past years" is unnecessarily wordy; the phrase "former students" says everything your reader needs to know.

Avoid expletive
sentences

Finally, work at pruning the expletive sentences out of your writing. Expletive phrases are those used to fill in a vacancy in a sentence; "It is" and "There are" are the two commonest ones. Such phrases are undeniably useful, but they are also bland and in most cases do little more than add two or three words that you do not really need. Why say, "It is obvious that the Redskins have a first-rate coach," when you could say, "Obviously, the Redskins have a first-rate coach"? "No one could study under such conditions" is both shorter and more concrete than "It is impossible to study under such conditions." "There were several reasons for the United States becoming involved in the war" is a sentence that postpones getting to the point; "The United States entered the war for several reasons" says the same thing more directly. Like passive constructions, expletive phrases are not bad in themselves, but when you use them too frequently they sap the vigor from your writing. Go over your first draft carefully; if "It is" and "There are" crop up more often than you realized, try to find better and more vigorous ways to express the same ideas.

ORGANIZING YOUR THINKING: PREWRITING

However carefully you may work out your sentences and polish your diction, you will still face major decisions about how you are going to put your paper together. You need to decide on the main point you are going to make, find ways to support it, and settle on a scheme for developing it; so you must have a plan. Granted, planning is a nuisance. Many of us are tempted just to start writing, confident that some pattern of organization will emerge as we go along. Such improvising may work for a few talented souls, but most of us need at least a rough blueprint to work from in order to turn out a coherent and halfway readable paper. A convenient term for this organizing process is "prewriting." There is more to it than simply drafting an outline. First you must sit down to think about what you want to do.

Choosing a Topic

Essentially, prewriting involves making choices, a whole series of them. The first may be choosing a topic. Let us be optimistic enough to assume, however, that your teacher has at least given some suggestions. He has assigned an argumentative paper on any of these issues: pollution, civil disobedience, legalized drinking for eighteen-year-olds, socialized medicine, the right of teachers to strike, or no-fault insurance.

1. Does it interest you?
2. Do you have an opinion?
3. Do you have information?

First, look over the list to find a topic that meets at least three criteria: it interests you, you have an opinion on it, and you have some information about it. Applying those standards immediately eliminates, let's say, civil disobedience and the right of teachers to strike. The topic of socialized medicine interests you because your brother is a doctor. You know he opposes it, but after thinking about the matter, you realize that you have only opinions and no real information. You know nothing about how the system works in countries where it has been tried, so you cross that one off. Then you consider writing about no-fault insurance since you have heard it would lower your insurance premiums, but again you realize you have no facts on which to base an argument; so that one is out. You give serious consideration to the proposal to legalize drinking for eighteen-year-olds. Since you are nineteen and last month paid a $20 fine on a "minor-in-possession" charge, you are definitely interested in it and have an opinion on it. But when you begin to jot down arguments to support your opinion, you get no further than, "If a young man is old enough to be drafted, he is old enough to buy a beer." You are aware how hackneyed that is but cannot think of anything original on the subject, so reluctantly you drop that one too.

Narrowing the Topic

By a process of elimination you have arrived at your topic, pollution. It meets the criteria, and it seems workable although you still must make several choices before you can start writing. An important part of the writing assignment is to narrow the topic you choose to a manageable size. First, what kind of pollution are you going to concentrate on? After mulling over your choices, you decide to write on water pollution because you know of several examples and it seems more visible and more drastic than air pollution. Now you are ready to start

Make notes

getting your ideas together. Begin by making notes, writing down any-

thing on the topic that comes to your mind. The result might look
something like this.

Places	*Causes*
Great Lakes, especially	chemical wastes
Lake Michigan	sewage
Chesapeake Bay	oil-spills
red tides off Florida	detergents
Houston ship channel	cattle feed-yards
Hudson River—other rivers	insecticides

Effects

dead fish

bad drinking water

damage to oyster and shrimp industry

terrible odors

ruins swimming and water skiing

hurts tourist industry

irrigation water ruined

When you stop and look back over your list, it is obvious that
you have far more material than you can use; thus, the next step must
be to start pruning. Looking at the list of places, you decide it would
be sensible to cut out the Great Lakes and Chesapeake Bay because
you have never seen them; the Hudson River goes for the same reason.
When you look at the note that says "other rivers," however, you
realize that not far from your home there is a polluted river you know
well. The topic is a natural. You have plenty of firsthand information,
and you can write about something you are genuinely interested in.
Now you check your list to pick out usable ideas. You choose "bad
drinking water," "dead fish," and "ruins swimming" and from the
list of effects and "detergents" and "sewage" from the list of causes.
Finally, you are in business and ready to start your outline.

Ask the three
questions again

Pick out the usable
ideas from your notes

Outlining

First, you think about the sequence you want to set up and decide
on Places, Causes, Effects. After reflecting a minute, you realize that
you should also mention what can be done about the pollution. As

the last division, you add Solutions. Now you can begin to rough out an outline. Unless your teacher requires that you turn in the outline with your theme, you don't need to worry too much about complete sentences and parallelism, but you should write down enough details and concrete examples to help you support the main points you are going to make. When you finish, the outline might look like this:

Place: San Gabriel River
 Description
     10 years ago water clear, bottom sandy, gravel bars clean. Now water murky and covered with patches of detergent foam, bottom slimy, gravel bars covered with rotting vegetation, water smells bad.
 Causes
     City of Georgetown dumps untreated sewage into the river—city growth—mobile homes along river, septic tanks seep into water.
 Effects
     Detergent scum choking off oxygen—fish dying—swimming ruined because of dirty water—water getting so bad cattle don't want to drink it—rural people can't use it for drinking even if chlorinated.
 Solutions
     Sewage treatment plant at Georgetown—strong laws controlling installation of septic tanks. State law prohibiting sale of detergents with phosphates or other harmful agents. Enforcement of existing laws controlling use of river for irrigation, watering cattle, etc.

If your mind is working well when you sit down to work out this outline, writing it may take you no more than thirty or forty minutes. The chances are, though, that prewriting will take an hour or more—maybe considerably more. However slow the process, time spent in organizing your paper before you start to write is worth it because once you have worked out a plan the hardest part of your writing job is done. Now the last preliminary step is to formulate a thesis sentence that will help you to control and focus your paper.

Thesis Sentences

Summarizes the main points

Refer to the thesis sentence as you write

A thesis sentence should be a succinct statement that summarizes the main points you are going to make in your paper. You do not have to begin the theme with it or even use it in your writing, but you need it as a working guideline. If you compose the thesis sentence carefully and keep referring to it as you write, it will keep you on the track and ensure that you fulfill the commitment you have made in it. For example, a thesis sentence for our hypothetical theme on pollution might read, "The careless and shortsighted handling of sewage is ruining the once beautiful San Gabriel River; we can stop the process and repair the damage only by eliminating the present sources of pollution and passing laws to see that new ones do not develop." This is not an exciting sentence, but a useful one; if you develop all the points mentioned in it, you will have done your job.

Here are some other samples of good thesis sentences from student themes:

> High school students should not be allowed the same freedom that college students have in matters of dress and hair style because such freedom would undermine the authority that school administrators must have to control students who are forced to be in school seven hours a day.

> The most annoying features of the place where I live are an overly efficient air conditioner, malfunctioning showers, and a main lobby packed with leering men.

> A typical member of the Establishment accepts the stereotypes of his society; this kind of person has rigid ideas about the profit motive, long hair, and patriotic duty.

These thesis sentences, if followed, virtually guarantee an organized paper.

In contrast, here are some thesis sentences that will give their authors little help in getting a paper together.

> I am going to describe a few of the many ways that women are oppressed throughout life.

This sentence is no more than a statement of purpose; it is too vague and brief to control a paper.

> The changes in drug laws proposed by the American Civil Liberties Union are unrealistic.

This statement is inadequate because it only introduces the topic and does not include the main points to be made: the reasons the proposals are unrealistic.

> Goldwater uses several rhetorical techniques to develop his argument and convinces his audience that he is right.

The sentence is so vague that it provides no guidance for the writer. He should have specified which rhetorical techniques he was going to discuss, what the thesis of Goldwater's argument was, and whether it was successful. For example, "Goldwater uses connotation, definition, and testimony to argue successfully that public welfare is a failure."

ORGANIZING YOUR WRITING: CONTROL

Topic Sentences

State the main idea in every paragraph

The topic sentence controls the other sentences

Put the topic sentence first

What the thesis sentence does for the organization of the whole paper, the topic sentence does for the organization of the paragraph. Most high school English courses cover the topic sentence thoroughly, but certain fundamentals bear repeating. Every paragraph should have a topic sentence that states the main idea; all other sentences in the paragraph should relate to the topic sentence, either supporting it or expanding on it. It might be compared to a magnet, which holds all the separate sentences together. The topic sentence of a paragraph is not necessarily the first one; the first may be a transitional sentence that leads into the topic sentence. Occasionally, the topic sentence will be the last in a paragraph, a summary of all the previous ones that led up to it. This variation in style, however, had best be left to practiced writers. Writers who are unsure of their writing skills do better to put the topic sentence first and devote the rest of the paragraph to developing it.

Here is an example of a paragraph that falls apart because the writer has no clear idea of his topic sentence:

> I fail to see how the length of a boy's hair can affect his school work. If a high school boy wants to have long hair, he should be able to. If restrictions are placed on a student, it should be done by his parents rather than by the school administration. Many boys are merely trying to stay in style, not letting their hair grow as a sign of rebellion. A little bit of hair never hurt anyone.

No sentence in the paragraph develops or supports any other sentence. The result is no more than a collection of random statements about long hair. Revising it to make the first sentence the controlling one would produce a coherent and unified paragraph like this:

> I fail to see how the length of a boy's hair can affect his school work. Being long on hair doesn't necessarily mean being short

on intellect. It might even mean the opposite. It may be that the boy who has the courage to let his hair grow down over his collar in spite of harassment from the school coaches and administrators also has the intelligence to think for himself in other matters. I suggest, therefore, that until the authorities who make so much fuss about hair can show by actual statistics that long hair leads to poor grades, they should not interfere.

The paragraph is no masterpiece, but at least everything in it focuses on the main point set forth in the first sentence.

Transitions

Another organizational problem, and one that bothers even experienced writers, concerns transitions, those useful words and phrases that tie the parts of writing together and keep a paper moving smoothly in the direction it should go. Transitional words are connectors, highway signs that guide us along the route by which an author develops his ideas. If you are driving from Dallas to Houston, you depend on regularly spaced indicators to keep you on the track: "Keep right for exit to U.S. 95"; "U.S. 95—Houston, 165 miles"; "Exit to Houston highway, 500 yards ahead"; "Take U.S. 290 east—Houston 65 miles"; "Exit to Houston business route—1500 yards ahead." If you watch the signs you will arrive at your destination without interruptions.

Repeat a key word

Transitional markers in writing are more varied and less obvious, but they work in the same way by establishing links between sections of the whole. One popular linking device has much in common with highway signs; it is the repetition of a key word. Look, for example, at this passage from Robert Ardrey's *The Territorial Imperative:*

> Through such unending panoramas of shifting, changing times, there passed like figures in a fragmented dream those little bands of struggling beings who someday would be men. They *survived,* like baboons, through recognition of a need, one for another; they *survived* through enormous selective pressure encouraging the expansion of normal primate wit. Above all, however, they *survived* through plasticity.[2] [Italics added.]

Inexperienced writers often worry about using the same word too frequently, but the purposeful repetition of words or phrases can be an effective linking device.

[2] Robert Ardrey, *The Territorial Imperative* (New York: Dell Publishing Co., Inc., 1968), p. 34.

Use demonstrative
pronouns

Other kinds of transitional words are pronouns, especially demonstrative pronouns, which provide links by referring to something already mentioned. The ones that recur most often are "this," "that," "these," and "those." For example, Ardrey goes on in *The Territorial Imperative* to say,

> Many—most without a doubt—were conservative creatures. *These* died by the dry, unanticipated stream beds, or numbed and froze in unanticipated storms. *These* quite obviously were not your ancestors. It was the others—the witty, the sensitive, the flexible, the ones who could recognize a changing environment when they saw one and incorporate new information into the program of their instincts—*these* were the ones to assemble, ever so slowly, a new and most remarkable genetic package: ourselves. [P. 34, italics added.]

Use connective words

Writers can use other kinds of connective words to tie ideas together within and between paragraphs. Here are the commonest:

- Conjunctions: "and," "but," "either," "or," "neither," "nor," and "for"; the words "when," "since," "if," and "although" also act as conjunctions when they are used to introduce subordinate clauses.

- Words used to introduce examples: "for example," "to illustrate," "for instance," "first," "second," and "it follows."

- Words used to introduce similar points: "moreover," "also," "in addition," "again," "furthermore," "similarly," and "same."

- Words used to indicate contrast or qualification: "however," "on the other hand," "nevertheless," "in spite of," "yet," "still," "even though," and "nonetheless."

- Words that indicate consequence: "therefore," "thus," "consequently," "the result is," and "so."

- Words that indicate order: number words such as "first," "second," and "third," "next," "finally," and "in conclusion."

- Words that point back: "previous" and "former."

Most of the time you will use words like these almost unconsciously; sometimes, however, you may conclude that a paragraph is choppy and that it could be improved by inserting a few connectives chosen from the list.

Finally, here are two examples that illustrate how a variety of connective devices work together to produce a coherent, smoothly flowing piece of writing. The first is by a professional writer, the second by a student.

Key words and phrases

No aspect of human life seethes with so many unexorcised demons as does sex. No human activity is (so hexed) by superstition, (so haunted) by residual tribal lore, and (so harassed) by socially induced fear. Within the breast of the urban-secular man, a toe-to-toe struggle still rages between his savage and his bourgeois forebears.

Key word

Like everything else, the images of sex which informed tribal and town society are expiring along with the eras

Pronoun reference

in which they arose. The erosion of traditional values and the disappearance of accepted modes of behavior have left contemporary man free, but somewhat rudderless. Abhorring a vacuum, the mass media have rushed in to supply a new code and a new set

Pronoun reference

of behavioral prototypes. They appeal to the unexorcised demons. Nowhere is the persistence of mythical and metalogical denizens

Key words and phrases

(more) obvious than in sex, and the shamans of sales do their best to nourish them. Nowhere is the humanization of life (more) frustrated. Nowhere is the clear word of exorcism (more) needed.

Key word   Order word
Key word
Demonstrative pronoun

How is the humanization of sex impeded? (First,) it is thwarted by the parading of cultural identity images for the sexually dispossessed, to make money. Those images become the tyrant gods of the secular society, undercutting its liberation from religion and

Order word
Key words
Contrast word
Key word

transforming it into a kind of neotribal culture. (Second,) the authentic secularization of sex is checkmated by an anxious clinging to the sexual standards of the town, an era so recent and (yet) so different from ours that simply to transplant its sexual ethos into our situation is to invite hypocrisy of the worst degree.

Order word/key word

Let us look (first) at the spurious sexual models conjured up for our anxious society by the sorcerers of the mass media and the advertising guild. Like all pagan deities, these come in pairs—the

Demonstrative pronoun
Pronoun reference
Repetition of key words

god and his consort. For our purposes they are best symbolized by The Playboy and Miss America, the Adonis and Aphrodite of a leisure-consumer society which still seems unready to venture into full postreligious maturity and freedom. The Playboy and Miss

Pronoun references

America represent The Boy and The Girl. They incorporate a vision of life. They function as religious phenomena and should be exorcised and exposed.[3]

High school is a time of growing up and maturing for most stu-

Repetition of key words

dents; therefore, the school administration thinks it should protect

[3] Harvey Cox, *The Secular City* (New York: The Macmillan Company, 1965), p. 167.

Key words	its students by making boys keep their hair short and their feet covered with socks. Such matters are not really the business of administrations, but of the students' parents. School principals,
Pronoun reference	however, do not see it that way. In their opinion they have the
Pronoun reference	right to dictate to students about everything they do.
Key word	High school administrators can usually give some reasons for restricting students' hair and dress styles, but they are not very concrete. The administration argues that boys cannot wear sandals or shoes without socks because it makes their feet smell.
Contrast word	On the other hand, girls are allowed to wear sandals; apparently
Demonstrative pronoun	*their* feet do not smell. This kind of paradoxical reasoning makes no sense.
Word showing similarity	Administrators also argue that long hair on boys is distracting.
Demonstrative pronoun	This opinion seems to be based on prejudice rather than any
Contrast word	specific cases, but the administration sticks to it anyway. Many promising students have been expelled from school because of their refusal to obey the administration's edicts on hair length;
Words showing consequence	as a result, their educations have ended. Such drastic consequences for minor infractions hardly seem justified.

MECHANICS

Why Bother?

So far we have been talking about the content and organization of your writing. Now we must deal with what are really matters of form and appearance, that is, the mechanics of composition: grammar, spelling, and punctuation. Learning all the hundreds of rules that govern writing the English language is no easy task, but you have been working at it for several years. By this time you should have a reasonably good grasp of the fundamentals. Now that you are writing on the college level, your teacher should be able to assume that he does not need to spend hours of class time reteaching punctuation or basic sentence structure. Most teachers, however, are realistic enough to know that many students have some persistent grammatical problems.

Use the handbook and glossary

For this reason, there is a short handbook and glossary of usage at the end of this text, to which you can turn for help with your specific problem.

Students who make major errors in writing most often do it not from ignorance, however, but from indifference, carelessness, or forgetfulness. They are simply not convinced that writing correctly is important enough to justify the amounts of time and effort it requires. It would be reassuring to agree with those who say that mechanics are really not important, that what you write and how you put your words together matter far more than details such as a comma fault or an occasional sentence fragment or a misplaced modifier. Such an assertion is partially justified. Focusing your attention on saying something worthwhile and saying it forcefully and clearly *are* much more important than devoting most of your energies to turning out an absolutely "correct" composition. A paper can be totally trivial even though the spelling, handwriting, and grammar are flawless. But it is poor logic to say that, because content is more important than mechanics, then mechanics do not matter. They do, and for several reasons.

First, poor grammar and punctuation in a paper draw a disproportionate amount of attention to themselves. In some ways the situation is analogous to that of running a household: more than one woman has complained that the most frustrating thing about housekeeping is that much of the time you are doing invisible work, that is, no one notices it unless it is *not* done. Both family and visitors take a neat kitchen, a clean floor, dust-free furniture, and meals served on time for granted; the housewife gets no compliments on those. But if she leaves the dishes in the sink and a coat of dust on the piano, everyone immediately notices and disapproves. Similarly, when reading your paper the college composition teacher seldom thinks, "What nice punctuation!" or "This student certainly spells well." He takes those skills for granted and concentrates his attention on other elements of your writing: clarity, coherence, and sound thinking. If, however, you have neglected the niceties of grammar and spelling, the errors will divert his attention from what you are doing right to what you are doing wrong—and that is certainly not where you want it. Both you and the housewife have a better chance of getting credit for the important things you do if you take care of the relatively unimportant ones as a matter of course.

The toleration level of teachers varies. Some are fairly permissive about the commoner lapses in grammar; some are very strict. Most college teachers, however, have reasonable standards. They no longer worry about such fine points as the difference between "can" and "may," "less" and "fewer," or the distinction between "different from" and "different than" or "among" and "between." Nevertheless, they still frown on comma splices and sentence fragments (two of their pet peeves), insist that you differentiate between adverbial and adjec-

Poor mechanics steal attention from content

tive forms, want subjects and verbs to agree and modifying phrases to come in the right place. And they care about spelling, not because they equate intelligence with good spelling, but because they know other people do.

Learning mechanics now costs less

The second reason you should be concerned about writing correctly is that you need to form good habits now when the penalties for writing incorrectly are not so severe as they will be later. In a freshman composition course, you will be writing several papers; if you have problems, you have a chance to solve them as you go along and gradually bring your work up to the level of standard English. In sophomore and upper division courses, however, your grade may depend on the one or two papers you turn in. Under those circumstances a poorly written paper can cost you dearly. The crucial test comes when you begin to write the letters and applications that could affect your future. At that point careless grammar and misspelling say to your prospective employer or to the admissions officer, "Here is a sloppy and irresponsible person who is totally indifferent to the impression he makes on me." Harsh and unreasonable as such a judgment may seem, it is a predictable one. People in authority do judge you by your writing.

Poor mechanics interfere with communication

The final hazard of bad grammar is that it can interfere with communication. The failure to put commas in the proper places can completely alter the sense of a statement. Misplaced modifiers can make sentences comically ambiguous. Run-on sentences or the failure to insert quotation marks where they are needed can confuse the reader. Thus, faulty mechanics not only distract and annoy your reader, they can also deceive him.

Spelling

Pay attention to your spelling. After eight or ten years of studying spelling, you should know whether you are a reasonably competent speller. If you are not, don't just shrug off your deficiencies by saying, "Well, I never could spell." If you had mastered all the skills required to drive a car except that of backing it, you wouldn't say, "Oh, I'll just settle for this. Backing up is too hard." You would practice backing until you mastered it because you would be handicapped in your driving if you did not. You will be equally handicapped in writing if you refuse to do whatever is necessary to correct your spelling. Remember that bad spelling is one of the main devices an author uses when he wants to play the role of the semiliterate hick. By using spellings such as "eddicate," "wuz," "mizerbul," and "bizness" he gives the impression that he is uneducated; you create the same impression when you turn in papers in which you write "comprimize" for "compromise," and "intergraded" for "integrated."

Use a dictionary

There are several steps you can take to improve your spelling. First, invest six or seven dollars in one of the standard dictionaries and keep it on your desk or work table. Get in the habit of looking up any word about which you have the slightest doubt. If you are not sure whether there are two *r*'s in "embarrass," look it up; if you are confused about whether "pursue" is spelled with a *u* or *e*, check it. Words with unaccented vowel syllables such as "sep-*a*-rate," "com-*pro*-mise," "mil-*i*-tant," and "ul-*ti*-mate" are frequent troublemakers because there is no way to be sure which vowel to use without checking; most word endings with an "ize" sound are spelled "ise" but "emphasize" is not, so you may have to check on those too. All of this is a nuisance, of course, but absolutely necessary if you are serious about improving your spelling.

Keep a list of words you misspell

You should also form the habit of keeping a list of the correctly spelled versions of words you have missed on papers. The flash card system is handy since it allows you to consult them in alphabetical order, or you may put the list in the back of your English notebook. In addition, make it a practice to pay particular attention to the spelling of key words in an assignment. Teachers have little patience with the student who is so careless that he consistently spells Hemingway with two *m*'s, writes a paper on John Stuart Mill and uses the spelling "Mills" throughout, or forgets to put in the second *l* every time he uses "syllogism."

Find a study skills program

Finally, there may be some spelling aids available on campus. Ask your teacher if your college offers a study skills program that includes instruction in spelling, if there is an English laboratory set up to help you, and if the bookstores carry inexpensive, programmed workbooks for improving your spelling. As a last resort, you can always find one of those fortunate souls who are natural spellers, and ask him or her to check over the final draft of your work.

Proofreading

The last reminder is one that you have probably heard as often as the admonition to brush your teeth. Proofread, proofread, proofread! Ten or fifteen minutes spent checking over your paper for commas, possessive marks, fragments, or omitted words can alter your image from a careless student to a conscientious one. Few teachers object to your making neat last-minute corrections or insertions. They would rather have you correct your own errors than leave them to be circled and sent back for revision.

THE FIRST ASSIGNMENT

Finally, here are some general suggestions that should help you get off to a reasonably good start on those first papers.

General Writing Hints

Reread the assignment

First, read the writing assignment over carefully at least three times and make a list of the main things you are required to do. When you have finished your first draft, check your notes to see if you have covered everything specified in the assignment. Be sure that you stay directly on the topic. If the assignment is to analyze connotation, discuss the connotation and not the ideas. Few things annoy a teacher more than receiving a theme, however good, on a topic quite different from the one he assigned. At best, you will probably have to rewrite it; at worst, it could bring an automatic *F*.

Allow enough time

Second, give yourself enough time. Almost inevitably the paper you thought you could write in two hours will take three or four for just the first draft; then you still have to make corrections and a clean copy, and proofread it. If by that time it is 2:30 on Friday morning and the paper is due at 10:00 A.M., you can hardly put your best efforts into the final copy. Moreover, you can improve nearly any piece of writing if you will do the first draft, set it aside for a day, and then take another look at it. Errors and rough spots that you missed the first time will become obvious on a second reading. You can correct them in the second draft and do some last-minute polishing as you make your final copy. It is time consuming, certainly, but not too arduous if you spread the task out over two or three days rather than jam it into one late-night, five-hour session.

Leave space for rewriting

The third point is simply a working technique. If you type, get some cheap paper and type your first draft with double or triple spacing and wide margins; if you write in longhand, write on every second or third line and again leave wide margins. The purpose of this apparently wasteful method is to enable you to *see* what you are doing. Words and phrases stand out better if there is plenty of space around them; an awkward phrase or misplaced modifier that might not be noticeable when it is crowded into a closely written paragraph may catch your attention if the writing is spaced out. You can also check the development of your sentences better if you can read them more easily. Also, the extra vertical space and wide margins give you more room to make changes or additions.

Length

Don't pad your writing. You will notice that the writing assignments in this book seldom specify the number of words you must have in a paper. That omission is deliberate, for in most real-life writing situations a person never stops to ask himself, "How long does this have to be?" Rather, he asks himself, "What points do I want to cover in this particular letter (or speech, application, or report) and how can I support them?" When he has written as much as he needs to make an effective presentation, he stops. Padding his writing with needless repetition and irrelevancies would only weaken his rhetoric. Students should follow the same policy: say what needs to be said clearly and concisely and then stop. Of course, this puts the burden of deciding how much is enough squarely where it belongs—on the writer, not the audience. If the student takes advantage of this freedom by turning in a two-paragraph paper to meet a complex writing assignment, he only demonstrates poor judgment.

While the traditional prescription of "500 to 700 words" may not make much sense as a minimum requirement for themes, in some cases setting a maximum number of words does make sense. After all, newspaper editorials have to fit into a two-column box, there are time limits put on speeches, and employers do not want to wade through a four-page letter of application. The question you need to ask yourself when writing is not "How can I put together enough words to fill up an impressive number of pages?" but "How can I be as concise as possible and still say everything that is absolutely necessary?" If you have something of consequence to say and support your statements with explanations and examples, you are not likely to run short of words.

By now, I am sure that you are thoroughly tired of reading about elementary writing. What we have covered so far are only the routine "housekeeping chores" involved in composition. Now we can move on to a more interesting topic, rhetoric itself.

Say what needs to be said

Be concise

1. *Revision of sentences* Criticize each of the following sentences. What specific writing problem or problems does each illustrate? Rewrite each sentence to make it stronger and more effective.

   a. Today the full use of individual liberty has not been given to the individual by society.

   b. It is voluntarily seen that pornography is in the area of private morality and scientific investigations have been made to show that obscenities in general does not have harmful effects on either society or individual.

   c. Assuming that the use and possession of drugs is not a crime per se, and under the assumption that behavioral effects cannot be determined when under the influence of drugs, then the only safe way to protect the user and those around him would be total isolation.

   d. It is through the effect of connotative words that the audience is persuaded that our world has been corrupted.

   e. It is logical to think that in our society we must endure such evils as the deception about selling products, brainwashing by television, or the slaughterings on the highways because establishing one idea among the entire society would be against the nature of a democratic society which we believe is the best possible society.

   f. When both husband and wife are working to keep their household going they feel needed by each other and this is one thing, the need for each other, that holds the family together.

   g. Because collectivism is defined as the socialistic principle of control by the people collectively, or the state, of all means of production or economic activities, or about the same idea as socialism, the average person immediately identifies this with Communism.

   h. It is the easiness of government to interfere into both phases of man's consciousness, material and spiritual, that is an invasion of privacy, and this privacy must be protected if man is to remain free.

   i. It is easily grasped by the reader that the basis upon which this opinion was formed is inadequate.

   j. The interference with civil rights by citizens is an eventual detriment to society as a whole.

   k. If you receive everything you ever wanted or needed, you would soon find yourself in a state of boredom.

   l. Through reading the student newspaper we have been able to examine international, national, and local events, in some instances evaluating their worth or affect, and as individuals draw some kind of conclusion.

2. *Prewriting*   Taking one of the topics given below, go through the steps of the prewriting process. Begin by choosing a subdivision of the large topic; then, write down all the points you can think of that might be useful in developing your smaller topic. Read over your list and decide which points can be grouped together to develop one of the divisions of your subtopic. Finally, arrange these points in a logical order and draw up a rough outline for a paper.

Topics
a. The generation gap
b. The need for election reform
c. The effects of television
d. Inequality of opportunity
e. Sex discrimination
f. Open-admission policies for colleges
g. The disadvantages of competition

3. The following examples give alternate versions of the same paragraph. In your opinion, which is the better written in each set? Give specific reasons for your judgments.

a. Because of a recent move made by my parents, my home has become a completely new environment: a small Southwestern town. The fact that only 5,000 people live in this town is very easy for me to understand for various reasons. Most of the people living there are very conservative and many times narrow-minded. As a result their children tend to follow in the same trends. Prejudices against blacks, long hairs, and other minority groups run high.

   For the past six months my home town has been in a small town, population only 5,000. I moved there not from any special desire to live in a small town, but because my father's business required that we move. Now that we are there, I can see why the town stays small. Certainly few people would choose to live in this town where bigotry and narrow-mindedness dominate. The citizens hate long hairs, consider blacks subhuman, and criticize anyone who does not think and act like they do.

b. Throughout their school careers women face discrimination. The athletic program in the average high school furnishes a concrete illustration. Although most high schools stress and actively support all sports activities, women, especially in the South, seldom get the chance to participate. If the women do manage to get a team together, the school district usually refuses to pay their expenses. For example, in my high school women could play only volleyball or tennis. Although our volleyball team went to state finals several years in a row, we got little support, either moral or financial, and almost no publicity.

Women are oppressed throughout their school careers. In high school this is probably most evident. Women, especially in the South, are discouraged from participating in sports. When they do, their teams are often lacking in financial support from the school district. For example, in my high school women could play only volleyball or tennis. While our volleyball team went to state finals several years in a row, very little was done to back it or even publicize its success.

c. Recently, as a university student, I was asked the question: "Should the university do away with all required courses and allow each student to design his own degree program?" Immediately I responded with an affirmative "Yes," but on later reflection, when I examined the reasons for my answer, I decided instead upon the negative response. Why? Because I feel that many students would eliminate too many of the basic required courses which are indispensable. They would skip the introductory lower level courses for being too dull, avoid the more difficult courses for being too time consuming, and would take only a sampling of the diverse intermediate courses; thereby not concentrating in any given subject.

A young man taking a poll among college students recently asked me, "Should the university do away with all required courses and allow each student to design his own degree program?" My first response was a quick "Yes." After thinking more about the question, however, I have decided that the answer should be "No." Why? First, I think that too many students would refuse to take basic courses that are necessary to a good education. They would skip elementary courses such as freshman English, algebra, and American government because they might find them boring. They would avoid the more difficult courses such as economics, physics, or the languages because such subjects would be too time consuming. Instead, students would choose at random courses that they thought would be fun and easy. At the end of their college career, they would have a collection of miscellaneous knowledge and no real training in or mastery of any particular subject.

4. Rewrite the following two paragraphs to make them smoother and more coherent. Begin each one with a topic sentence that will serve as a guideline for developing the rest of the paragraph.

a. All too often young people enter into the bond of marriage without considering future financial situations that can arise. One such problem is self-supported education. College educations are expensive and one or both partners may have to work. This results in separation of the couple. Further separation is caused by the many hours that have to be spent studying and doing homework. Working eight hours a day, going to school and studying leave very little time for the couple to spend together. Most jobs require the student to devote his full attention to the work being done. Little time is left, therefore, for his studies.

b. "I did not know I was eligible to enter the university." This is what Eddie Jones said to his high school counselor when he was told his grades met the university entrance requirements. Eddie is an average student who believed the myth that our university is only for smart people. Many students fail to apply simply because they are uninformed about its requirements. Minority students are the most uninformed about their opportunities. I think all minority students would be able to attend the university. At other colleges drives to enlarge enrollments always succeed in increasing the number of students. Therefore, concerted drives should be made to bring more minority students to this university.

5. Proofread the following student paper carefully and correct any errors in spelling, punctuation, grammar, or word choice.

Thesis sentence: Thos people in society who stand pa-sively while members of their kind are robbed and beaten illustrates John Stuart Mill's point that a person does harm to his fellow man not only by his actions, but also by his inactions.

At around midnight on a slum district street, an old man is robbed and slowly beaten to death by a group of thugs. Several people observe the incident from an apartment building directly above and also from about seventy-five yards down the street. But no one charges to the victum's rescue. Instead they seem to sink into the dark shadows that the night provides them with. The thugs do not even seem to rush away from the incident. They seem assured that no one will even make a move to stop them. Later when the police arrive, questions are asked to people living in the immediate area of the crime. But all of the people interrogated are reluctant to admit that they even saw the crime.

The preceding incident is a perfect example of what Mills refers to in his essay as harmful inaction. Mills states that while people may be harmed by another's actions, they may also be hurt by one's lack of action. By this Mills means that man has certain obligations to help his fellow man in time of need. He feels that it is not enough just to avoid harming other people, but it is also a moral obligation to help save another's life or to join in assistance for other reasons where another may need help. Other areas where it would be a moral sin to remain inactive are such things as military servitude, paying taxes, or to give evidence in a court of justice. Mills believes it is man's duty to indulge in these responsibilities because man also reaps security and safety from these very items.

Those people who watched an old man be murdered are guilty of inaction. In a sense they are just as responsible for the crime as the thugs who actually did it because they could have prevented a terrible event from taking place.

6. Look through several magazines and/or newspaper articles to find two or three sentences that seem particularly effective to you. Copy them, bring them to class, and be prepared to say why you think they are good sentences.

SUGGESTED
WRITING
ASSIGNMENT

Purpose: To give you practice in writing unified, carefully focused, and responsibly developed paragraphs.

Procedure: First, carefully reread the section on topic sentences. Then, choose *two* of the topic sentences given below and for each one write a paragraph of 150–200 words, that develops and supports the topic statement. Begin your paragraph with the sentence given and be sure that everything you write relates to and supports that sentence. Use a separate sheet or sheets for each of your paragraphs.

1. The student who comes to college on an athletic scholarship assumes a tremendous responsibility.
2. A minority student at this school faces certain problems that other students do not have.
3. The term "radical" provokes strong reactions in many people. (You may substitute the term "freak," "jock," "liberated woman," or "male chauvinist.")
4. The Supreme Court decision banning capital punishment has major implications.
5. An ex-serviceman who returns to college has certain advantages [or disadvantages].

2

The
Components
of
Rhetoric

The introduction presented rhetoric in general terms: what it is and why it is worth studying. Now it is time to separate the whole into its components, identify each part, see how each is related to the other, and examine the way each contributes to the total effect.

We can break any example of rhetoric down into four parts: the persuasive purpose, the audience, the rhetorician's persona, and the content of the argument.

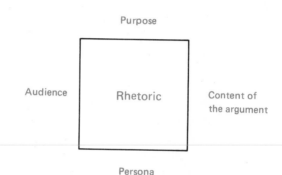

Seldom will we find an example of rhetoric so neatly structured that the diagram of it will have the symmetry of a square. The persona by force of character may dominate the presentation; the argument may be so carefully worked out and supported that we are unaware of the appeal to an audience; or the attempt of the author to ingratiate himself with his audience may be so blatant that we are less aware of what he is saying than of the way he is saying it. What we visualize in the abstract as an ideal square may turn out in reality to be a lop-sided quadrangle; nevertheless, each part of the structure must be there or the whole will come apart. Thus, the writer who sets out to construct an effective piece of rhetoric must keep the following points in mind.

Questions to ask when constructing rhetoric

1. What am I trying to do?
2. Who is my audience and what are its main characteristics?
3. How should I present myself to the audience?
4. What kinds of arguments should I use?

When the situation is reversed and the student wants to make a reasoned evaluation of the rhetoric of others, he must ask the same kind of questions.

33

1. What is the author's purpose?
2. Is he aware of his audience and does he show a sensitivity to its interests?
3. Is his persona convincing?
4. What are his arguments and are they suitable to his audience?

Only when you have considered each of these components of a piece of persuasion can you make a supported judgment about whether it is successful and why it does or does not work.

PURPOSE

The answer to the question "What is the purpose?" is often simple, even obvious. For student themes the rhetorical purpose may be stated in the assignment as it is in the first suggested theme at the end of this chapter. Or you may be asked to choose one side of a current issue and write a persuasive paper; for example, "Construct a reasoned argument either for or against an open admissions policy for your college." Here you establish your purpose as soon as you decide which view you want to support. Similarly, with much of the rhetoric we read or hear we can tell immediately what the writer's or speaker's purpose is. Candidates for office seek to discredit their opponents and gain support for themselves and their programs; crusaders for causes such as prison reform or more public housing quickly make their purposes known; public relations firms try to promote good will for the organizations they represent; and advertisers want to sell products.

But it is not always easy to pinpoint rhetorical purposes, either one's own or someone else's. Suppose your freshman sociology professor assigns a paper on "Class Distinctions in Your High School." Before you begin to write such a paper, you need to decide what your purposes are. First, of course, you would want to enumerate and define the various groups within the high school in a way that would illustrate to your professor that you understand the concept of social stratification. If you limit yourself to this purpose, you will do a paper that is purely descriptive and analytical; you will make no value judgments. If, however, you also want to talk about the effects of the class system on the students, you have expanded your purpose and must plan your paper accordingly. If you want to maintain that the effects of the system are beneficial for students, you will gear your paper to move in one direction; if you want to show that they are detrimental for students, you will gear it to move in another.

Purpose controls the
thesis sentence

Your purpose will control the thesis sentence for your paper. A thesis for the first point of view might be:

> The student body of Jefferson High School is divided into the leaders of various student activities, their followers who emulate them, a large middle group who conform to the patterns set by the leaders but do not participate in school affairs, a small group of nonconforming student activists, and a class of poor and indifferent students who are the potential dropouts; the division is a healthy one because it reflects the class structure of the community and is useful because it gives each student a group with which to identify.

If you want to write from the second point of view, your thesis sentence might be:

> If you are a student at Jefferson High School, you are a Big Wheel, one of the Big Wheels' hangers-on, a member of the great mass of invisible nothings, or one of the peons who hate being there and will not stay any longer than they have to; this class system is vicious because it promotes snobbishness, rewards superficial accomplishments, and gives most of the students who are caught in it a lasting sense of inferiority.

When you have drafted a thesis sentence like either of these, you are off to a good start on your paper; you now have a clear sense of what you want to do and can go on to expand and support your ideas.

This technique of articulating your purpose before you begin to write is useful whether you are writing papers or essay exams for one of your courses, writing a congressman to persuade him to support a bill, drafting a statement of your personal goals in order to apply for a scholarship or admission to an honors program, or composing a campaign speech to be used in your race for the student senate. Knowing precisely what you want to do will help you to shape your argument, eliminate extraneous material, and make the most efficient use of the limited time and space you have. Under some circumstances —writing an essay exam, for example—you may have to make a quick decision about purpose; at other times, you may have the leisure to think out your goals well ahead of the time you write. In either case, the time it takes to choose a purpose is well spent. Too often students will spend thirty minutes of a fifty-minute exam writing at random before they begin to focus on the real issues; their reasoning seems to be that showing the teacher they have a lot of information will bring rewards. Usually the teacher's response is, "This is all very interesting, but you haven't answered the questions." If you are writing an out-of-class paper, starting to write before deciding what you intend to do can produce a disaster like the paper from which the jargon paragraph on pages 75 and 76 was taken.

Set reasonable goals for your writing

Finally, you should learn to set reasonable goals for your writing. You are, after all, not a professional writer or rhetorician, and no one expects you to produce brilliant arguments or profound judgments that will dazzle your audience. In a discussion you are accomplishing enough—indeed, a great deal—if you convince a skeptical audience that you have some good points and that they should think about them. When you are writing term papers, your philosophy professor will be satisfied with a paper that shows you have a decent grasp of a philosopher's theories, and your biology professor will be pleased with a report that is clear and accurate. If you set for yourself goals that are too ambitious and unrealistically high, you will defeat yourself before you start. "A man's grasp should exceed his reach" is not necessarily good advice.

AUDIENCE

How to Analyze Your Audience

Once you have your purpose clearly in mind, your next task is to define and analyze your audience. A sure sense of your audience— knowing who it is and what assumptions you can reasonably make about it—is crucial to the success of rhetoric. In practice, you have probably been making sound inferences about audience for a long time and putting those inferences to good use in your personal rhetoric. Tailoring your appeal to suit your audience is, after all, primar-

Start with common-sense psychology

ily a matter of using everyday, common-sense psychology. Most young people know almost instinctively what tack to take when they want something from their parents. They know too that what may work with one parent may not succeed with the other; thus, they modify their arguments accordingly. They are equally skillful in varying their language, their tone, their modes of appeal to fit other audiences: teachers, friends, teammates, coaches, brothers and sisters, or prospective employers. By drawing on experience and information accumulated over a period of time they know, almost without thinking about it, how to approach a particular audience.

The techniques you use to appeal to a larger, more remote, and

Catalog the traits
of your audience

less well-known audience are no different from those you would use with a small group that you know intimately. You base your rhetoric on what you know about your audience. You must keep in mind the concerns and values of the people you want to reach; you should have some knowledge of their educational and social backgrounds, how old they are, what kind of work they do, and whether they are, on the whole, liberal or conservative about religion, sex, and politics. Given this kind of information, you can decide what to include in your arguments and what to leave out, what kind of vocabulary to use, and what shared experience you and your audience may have that you can draw on for examples.

The problem is, of course, that you cannot have this kind of information about an audience you do not know, a group of readers or listeners that is nebulous, faceless, without substance or identity. Once you realize who your audience is, however, it will begin to take on form and character, and you can start to fill in some of the unknowns. You will have to analyze your audience consciously, specify its traits, and decide what conclusions you can legitimately make about an audience with those traits.

Suppose, for example, that you are one of six students who have been chosen to meet with a board of teachers and administrators of your college to work out a new set of rules about visiting hours and privileges in the dormitories. You are the one who is going to write up the proposal agreed upon by the students for presentation to the board. What do you know about your audience? First, they are middle-aged, from thirty-five to fifty-five; when they went to college, strict rules about hours for visiting were taken for granted as necessary and beneficial limitations on students. Second, they are well-educated, probably intelligent, and like to think of themselves as open-minded and amenable to reason. Third, they are concerned about the morale of the students, but they are also concerned about their study habits and grades. Fourth, they are sensitive to the opinions of the students' parents and of the alumni and trustees. Armed with this kind of information, which is no more than an accumulation of common-sense observations, you should be able to shape the kind of argument that is likeliest to succeed.

Advantages of Analyzing Your Audience

Even though drawing up this kind of catalog of your audience's traits is no more than an exercise in common sense, it can be an extremely useful kind of exercise, one that you ought to do as a routine step in any prewriting process. First, it forces you to think specifically about what group or groups you want to reach and helps you to keep your attention focused on that segment of the population. For example, if you are arguing for a liberalization of enrollment standards for your college, your real audience is the faculty and the administration. They are the ones who have the power to make the change and who must be convinced of its merits. The students who may be in your audience are relatively unimportant. Second, knowing your audience and its characteristics helps you to eliminate extraneous material from your argument and to concentrate on the key points. In the example just given, you might be able to think of half-a-dozen reasons for lowering admission requirements. First, it would increase the size of the student body, and consequently bring in more money; second, it would bring a greater variety of students to campus; third, it would make it easier for the students to get good grades; fourth, the fraternities and sororities would have fewer financial problems; fifth, it would increase the proportion of students from minority groups; and, sixth, there would be more material for the football team. If you keep in mind that your audience is teachers and administrators, not students, you will stress reasons one, two, and five, and will prudently not mention three, four, and probably six.

A third reason for fixing your audience firmly in mind before you start writing is that by doing so you avoid wasting time with unnecessary explanations and definitions. If you are writing for your fellow students, you do not need to repeat what is common knowledge to all of you. If you are writing a paper or exam for a course, and your audience is just your professor, you will only irritate him if you stop to define terms that he takes for granted as a part of the working vocabulary of the course: for example, "ethical systems" in a philosophy course; "imagery" and "prosody" in a poetry course; "learning behavior" or "feedback" in an educational psychology course.

It is virtually impossible to frame an appeal that will work with large, undifferentiated masses of people, and you would do better not to try. The attempt to do so can produce little but bland and vapid generalities that would annoy any perceptive audience. The wiser course is to set the boundaries to your audience as precisely as you can, decide what major characteristics the members of that audience are apt to have in common, and keep those characteristics in mind when you frame your appeal. If you are addressing a group of medical doctors, you can reasonably assume that they are, as a whole, affluent,

Focuses your attention

Promotes concentration on key points

Eliminates unnecessary material

conservative, intelligent, and socially prominent. Some of them do not fit in these categories, of course, but reading the newspapers, knowing the legislative record of the American Medical Association, and drawing on your personal experience will support such a general judgment. Using the same process of reasoning, you can legitimately make comparable generalizations about farmers, teachers, blue-collar workers, military men, and other relatively homogeneous groups. In any group you characterize there will be numerous exceptions, but they are not the ones who set the patterns you must have to work from.

The Importance of Sincerity

At this point, some of you are undoubtedly thinking: "But this is a sellout. You're suggesting that we compromise, that instead of saying what we think we should figure out what will please the audience and say that instead. That's dishonest." Such a reaction is understandable, but it misses the point. No one is recommending that you be insincere or pretend to attitudes and beliefs in order to curry favor with your readers. In fact, that kind of approach will soon prove self-defeating because words have a way of catching up with one and because the writer or speaker who proves himself to be strictly an opportunist may lose every segment of his audience.

There is a distinct difference between pandering to your audience's biases and weaknesses and appealing to their legitimate interests and concerns. The rhetorician who does the first shows contempt for his audience by assuming that they can be manipulated without resistance through their emotions and do not have the intelligence to think for themselves. When you use the second approach, you can say honestly what you think but say it in such a way that you show regard for your audience's convictions as well as your own. For example, suppose you are helping to raise money for your local symphony. If you have no scruples about how you do it, you could suggest to Mrs. Jones, who in fact cares nothing about music, that you know she will want to contribute $500 to the cause because she is a person of unusual refinement and culture and a lover of the arts. You might also appeal to her vanity by pointing out that contributors of $500 will have their names printed on the program in gold letters—so everyone will know how *much* she gave. That is pandering to your audience. You could, however, make an honest attempt to persuade by appealing to her genuine civic pride, pointing out that the symphony is a cultural asset to the town, attracts visitors who spend money, and provides opportunities for young people to develop their talents. But honesty here does not mean that you have to start out by saying, "Mrs. Jones, I know you don't care anything about music. . . ."

Keeping Your Audience in Mind

Probably the most frequent breakdowns in establishing rapport with your audience come from neglecting to identify your audience before you start to write or from just forgetting to keep it in mind once you have begun. If you are going to argue that women should no longer settle for the secondary roles in the professions—nurse instead of doctor, bookkeeper instead of investment counselor, secretary instead of executive—you are not likely to make an effective argument unless you decide ahead of time whom you are going to address: women themselves, leaders in the professions, or the faculties of professional schools. Say you determine that your audience is predominantly conservative and practical; if you then allow yourself to go off into an idealistic and emotional argument—and this frequently happens with issues on which people have strong feelings—you are defeating your own rhetorical purpose.

At the worst, the failure to consider your audience and its characteristics can twist attempts at persuasion into what is actually a form of *anti-rhetoric*. Take, for instance, an ardent champion of civil rights who says he wants to improve job opportunities for blacks in his community. In a speech to a local civic service club he berates local employers for their exploitation of blacks and their discriminatory hiring practices while pointing out that he was putting blacks into key positions ten years ago and, in addition, financing scholarships to help them. This speaker may be sincere about wanting to open more jobs for blacks, but he is not likely to do it by attacking those who could help and then further alienating his audience by holding himself up as a model of noble behavior. This kind of rhetoric does more to boost the speaker's ego than to persuade anyone. His audience will become defensive and hostile and is likely to reject anything he suggests. Sociologists call the reaction "backlash." The student radicals of the late 1960s, with their obscenities and "nonnegotiable demands," were really practicing anti-rhetoric.

There is, of course, a need for rhetoric that attacks, accuses, and agitates for change. You cannot and should not always try to be pleasant. Nevertheless, before you begin to criticize and denigrate people or institutions, you should stop to think who your audience

Watch out for anti-rhetoric

is and what you are trying to do. Maybe you really don't have any audience; you are just blowing off steam, which is all right. But if you really want to change something—say, the marijuana laws—you are not going to do it by making the legislators who are responsible for them angry. Condemnations and expressions of outrage are effective rhetorical tools only if they are used with the right audience.

Use outrage on the right audience

Audiences for Student Writing

A student may go about finding his audience in several ways. Often he has no problem because the audience is explicitly or implicitly designated in the assignment. You may be asked to prepare for a class a particular report or to submit to a committee a statement of your reasons for wanting to participate in an honors seminar in history. If you are writing an essay exam or a term paper, obviously the audience is your professor or his grader; if possible, it may be a good idea to find out which. If, however, your only instructions are to write a paper about your views on Women's Liberation or an argument for or against abolishing the English requirement in your college, you need to find your audience before you begin. One question you might ask yourself is, "Who would be interested in these topics?"; that will give you a starting place. From there, you can narrow your audience further by concentrating on a group of people about the same age or of a certain educational level. In most cases, it is probably easier and more natural for you to write to other young people. The simplest device for finding your audience for freshman papers, and one that many teachers recommend, is to address your paper to your class. Doing this solves your problem about vocabulary and terminology and gives you a basis of common assumptions and experience from which to work. It also eliminates the artificial and intimidating situation of writing solely for your teacher. Whatever audience you decide on, you will produce a better paper if you write in capital letters at the top of your rough draft "AUDIENCE: ———" and specify your readers and their characteristics.

The assigned audience

The unassigned audience

Writing to your class

PERSONA

Once you have defined your audience, your next task is to decide the role that you, as rhetorician, are going to play for your audience. The term "persona" best describes that role because it is a comparatively neutral term. "Persona" derives from the Latin word for the masks worn by the actors in ancient classical drama, masks that immediately classified their roles for the audience: a smiling mask for a comic character, a sorrowful one for a tragic character. Thus, "persona" is an apt word to describe the identity assumed by a writer or speaker.

Now, only one paragraph into this section, I know I am already in trouble with my audience. For rather complicated psychological reasons that I will not try to go into here, almost all of you put a premium on "naturalness" and "being yourself," even though you may not have a precise idea of what you mean by those terms. Thus, the words "masks," "role playing," and "assuming an identity" have bad connotations for you. Once more, you may suspect that you are being advised to be insincere and artificial in order to persuade people. And once more, I will try to convince you that the techniques we use in rhetoric are really natural ways of behaving that all of us employ constantly without even thinking about it.

Psychologists have long known that the normal person plays many roles.[1] As a person who lives in a complex and sophisticated culture, you find yourself in a variety of different situations during the course of a day, and you adjust your behavior accordingly. You wear no mask when you are grousing at the alarm clock in the privacy of your room, but you assume one when you get to the breakfast table and want to be at least civil to your companions. In class you assume the role of student; you pay attention, take notes, ask questions. Your instructor is playing the role of teacher, acting quite differently from the way he did in his office talking to a colleague ten minutes before. Late in the afternoon you may shift to the role of son or daughter when you are talking over the phone with your parents, and that evening show another facet of your personality when you are drinking beer with your friends. All of this behavior is unaffected and sincere; you are being yourself, but in a flexible way that allows you to choose responses appropriate to your situation and your audience.

How to Decide on Your Persona

Such flexibility is precisely what is involved in establishing your persona in a rhetorical situation. The only difference is that when you are not familiar with your audience, you need to think ahead about **Purpose and audience** your purpose, the makeup of your audience, and the image of yourself that you want to project. In face-to-face situations, you can still rely largely on instinct; common sense tells you that it is all right to act

[1] See Kenneth J. Gergen, "The Healthy, Happy Human Being Wears Many Masks," *Psychology Today,* May 1972, pp. 31 ff.

casually at a meeting of student advisers, but foolish to do so at a hearing before the dean of students. When you are writing, however, you have fewer clues to guide you; therefore, it is a good idea to think about your persona before you frame an appeal on an important issue. For example, suppose you are writing to the city council to request that the city elections be held when college is in session in order that more students can participate. Before you start, ask yourself how you want to appear to the council members. Your answer will probably be something like this: young voter—responsible, mature, eager to participate in civic affairs. If, however, you are writing to set up a job interview, the line after "PERSONA" might be: environmental engineer—intelligent, serious, hardworking, optimistic about opportunities in the field. For a rhetorical situation in which your purpose is to protest college plans to build a new swimming pool when the campus needs more classrooms, you could take on the role of the angry young man who is concerned about the quality of education and distressed about misplaced priorities in spending. There is no reason why all of these roles cannot be quite honestly assumed by one person; a variety of roles does not necessarily reflect any conflict, deceit, or insincerity.

The ethical appeal

Integrity and competence

Your ability to establish a credible persona worthy of the respect and attention of the audience is the crux of the ethical appeal, the appeal that convinces because of the speaker's integrity. Obviously, as Aristotle and the other classical rhetoricians continually pointed out, the best way to *seem* like a person of integrity and competence is to *be* a person of integrity and competence. So be yourself; don't try to fake a pose that is not really you. Yet remember that there are many poses which you can assume with no dishonesty or pretension. You can be a calm and rational advocate of capital punishment, an impassioned supporter of the Campus Crusade for Christ, or a detached and amused observer of the latest dress fad. Remember too that you cannot actually *prove* you are honest; the best you can do is to be straightforward and to depend on the good will of your audience. You can, however, demonstrate competence by having the evidence you need to support your arguments and by showing familiarity with your topic.

The Damaging Effects of Carelessness

Insufficient evidence

The writer who has obviously not taken the trouble to do his homework on an issue sacrifices the respect of his audience. Other kinds of carelessness can also seriously damage the image you want to present.

Mechanical errors

Suppose, for instance, that you are applying for a scholarship. You can demonstrate your financial need, show that you are both bright and ambitious, and produce excellent letters of recommendation. You put a lot of thought into the letter of application, but you do not take the time to check the spelling of Optimist Club; so you address the letter to the President of the Jonesville Optomist Club. You will make a bad impression even before the envelope is opened. In the body of the letter, you use "except" when you mean "accept"; you speak of your ambition to be a veterinarian, but spell it as most people pronounce it, "vetinarian"; when you mention a college's fine reputation, you write "it's" instead of "its"; you conclude the letter by saying, "I appreciate your consideration irregardless of your decision."

This letter may well ruin your chance of getting a scholarship because, without your being aware of it, you have established a persona quite different from the one you intended. By careless spelling and grammar you have created the image of someone who is too lazy to look up words and too sloppy to check his letter for errors. You have characterized yourself just as surely as you would by appearing for a formal interview with mud on your shoes, a button off your shirt, and grease stains on your coat. You may be an admirable person in spite of your dirty clothes and a promising student in spite of your bad spelling and faulty diction; but, if you start off by establishing an image that annoys people, you will probably never have the chance to demonstrate your real abilities.

You may protest that such criteria are ridiculous, that only small-minded and shortsighted people would base important decisions on trivial details. You have a point. Most teachers realize that many poor spellers are good thinkers and that the student whose spelling, punctuation, and sentence structure are almost perfect may be incurably shallow. Nevertheless, the people in authority who decide who will be accepted in medical school or in the foreign service, who will get scholarships or be chosen for graduate school, do make judgments on the basis of the way people write. You cannot change that. And they have so many applications from well-qualified people that the carelessly done letters will not survive the first screening.

Other elements of persona

In other kinds of writing situations, observing the mechanical niceties of the language may not be as important as adapting your vocabulary to your audience or establishing the right degree of formality or familiarity. These elements of your persona and others, such as your approach to your topic and your distance from the audience, all combine to set the tone of your rhetoric, an important matter that we will take up in detail in Chapter 5.

THE CONTENT OF THE ARGUMENT

The ingredients of rhetoric that we have been discussing so far—persuasive purpose, audience, and persona—are, in one sense, essential parts of any argument. In another sense, however, they are trimmings or, if you like, superstructure; the real substance of rhetoric is, finally, the argument itself.

This last side of the rhetorical square is too complex to explain in a few pages at the end of a chapter. In fact, the rest of this text concentrates on the analysis and evaluation of arguments, on the ways in which people seek to persuade, and on suggestions that will help you incorporate those techniques of persuasion into your own writing. Thus, the brief discussion here will be no more than general definitions and a description of the two categories into which argumentative techniques fall.

The two categories of argument: 1. logical

The simplest way to describe these categories is to label them "logical" and "nonlogical." The logical modes of argument are those that appeal to the intellect, that try to persuade by setting in motion thought processes that will culminate in the audience's reaching the desired conclusion. The chief forms of logical argument, or what Aristotle called the appeal to reason, are deduction, induction, cause and effect, definition, arguments from comparison, and the use of evidence

2. nonlogical

and testimony. The nonlogical methods most commonly used in persuasion are connotation, figurative language, tone, and diction. The classical rhetoricians classified these techniques under the appeal to emotion.

Rhetoric combines the two categories

This classification looks attractively neat, but like most pigeonholing it oversimplifies and distorts the real article. In practice, almost any rhetorical appeal combines the logical and the nonlogical; sometimes, it is nearly impossible to separate the two elements. For example, a sociologist making an inductive argument may have a respectable number of samples, but may describe them in connotative language. Is he being logical or nonlogical? A philosopher may build an impressive argument on analogy, but that analogy may be a persuasive metaphor. On close analysis we usually find that the skeleton or frame of any argument will be logical, that is, it will be built on induction, evidence, definition, or some combination of logical devices. The substance or body of the argument, however, will contain substantial amounts of nonlogical material such as figurative language or connotative adjectives. To understand and evaluate the complete argument we need to analyze the parts. We shall do that when we study the language of rhetoric and how it works.

1. Write sample thesis sentences that could serve as statements of purpose for the following writing assignments:

a. An essay on the benefits (or disadvantages) of living in a co-ed dormitory.

b. An essay for (or against) Zero Population Growth.

c. A letter persuading your parents that you should be allowed to move into an apartment.

d. A report on the results of an experiment that you have recently done in your psychology class.

e. A letter to the editor of the student newspaper complaining about study conditions in college dormitories.

f. A letter to the board of regents asking for more subsidized housing for married students.

2. State briefly what your main purposes would be in the following writing assignments:

a. A statement of personal goals to accompany your application to law school (or to a theological seminary).

b. An application for a grant from a foundation in order that you may spend part of your sophomore year in field work doing an independent study in a subject of your choice (for example, nutrition for welfare clients, conditions in a mental hospital near your home, voting patterns within the eighteen- to twenty-one-year-old age group, or racial attitudes among junior high school students in your town).

c. A letter to the dean of your college asking for reinstatement in school after you have been expelled for getting drunk and taking a midnight swim in the Memorial Fountain.

d. An application for a job as the recreation or waterfront director at a well-known and expensive summer camp.

3. In the fourth century B.C. Aristotle wrote what is probably the most famous of all rhetoric texts. In it he counseled his readers to adapt their rhetoric to the character of their audience and gave them the following guidelines to help them. What do you think of his analysis? Are his assumptions about the young and old still valid? Would you use them if you were addressing audiences in that category? What specific criticisms would you make of his generalizations?

Young men have strong desires, and whatever they desire they are prone to do. Of the bodily desires the one they let govern them most is sexual desire; here they lack self-control. . . . The young are passionate, quick to anger, and apt to give way to it. . . . Fond of honor, they are even fonder of victory, for youth likes to be superior, and winning evinces superiority. They love both honor and victory more than they care for money. Indeed, they care next to nothing about money, for they have not yet learned what the want of it means. . . . The young think no evil, but believe in human goodness, for as yet they have not seen many examples of vice. They are trustful, for as yet they have not often been deceived. . . . They are high-minded; first, because they have not yet been humbled by life, nor come to know the force of circumstances; and secondly, because high-mindedness means thinking oneself fitted for great things. In their actions they prefer honor to expediency; for their lives are rather lives of good impulse than of calculation. . . . They carry everything too far; they love to excess, they hate to excess—and so in all else. They think they know everything, and are positive about everything.[2]

Of the elderly Aristotle says,

The Old have lived long, have been often deceived, have made many mistakes of their own; they see that more often than not the affairs of men turn out badly. And so they are positive about nothing; in all things they err by an extreme moderation. . . . They think evil; that is, they are disposed to put the worse construction on everything. Further, they are suspicious because they are distrustful and distrustful from sad experience. As a result, they have no strong likings or hates. . . . They are mean-souled, because they have been humbled by life. Thus they aspire to nothing great or exalted, but crave the mere necessities and comforts of existence. And they are not generous. Property, as they know, is one of the necessities, and they have learned by experience how hard it is to acquire, how easy to lose. They are cowards, apprehensive about everything . . . the old are not characterized by passion, and their actions are governed not by impulse, but by love of gain. . . . Their lives are rather lives of calculation than of moral bias. [P. 135.]

4. Imagine that you have been asked to write articles for any three of these publications. Examine a copy of each of the three you choose; and, in a sentence of no more than twenty-five words, specify who

[2] Aristotle, *The Rhetoric of Aristotle,* trans. Lane Cooper (New York: Appleton-Century-Crofts, 1960), p. 133. Copyright © 1960 by Appleton-Century-Crofts.

your audience would be in each case and what important characteristics that audience would have.

Seventeen	*The Reader's Digest*
The New York Times	*The Christian Science Monitor*
Glamour	*U.S. News & World Report*
Playboy	*Family Circle*
Ebony	*Psychology Today*
Time	

5. What assumptions about his audience is the writer of each of the following advertisements making?

a. THE DURABLE ONE   Our car may not be the prettiest and shiniest on the market, but it's the toughest. We built it to last. And not to cost you a fortune.

We start with a simple car that doesn't have an ounce of wasted space. Then we refuse to put on any frills. Instead, we make a tight car that doesn't rattle, doesn't rust, doesn't gobble gas.

And we test every car before it leaves the factory. No lemons allowed.

If you care more about durability than you do about decor, Bulldog is the car for you.

b. BAHAMA ADVENTURE   Guided tours you don't want—they're stuffy and dull. But how about an adventure, a real ADVENTURE? A fun tour of the Bahamas with exciting nights and leisurely, sun-baked days?

Discover new people, new places, new things to do. You'll find the excitement of extraordinary places, off-the-beaten-path nightclubs and restaurants.

Only a few lucky souls find ways to put zest in their lives. You can be one of them if you join this fabulous Cruise of Adventure that only Bahamas, Unlimited, offers you.

c. MINDPOWER: YOUR KEY TO SUCCESS!   Most people drudge along in life using only a fraction of their real capacities. They feel—know—that they have potential that has never come to the surface. Buried in them somewhere is power, the power to do the things they dreamed of once. Are you one of these unhappy ones? Do you want to find the key that will release those vital forces?

Our new, scientifically based course in MINDPOWER will show you the way. By learning ten simple rules for awakening the hidden dynamics of your brain, you can throw off that inertia that has kept you from being the man you deserve to be. Write today!

6. Here are the opening paragraphs from a column called "Stuff and Thangs," which appears regularly in a farm newspaper. The column is always signed, "Ever thine, The Edditar."

> Since th' attempted assassination of Gov. George Wallace we hear again th' weepin' & wailin' and gnashin' of teeth as the fanatics start tryin' to control violence by legislation instid of law inforcment. This exercise in futility ort to be obvious to anybody, but when you get headline hunters like Senator Bayh and Teddy Kennedy tryin' to make th' front pages every day, almost any old excuse will suffice.
>
> How anyone can figger any gun law would keep a would be assasin from makin' his try is difficult for a normal person to understand. After all, assassination is carried out in international circles with more than a little success.
>
> Some of the provocateurs in print like to compare crime rates in America with other countries around th' world, and on the face of it the percentages do seem to be in favor of most other countries, but you caint blame this on the fack that most Americans have th' money to buy fire arms, and also th' guts to demand they have some protection other than bleeding heart judges and a passle of people wringin' their hands. [From *The Weekly Livestock Reporter,* May 25, 1972.]

What is the persona this writer is trying to establish? How do you know? What assumptions about his audience does that choice of persona reveal? Is he consistent? Do you find his ethical appeal convincing?

7. Clip one of the columns of a well-known journalist—for example, Russell Baker, Tom Wicker, William F. Buckley, Art Buchwald, Marianne Means, or James Reston—and tape it to a sheet of paper. Under it write a short description of the persona the writer is assuming and give some evidence to support your analysis. Keep it short, not more than 100 words in all.

8. Describe very briefly the persona you would want to adopt in each of the following rhetorical situations:
a. You are participating in Operation Outreach, a project in which stu-

dents and faculty visit high schools throughout the state to encourage members of minority groups to enroll in your college.

b. You are editor of a student newspaper, replying to a letter from an outraged alumnus that begins with this paragraph:

> The entire university swarms with hippie types. Unbathed, unshaven, barefooted, beaded, etc., hunkered around in little groups all over campus and the surrounding area like bewildered animals. One pathetic little creature in the Student Union—a girl —boldly walked up to me and asked, "Do you have an extra dollar on you?" The lethargic characters barely look as though they might in some remote way belong in the human race.

c. You are trying to borrow thirty dollars from your roommate so that you can impress your date by taking her to Trader Vic's for dinner.

SUGGESTED WRITING ASSIGNMENTS

Theme 1

Purpose: To make you aware of the importance of establishing a balanced rhetorical stance when you want to present an effective argument.

Procedure: Choose one of the topics given below. Before you begin to write, consider these points. (1) Who is your audience and what important characteristics does it have that will affect the way you present your argument? (2) What is your persona?; how do you want to appear to your audience? (3) What are the principal points of your argument?

In a separate section at the beginning of your paper, put down these labels:

AUDIENCE: _____

Relevant characteristics: _____

PERSONA: _____

Character traits: _____

CHIEF POINTS OF ARGUMENT: _____

_____

After filling in this section, drop down a few lines and begin your theme.

Topics

a. You are applying for admission to veterinary or medical school. One of the requirements is that you write a short autobiography to submit along with your college transcript and letters of recommendation. Your audience is a board of doctors, either medical or veterinary, who receive about three times as many qualified applicants as they can admit. Assume that your grades and letters of recommendation are good.

b. You would like to work next summer in some federally financed project in your field (nursing, environmental engineering, a wild life refuge, Vista, Head Start, or something similar). Such jobs are usually given by a congressman or senator, so you are writing to your representative. Compose a letter that you think would help you get the job.

c. You cannot return to school next year unless you receive a substantial scholarship. Possible sources are one of the service clubs in your home town, such as Lions, Optimists, or Rotary, one of the national foundations such as the Ford Foundation, or a church scholarship that has been set up to help deserving young people. Assume that you have a good high school record. Compose a letter that you think would help you to receive such a scholarship.

Theme 2

Purpose: To help you understand how the rhetorical components of purpose, audience, persona, and argument operate by doing an analysis of them in poetry, a genre that is not usually thought of as rhetoric.

Procedure: Take one of the two poems that follow and do a full, but reasonably concise rhetorical analysis of it. Begin by stating what you think is the role or persona that the speaker is assuming and what image of himself he wants his audience to accept. Then state what seems to you to be his persuasive purpose. In the next paragraph, describe the way in which you think the speaker views his audience and state what assumptions he is making about it. Give your reasons for thinking so. Complete your paper with an evaluation of the argument the speaker is making. Is it chiefly logical or nonlogical? Do you find the argument convincing? If so, why? If not, where did the rhetorician go wrong?

Dover Beach

The sea is calm tonight,
The tide is full, the moon lies fair
Upon the straits; —on the French coast the light

Gleams and is gone; the cliffs of England stand,
Glimmering and vast, out in the tranquil bay.
Come to the window, sweet is the night-air!
Only, from the long line of spray
Where the sea meets the moon-blanched land,
Listen! you hear the grating roar
Of pebbles which the waves draw back, and fling,
At their return, up the high strand,
Begin, and cease, and then again begin,
With tremulous cadence slow, and bring
The eternal note of sadness in.

Sophocles long ago
Heard it on the Ægæan, and it brought
Into his mind the turbid ebb and flow
Of human misery; we
Find also in the sound a thought,
Hearing it by this distant northern sea.

The Sea of Faith
Was once, too, at the full, and round earth's shore
Lay like the folds of a bright girdle furled.
But now I only hear
Its melancholy, long, withdrawing roar,
Retreating, to the breath
Of the night-wind, down the vast edges drear
And naked shingles of the world.

Ah, love, let us be true
To one another! for the world, which seems
To lie before us like a land of dreams,
So various, so beautiful, so new,
Hath really neither joy, nor love, nor light,
Nor certitude, nor peace, nor help for pain;
And we are here as on a darkling plain
Swept with confused alarms of struggle and flight,
Where ignorant armies clash by night.

Matthew Arnold, 1867

Death Be Not Proud

Death be not proud, though some have called thee
Mighty and dreadful, for, thou art not so;
For those, whom thou think'st thou dost overthrow,
Die not, poor death, nor yet canst thou kill me.

From rest and sleep, which but thy pictures be,
Much pleasure, then from thee, much more must flow,
And soonest our best men with thee do go,
Rest of their bones, and souls' delivery.

Thou art slave to fate, chance, kings, and desperate men,
And dost with poison, war, and sickness dwell,
And poppy, or charms can make us sleep as well,
And better than thy stroke; why swell'st thou then?

One short sleep past, we wake eternally,
And death shall be no more; death, thou shalt die.

John Donne, c. 1617

3

Where Rhetoric —and Stops

The first section of this book has been frankly rhetorical, an attempt to persuade you that you will benefit from the study of rhetoric—to convince you that understanding how it is used and how to use it yourself is an essential part of your education. If the rhetoric has succeeded, at this point you have developed at least a mild interest in going on to see how rhetoric works and what good it can be to you.

Before we proceed, however, we need to decide when rhetoric is relevant and when it is not and what limitations we are working under. However much we may enjoy arguing and exercising our wits, there are times when it is pointless.

Varieties of Propositions

Consider, for example, the following statements:

A. Chocolate cake is a wonderful dessert.
B. Democracy is a good form of government.
C. The Dallas Cowboys were the NFL champions in 1971.

Strictly speaking, all three are what the logicians call "propositions," that is, they are statements that can be affirmed or denied. Only one of them, however, is really arguable and, therefore, a proper topic for the exercise of rhetoric; that is the second one, "Democracy is a good form of government." It alone is a legitimate assertion: a statement of belief or judgment that can be logically supported with reasons.

Legitimate assertions

Proposition A is simply an expression of taste; the writer is saying, "I like chocolate cake." It is not debatable because there is no arguing with taste, a subjective reaction to an experience. You cannot convince a person through reasoning that he does not feel what he feels. If you like horror movies and your roommate hates them, it is fruitless to try to persuade him that he will enjoy a double bill featuring "The Blob Strikes Again" and "The Bride of the Vampire." Nor can emotional reactions be reasoned away with facts and logic. For example, a driver might try to refute his passenger's complaint that he is driving recklessly by saying that he is not exceeding the speed limit. The pattern of reasoning goes like this:

Subjective reactions

> Anyone who is not exceeding the speed limit is not driving recklessly.
>
> I am not exceeding the speed limit.
>
> Therefore, I am not driving recklessly.

55

The syllogism is perfect, *but* the major premise is a statement of personal reaction; therefore, the logic is irrelevant. (The syllogism, a logical device for deriving a conclusion from two premises, is discussed in Chapter 7.)

Similarly, it is pointless to use rhetoric to determine whether water skiing is a better sport than surfing if by "better" you mean more enjoyable. People do or do not like raw oysters; they love, hate, or are indifferent to cats; they prefer blondes to redheads and science fiction to mystery stories. It would be silly to challenge their preferences. On such matters we ought to relax and enjoy human diversity; we can agree to disagree and not waste energy on rhetoric intended to change tastes. While it is true that people's tastes sometimes do change, it is usually because of experience, not the force of someone's persuasion.

Proposition C, "The Dallas Cowboys were the NFL champions in 1971," may or may not be true, but it is not a matter of opinion or judgment. It is a matter of fact that can be verified, and all the rhetorical powers that you can summon will not alter the truth. Only small children or very foolish adults waste their breath in debating such a point. A problem arises, however, when someone makes a statement that must be either true or false, but cannot be verified. On such occasions, many people argue furiously and eloquently without realizing the futility of their rhetoric. This kind of argument often involves issues such as whether there is intelligent life on other planets or whether flying saucers really exist. Or, the argument may be about whether man has free will or whether some people have extrasensory perception. Presumably, there are definite answers to such questions, but we have no way to learn them. Therefore, although it may be entertaining to speculate about such hypothetical matters, allowing yourself to become embroiled in rhetoric about them is about as ridiculous as engaging in the old theological dispute about how many angels could dance on the head of a pin.

Preferences (margin note)

Matters of fact and unverifiable statements (margin note)

Characteristics of Assertions

Engaging in rhetoric is worthwhile only when there is a possibility of throwing new light on a topic, bringing people into closer agreement, persuading them to alter their attitudes, or getting them to take action. Discussing proposition B, "Democracy is a good form of government," offers such possibilities. So does arguing about such statements as "Journalism is a more rewarding career than advertising," "The future of farming in this country is in serious jeopardy," "The study of poetry is a waste of time," or "Every high school graduate should spend two years working or in the service before he decides whether he wants to go to college." All these declarations —and it would be easy to think up dozens of similar propositions— have elements in common. First, they are assertions, that is, judgments and/or expressions of opinion. Second, although they reveal preferences, they do more than simply express likes and dislikes; the concept of "ought" or "should" is implicit in the way they are stated. Third, they require support because as they stand they have little force. The immediate reaction of a listener, even if he is sympathetic, is, "Why do you say that? I want to hear your reasons." Because such assertions can be supported with concrete evidence and examples, fruitful discussion is possible.

Thus, assertions, statements that can and must be supported, form the basic framework of expository and rhetorical writing. You need to construct your own assertions carefully and cautiously because once you have made one you have the responsibility of supporting it. Don't, in a fit of enthusiasm or outrage, set out to prove far more than you can manage in one paper or make statements that you cannot possibly support. "Democracy is a good form of government" is a reasonable declaration, one for which you can find evidence; but "Democracy is the best form of government that the world has ever devised" is unsupportable even in a five-hundred-page book. To make a convincing argument for that sweeping generalization, you would have to compare democracy with all the other forms of government that ever existed. Only an expert would have enough information even to attempt such a comparison. You could make yourself look foolish if you tackled such a gargantuan task. Equally foolish are such extreme assertions as "People on welfare are parasites who want something for nothing" or "In these days a person without a college degree cannot hope to make a decent living or be respected in society." Both statements put a nearly impossible burden of proof on the arguer. He has claimed more than the evidence will support, and if his reader thinks of even a few exceptions to the assertion, his case is irreparably damaged. Such statements mark the rhetorician as naive or irresponsible—or both.

Judge rhetoric by
the assertions it
proves

When you are analyzing the rhetoric of others you need to be equally alert to the way in which the author's main assertions are stated. What claims does he make, and what positions does he undertake to support? If he takes on more than he can handle, he has weakened his rhetorical position from the beginning. One of the chief flaws in the arguments of extremist groups in this country has been their unbelievable assertions. Militant blacks, for example, often assert that the United States is the most racist country in the world. Anyone who is aware of the apartheid policies in the Union of South Africa knows that such a statement is a gross exaggeration. Thus, the writer immediately loses credibility with a large portion of his audience. In general, you should be skeptical of rhetoricians who load their assertions with superlatives such as "most," "best," "worst," and "greatest"; their tactics are likely to be as shaky as their claims because such statements can rarely be supported with legitimate and sensible arguments.

ASSUMPTIONS

Definition

If assertions form the framework of rhetoric, assumptions are its foundation. An assumption is the supposition that something is true, the taking-it-for-granted that a statement or belief is so obvious that there is no need to explain it or support it.

Necessary Assumptions

In discourse we all make two kinds of assumptions: first, that our audience shares with us certain knowledge and experience; second, that it shares certain values, beliefs, and attitudes. We must make such assumptions, or we could not begin to communicate; we would spend so much time laying the basis for an argument that we would never get to the main point.

Assumptions about knowledge

The first kind of assumption causes relatively few problems for anyone who is reasonably alert and sensible. We know without actually thinking about it that most of the people we have contact with share our experience of living in a complex industrial society and of having gone to public schools; that they know what Christianity is and are familiar with American history and traditions; that because they are exposed to radio, television, and the newspaper, they have some idea of what goes on in the world. We base our conversations with people on these shared experiences. If you have ever tried to make conversation with someone who speaks English but comes from a radically different culture, you know how frustrating it can be to talk with a person about whom you cannot make the ordinary assumptions. When you know very little about your audience, communication is difficult. Under such circumstances persuasion is virtually impossible.

Assumptions about values

Making assumptions about what people feel and believe is considerably more hazardous than making assumptions about what they know, yet we must do it. We can and do generalize about the values of age groups, sexes, professions, and various economic, educational, and social classes. If we think carefully and objectively about what assumptions we are warranted in making about our audience's attitudes and convictions, there is a good chance that they will at least listen to us sympathetically. If, however, we make a series of unwarranted assumptions, whatever we say is likely to fall on deaf ears.

Unwarranted Assumptions

Projecting personal values

Making faulty assumptions has many causes—carelessness, bad judgment, and laziness are a few—but the primary source of unwarranted assumptions is the common habit of attributing our own values to other people. We all have our biases, and we forget that others do not share them. Undoubtedly you have had the experience of being present when someone told a joke or story that you found offensive. If you think about it, you will realize that the reason you were offended was that the narrator made unwarranted assumptions about you. If he told a derogatory joke about blacks, Jews, or some other minority group, he assumed that you shared his prejudices; if he used obscene language, he assumed that you did not mind hearing it; if he told unsavory anecdotes about friends or public figures, he assumed that you shared his taste for ugly gossip. And as a result of his bad assumptions, you have probably avoided future conversation with him whenever possible.

Although your decency or good manners would probably keep you from making that particular kind of mistake, you might unwittingly make other unwarranted assumptions less insulting but almost as damaging to your rhetoric. For instance, a man might argue quite forcefully that it is not worthwhile for most married women to hold down jobs; because of the added money spent for clothes, the cost of transportation, the higher expense for lunches and eating out frequently, and the elevation into a higher tax bracket, the average woman's net profit is so small that it is pointless for her to work. The person who reasons along these lines reveals his assumptions that women's only reason for working is to make money and that they do not take pride in their work or get a sense of accomplishment from it in the same way that men do.

Making hasty judgments: about people

Our assumptions can also lead us to make hasty judgments about other people. As the psychiatrist Robert Coles points out, "The assumptions we make about a person's social and political behavior have to do with the kinds of lives we ourselves live." Thus, the person who remarks that it is a pity that a woman of thirty-five isn't married reveals his assumption that all women need a husband; the individual who labels people who criticize the government as "malcontents," "un-American," or "antisocial" reveals his assumption that all "normal" people endorse the status quo.

about problems

The way we view certain problems is also controlled by our assumptions. You have probably heard the argument that we are unduly alarmed about air and water pollution or about the depletion of our natural resources; by the time the lakes are stagnant, we will have found a way to purify them. A similar claim is that if our energy sources run out, we will find new ones. This kind of thinking is based on the assumption that there are technological solutions to every problem. A closely related assumption is the common belief that spending more money will alleviate our social ills: poor education, slums and ghettos, lack of adequate medical care, and juvenile crime.

Recognizing unwarranted assumptions

The tricky thing about these kinds of assumptions is not that they are necessarily wrong—some of them may prove to be sound—but that so often we are not aware that we are making them. We do not see the basis of our arguments because our opinions are so entrenched that we cannot see our own line of reasoning. Nevertheless, anyone who constructs an argument without thinking about his assumptions is building everything on a foundation that could cave in under him. Your opponent may say, "Ah ha! You assume that if you spend enough money, you can teach children to read; but they tried that in Chicago two years ago and it didn't work." If, however, you realize that this is your major assumption, either you might have the wisdom not to try to base your argument on it, or you might anticipate the objection ahead of time and be prepared to meet it. There is nothing wrong with making assumptions; they are indispensable to rhetoric, exposition, and all forms of logic. What is necessary is that you recognize and evaluate both your own and those of other people.

A PRIORI PREMISES

Many arguments, especially deductive arguments, as we shall see in Chapter 7, are based on a special kind of assumption that is even more deeply rooted in the emotions and intuition than are the common beliefs and attitudes that we were talking about in the last section. We call these particular kinds of assumptions a priori premises; the term "a priori" means "based on a hypothesis or theory rather than on experiment or experience; made before or without examination; not supported by factual study."[1] Now obviously we cannot always make clear distinctions between a common assumption such as "All poor people are Democrats" and an a priori premise such as "Slavery is wrong"; the two categories are going to overlap and merge into each other occasionally. In general, however, we can say that a priori

Definition

premises are beliefs that are so deeply and fervently held that for the people who subscribe to them they have the force of facts, immutable truths. A priori premises do not need proof; in fact, by their very nature they *cannot* be proved. A person cannot marshal evidence to demonstrate an a priori premise in the same way that he could gather data to prove that the speed of light is 186,000 miles per second or that the world is round.

One of the most famous a priori statements comes in the introduction to our Declaration of Independence: "We hold these truths to be self-evident: that all men are created equal, that they are endowed by their Creator with certain unalienable rights, that among these are Life, Liberty, and the Pursuit of Happiness." The key word here is "self-evident"; the term suggests that the authors are positive that everyone agrees with their premises. But are these universal and eternal

[1] *The American Heritage Dictionary of the English Language,* s.v. "a priori."

truths? A Japanese or Indian who has been raised in a caste society might claim that it is self-evident to him that all men are *not* created equal, and that God ordained that there should be the high and the low. Proponents of totalitarian governments could claim that no one has inalienable rights that may not be taken away from him by some power, and that the idea that everyone is entitled to pursue his happiness is nonsense. To nearly all Americans, however, the original statement stands as an article of our faith, unshaken by the most vigorous challenge. We cannot *prove* our belief is true, nor can anyone else *prove* it is false.

They often concern
human nature

A surprising number of a priori premises are statements about the nature of man. Romanticists such as Rousseau, Emerson, and Thoreau held that man is naturally good; the Calvinists held that he is naturally sinful. Each side based its entire philosophical system on its premise, which is unproved and unprovable. In modern times, one school of psychology and anthropology argues that man is naturally aggressive and acquisitive; another argues that he is basically peaceful and cooperative. Each side can cite historical evidence to support its theory, but neither side can prove the other is wrong. Among the oldest of our a priori premises are those concerning the nature of woman. For centuries, theologians and psychologists have been saying that there are basic and crucial differences in the personalities of men and women and confidently assuming that different activities and traits are "natural" to each sex. Now, people like Betty Friedan, Germaine Greer, and Gloria Steinem are challenging these long held beliefs by claiming that what is thought of as the "feminine nature" is entirely the product of cultural influences and expectations, not "natural" at all. They argue cogently, but it is unlikely that they will convince their opponents.

They are the foundation
of moral discussion

A priori premises about right and wrong, about good and bad, are the foundation of all moral discussion. If you hold that killing is wrong, you assume a priori that life is valuable and /or sacred. When you condemn discrimination and injustice, you are basing your argument on the belief that everyone should have equal rights. If you oppose wiretapping under any circumstances, you hold that privacy is an absolute right. Arguments against lying, cheating, and stealing come from the conviction that honesty is a basic good; those against violence and brutality come from the belief that hurting others is evil. Such ethical attitudes are so strongly rooted in us that we forget that they cannot be proved or tested without falling back on other convictions that are also held a priori. Our not being able to prove them, however, need not in any way detract from their significance for the believers. Any person has the right to say that because of training, experience, and intuition, he holds certain convictions, that they are true for him, and that he will act on them. Such an attitude is and must be the basis of morality.

Not everyone shares the same premises

Difficult as it may be for us to realize, not everyone shares our a priori premises about what is right and wrong. Suppose, for example, that you find yourself in a discussion with a person who insists that our political system is a failure and that we must make radical changes in it if we are to give the common people their rights. You ask him what kind of changes he has in mind. He replies that no reactionary group should be allowed to buy political advertising in the press or on television, and that anyone who makes derogatory remarks about a minority group should be put in jail. Shocked, you point out to him that such laws would violate the Bill of Rights. His reply is that such violations do not matter; certain constitutional freedoms must be sacrificed in order to attain the goals of his movement. At that point, you might as well quit talking. Your basic premises are so different that fruitful discussion is impossible.

The point to keep in mind is that the wise rhetorician recognizes when he and his opponents have irreconcilable a priori premises and says simply, "We cannot have a productive discussion because we have no basis from which to start." Too many arguments proceed in parallel lines because both opponents are so busy expounding their views that they have not stopped to articulate their primary assumptions. If they did, they would find that agreement is impossible. A person who believes that men are naturally peaceful and cooperative is wasting his time to argue for disarmament with someone who thinks that men are basically aggressive and acquisitive. If you are a sensualist, a person who holds that physical pleasure is the chief good, you would be naive to discuss the good life with one who believes that people get the most out of life by developing the powers of the intellect. When you find yourself at an impasse in a discussion, you should stop and examine the a priori premises that you are bringing to it. If upon reflection you find them sound but radically different from your opponent's, you might as well desist and start talking about the latest movie you've seen.

1. Which of these statements are legitimate assertions? Give your reasons for rejecting those that you do not find arguable.
a. Helen of Troy was the most beautiful woman the world has ever known.
b. Football is my favorite game.
c. Honesty is a good policy.
d. Mt. Everest is the highest mountain in the world.
e. Fifty percent of teen-age marriages end in divorce within five years.
f. Chocolate ice cream is better than strawberry ice cream.
g. The Washington Redskins will win the Eastern division championship this year.
h. All women drivers are bad drivers.
i. Women drivers have a greater number of accidents than men drivers.
j. All women drivers should take a course in defensive driving.
k. The love of money is the root of all evil.
l. Power tends to corrupt.

2. Rephrase the following assertions into statements that you could support in a paper of about 1,000 words.
a. In another ten years fraternities will cease to exist on this campus.
b. Multiple choice tests are the worst kind of examination.
c. A woman cannot be elected president of the United States.
d. Violence on television is corrupting the young people of this country.
e. Dope addiction is the cause of the growing crime rate in our cities.
f. Nowadays there just isn't any good old-fashioned home cooking.

3. What assumptions underlie the following statements? Do they seem warranted?
a. We should stop spending billions on defense so that we can clean up the environment, build hospitals, and eradicate the slums and traffic congestion that plague our cities.
b. Oh, you're an English teacher. I'll have to watch my grammar.
c. Joe and Harriet must be getting a divorce. Yesterday I saw her having lunch with George Williams.
d. With the kind of grades Stanley gets, he'll never amount to much.
e. Of course, you'll prefer this painting. It's an original.
f. Vivian is thirty-five and starting back to college. It's certainly going to be hard for her to keep up with those young kids.

g. Those doctors in public health can't be very good or they'd be out in private practice where the real money is.

h. Well, Jack's nervous breakdown doesn't surprise me. He has such a high IQ.

i. I know Jane is awfully bright, but I still think she's making a terrible mistake by going into engineering.

4. It is both useful and enlightening to examine one's own assumptions from time to time. After mulling it over and perhaps talking with some friends, jot down the assumptions that you find you have on one or two of these topics. Try to be candid. What effect do these assumptions have on your thinking?

Topics

a. The relationship of money to success

b. The relationship of money to happiness

c. The relationship of money to political opinion

d. The relationship of intelligence to success

e. The relationship of intelligence to physical attractiveness

5. What are the a priori premises that underlie these statements?

a. What's good is what you feel good after.

b. If people cease to believe in God, there will be a collapse of morality in this country.

c. Under a system of socialized medicine, doctors would lose their incentive to practice.

d. An administration that has permitted twenty million people in this country to live in poverty does not deserve another four years in office.

e. If the voters have all the facts, they will invariably choose the best man.

f. With his upbringing, Charles was bound to get in trouble sooner or later.

g. Government sponsorship of birth control clinics is an unwarranted interference in the lives of private citizens.

h. If we established a guaranteed annual income in this country, millions of people would just quit working.

i. Don't make a thief out of this young man. Lock your car!

j. A person who would plagiarize his Master's thesis should not be allowed to teach in this school.

6. Decide what a priori belief you hold on one of the issues given below; then, write a paragraph of about 100 words that is developed from your premise. Write your premise at the top of the page before you begin.
a. Strict proctoring versus the honor system for final exams
b. Tight discipline versus a relaxed attitude in raising children
c. Ability versus luck as the determining factor in getting a job

SUGGESTED
WRITING
ASSIGNMENT

Purpose: To make you aware of your own a priori premises and how they control the stands you take on controversial issues.

Procedure: Pick one of the topics listed below, preferably one on which you have strong opinions, and write a short paper in which you argue for one side of the issue. Before you begin to write think carefully about what belief or beliefs you hold a priori that determine the thrust and focus of your argument. Write those beliefs in a separate section at the beginning of your paper, and refer to them for guidance as you build your rhetorical appeal. Remember that your a priori premises will almost certainly be statements about the nature of people or moral pronouncements about right and wrong, for example, "People are basically selfish" or "People are basically altruistic"; "The government should ensure adequate food, clothing, and shelter for everyone" or "Government handouts damage character."

Suppose you had to write about a proposal to furnish free contraceptives to anyone who applied to a public health center. Your first reaction might be one of revulsion and outrage. All right, stop and ask yourself why you feel that way. First, you probably believe that birth control should be a private, not public concern; second, that illicit sexual activity should not be encouraged, especially by the government; third, that giving things away free hurts business. If, however, you take the other side of the issue, your a priori premises would probably look something like this: first, no unwanted children should be brought into the world; second, that control of pregnancy should not depend on the ability to pay. There could also be others.

Apply this process to one of these topics:
a. We [should, should not] have free, tax-supported hospitals just as we have free, tax-supported schools.

b. All pornography [should, should not] be banned.
c. Dress and grooming codes [should, should not] be abolished in high schools.
d. Unwed mothers [should, should not] receive government subsidies.

Your controlling thesis sentence for such a theme could take this form: __(statement of a priori premise)__ ; therefore, __(conclusion)__ .

4

Controlling the Explanatory Power of Words

A convenient way to begin talking about the vocabulary we use in rhetoric is to distinguish between abstract and concrete words. Abstract words are those that describe ideas, qualities, attitudes, and characteristics. They refer to concepts that we know only intellectually, not through any of our senses. The term "loyalty" is abstract; so are "love," "tolerance," "misery," "dissatisfaction," "philosophy," and any other word that stands for something we cannot see or experience. Concrete words, on the other hand, refer to objects, living things, and activities that we know through our senses. "Swimming" and "running" are concrete terms; so are "kitten," "girl," and "tree," or, "shiny," "rough," "blue," "pink," and other image-producing words. In general, we *perceive* the concrete through our senses; we *conceive* the abstract through our minds.

Definitions like these are useful, but they are also oversimplified. We cannot just call a word "abstract" or "concrete" and be finished with it; we must also recognize degrees and levels within each category. For example, "house" is a concrete term, but it is much less concrete than "two-story red-brick Colonial home"; "illness" is a concrete word, but it is not as concrete as "typhoid fever" or "pneumonia." "Philosophy" is more abstract than "existentialism," and "literature" is more abstract than "poetry" or "drama." In his book *Language in Thought and Action,* the semanticist S. I. Hayakawa illustrates the concept of word levels by setting up a ladder of abstraction with steps moving from the most concrete to the least concrete and simultaneously from the least general to the most general. Such a ladder looks like this:

The concrete and the abstract overlap

6. ethical philosophies
5. religion
4. Christianity
3. Protestantism
2. the Baptist Church
1. the First Baptist Church of Canton, Ohio

Using Abstract Words

Despite the repeated advice to writers to "Be concrete" and "Try to be more specific," obviously we must often use abstract language if we are to talk about anything weightier than the weather or the price of groceries. To discuss values, beliefs, and theories, we have to employ conceptual language. Thus, sentences like "An unshakable

Abstract words express values, beliefs, and theories

69

belief that private enterprise leads to the exploitation of the working class is fundamental to Marxist theory" and "Most aesthetic theories stress that form and structure are necessary to any art form" are necessary kinds of statements. Furthermore, it is broadly true that the more knowledge we have and the more complex our thinking becomes, the more we have to depend on abstract words to express ourselves. We must expect, therefore, that much of our communication about ideas will use words taken from the upper levels of the abstraction ladder.

Using Concrete Words

Concrete words

Help hold readers' attention

Give substance to generalities

Give examples of the abstract

The problem is, however, that a distressing number of writers, both amateur and professional, come to equate abstract language with erudition and high rhetorical purpose. They forget that to hold their readers' attention they must work through the senses as well as the intellect; that they must give their generalities substance by reinforcing them with examples and that they must make their abstractions concrete by appealing to the senses. In the following passage, the poet and critic John Ciardi illustrates how effectively a writer can communicate an abstract concept if he supports it with a vivid concrete example.

> It is certain that man has put an enormous amount of his psychic energy into shaping language, and that language has, in turn, powerfully affected his behavior. In most primitive languages, for example, . . . the same word does for both "stranger" and "enemy." If I have separate words for these two ideas, I can look at an unknown person without an alarm signal. If I have one for them, I will be less ready to let the man pass unmolested. I am already in Oedipus' chariot en route to Thebes and half-cocked to kill my unknown father when his chariot blocks mine on the road. The language my fathers made, made me my father's killer.[1]

On the other hand, this paragraph from a book by a well-known contemporary psychologist demonstrates the shortcomings of writing that is completely abstract.

> Attacking controlling practices is, of course, a form of countercontrol. It may have immeasurable benefits if better controlling practices are thereby selected. But the literatures of freedom and

[1] John Ciardi, "Tongues," *World,* February 27, 1973, p. 6.

dignity have made the mistake of supposing that they are suppressing control rather than correcting it. The reciprocal control through which a culture evolves is then disturbed. To refuse to exercise available control because in some sense all control is wrong is to withhold possible important forms of countercontrol. We have seen some of the consequences. Punitive measures, which the literature of freedom and dignity have otherwise helped to eliminate, are instead promoted. A preference for methods which make control inconspicuous or allow it to be disguised has condemned those who are in a position to exert constructive countercontrol to the use of weak measures.[2]

The paragraph is by no means incomprehensible to an intelligent reader who is willing to work at it, but it is difficult and dull, primarily because there are no concrete examples in it. As you read it, your mind wanders because nothing in the passage appeals to the senses or calls up an image. Writing like this is not merely dull, it is literally lifeless. Except indirectly, by the references to "the literatures of freedom and dignity," there is no indication that the author is talking about people. A reader who runs across this passage out of its context, as here, and who is unfamiliar with the author's theories on human behavior might conclude that his comments on controls and countercontrols refer to machinery. Notice too that the passage does not contain an example that would clarify what is meant by "control" and "countercontrol."

Concrete words: help avoid lifeless writing

Help achieve plain writing

Fortunately, student writing seldom reaches an extreme level of impersonality and dryness. Too many students, however, succumb to the notion that college writing should use stiff, abstract language. Thus, in their effort to be formal and rise to new expectations, they produce sentences like these:

It is required that regular school attendance be observed by everyone.

Compulsory school attendance is a general law that is nationally observed.

The concept of compulsory school attendance is accepted throughout the educational system.

Grammatically, the sentences are acceptable; rhetorically, they are a flop. They are lifeless; they bring to mind no images, not even a

[2] B. F. Skinner, *Beyond Freedom and Dignity* (New York: Alfred A. Knopf, Inc., 1971), p. 181.

school. Moreover, there is no point in their being written so abstractly since the idea expressed in them is not complex or difficult. To say, "In most states everyone has to go to school until he is seventeen" would do the job simply and effectively.

The sample sentences above illustrate an additional problem that writers create for themselves when they depend too heavily on abstract words. By choosing abstractions as the subjects of their sentences, the authors have sharply limited the kinds of verbs they may combine with them. Abstractions such as "attendance" and "concept" cannot, logically, *do* anything; to follow them, therefore, a writer almost instinctively chooses a form of "to be," or some other comparably weak verb. Although you can sometimes overcome this tendency if you use imagination (for example, "loyalty" may "demand" and "tyranny" may "crush"), avoid boxing yourself in in the first place; choose a concrete subject and an active verb. Notice how much difference such choices can make.

Abstract   Publication is the prerequisite of promotion at this university.

Concrete   At this university only the professor who publishes earns a promotion.

Abstract   Treason is a crime for which there is no sympathy.

Concrete   The traitor forfeits all sympathy from his fellow countrymen.

Abstract   The discrepancy between the American dream and the American experience is the central theme of American literature.

Concrete   For two centuries the American writer has dramatized the discrepancy between the American dream and the American experience.

Concrete sentence subjects help avoid weak verbs

Combining the Abstract and the Concrete

Nearly all writing requires that we discuss abstract ideas: they form the basis of expository prose. A good way to cope with the problem of combining the abstract and the concrete is to end the prewriting process by roughing out an outline in which you use abstract statements to express the main points and concrete supporting details to express the subdivisions. Suppose that you are going to write a paper to argue that your college should give full scholarships to students

Outline with abstract main points and concrete subdivisions

who excel in the sciences as well as those who excel in athletics. Your main points will be value statements that you must express in abstract terms; your supporting evidence, however, should be concrete, vivid, and personal. An outline for your paper might be:

I. The present practice discriminates among students on the basis of physical ability and sex.
    A. Thousands of high school athletes receive full scholarships.
    B. No women athletes receive scholarships.
    C. Bright science students must compete for only a few National Science Foundation grants, grants often quite small.
    D. College athletes get extras: tutoring, fraternity dues, summer jobs.
II. Present practice discourages scholastic achievement among high school students.
    A. High school athlete works hard to develop talents because rewards are substantial.
    B. Science students have little incentive to spend extra hours and effort on developing abilities because there is no tangible reward.
    C. Scholarships reinforce high school value system: worship of athletes, indifference to studies.
III. Over a long period of time the present practices will prove short-sighted.
    A. Subsidized college athletes usually become professional football players. Earning years are relatively short; contribution to society relatively minor.
    B. Subsidized students in science would become doctors, biologists, research scientists, or teachers. Earning years long; contributions to society potentially great.

When you have an outline like this, you are not likely to write a theme that is simply a collection of generalities. Moreover, in the process of writing, you will probably think of actual incidents that illustrate your points and thus can add a personal note to the paper.

Writers who contribute to the better popular magazines—*Harper's* and *The Atlantic Monthly,* for example—seem to know instinctively that they must reinforce the abstract with the concrete. Certainly no one requires you to produce writing of the caliber found in those periodicals or in the anthology your teacher may have assigned to accompany this text, but you can learn from analyzing it. Look at these samples:

[John is the] prototype of the bigot. . . . I first met him when he was protesting the archbishop's decision to admit some children who were Negro but also Catholic to the parochial schools of New Orleans. . . . Up and down he walked, picketing, tall, husky from the rear, an incipient paunch in front. He wore a brown suit, slightly frayed at the cuffs, and on its right shoulder rested his sign, wrought and lettered by himself: "Fight Integration. Communists Want Negroes With Whites." . . .

He is a passionate segregationist. . . . He has plans. He would like to exile most Negroes to Africa, perhaps sterilize a few quiet ones who would work at certain jobs befitting their animal nature, itself the work of God, he would emphasize. He would strip Jews of their fearful power, sending them off also, but to Russia, where they came from and yearn to return.[3]

As if through a one-way mirror, the urban poor watch the outside world speed by in expensive automobiles. They see steel and glass skyscrapers of affluent America rise from the slums where they used to live. Television reminds them all day long that most opportunity is barred to them. They see out from the slums, but few see in. The first generation to suffer poverty in the midst of plenty, they are the first to be stigmatized by poverty.[4]

Although neither Coles nor Clark is a professional writer—Coles is a psychiatrist and Clark, a lawyer—each has the gift of making his audience *see*. It is an invaluable asset in any writer.

To summarize: in order to make your writing as clear and forceful as possible, keep in mind these three guidelines.

Three guidelines for using abstract and concrete words

1. Use abstract language to express ideas, but whenever possible reinforce and clarify it with concrete and specific examples.
2. Try to avoid using abstractions as sentence subjects, particularly those overworked words "aspect," "factor," "element," and "concept."
3. Keep in mind that excellent advice that Hayakawa gives in his book: "The interesting writer, the informative speaker, the accurate thinker, and the sane individual operate on all levels of the abstraction ladder, moving quickly and gracefully and in orderly fashion from higher to lower, from lower to higher, with minds as lithe and deft and beautiful as monkeys in a tree."

[3] Robert Coles, *Children of Crisis: A Study of Fear and Courage* (Boston: Little, Brown and Company, 1967), p. 300.
[4] Ramsey Clark, *Crime in America* (New York: Simon and Schuster, 1970), pp. 56, 57.

"... to have and to hold in counterproductive as well as productive time frames, so long as you are bilaterally capable of maintaining a viable life-style. ..."

JARGON

Definition

Jargon is a style of writing characterized by wordiness, a preponderance of abstract terms, excessive and irresponsible use of the passive voice, euphemisms, weak verbs, pretentious diction, and clichés, excessive caution, and the absence of strong words and statements. A piece of writing does not have to have all of these qualities to be labeled as jargon. Even a few jargon phrases, if overused, can turn decent prose into gobbledygook. Writing that is weighted down with jargon is, at its best, dull and confusing. At its worst, it is pretentious, evasive, and incomprehensible. Any level of jargon is a nuisance to the reader, who must unwrap a cocoon of verbiage to extract the meaning. Take, for example, this paragraph from a student theme on *Brave New World*:

> Through sex, pleasure achieves its maximum capabilities. Without reproduction, man would fail to exist. Reproduction is creation and creation is reproduction. Man is the instrument of reproduction and what man reproduces determines what man is. In creating attitudes about sex, man also creates attitudes about himself. The

attitude man takes toward sex takes a part in determining how much man cares about himself. Sex can teach man to care about existence. However, when other values are added to sex, then sex can be used to control desire and ambition. . . . If a man wants to remain free, then he must retain his desires and ambitions. If we use sex to care about life, then we are able to keep desire and ambition as qualities of life.

My guess is that the writer is trying to say that if we, like the people in *Brave New World*, come to consider sex only as entertainment, we shall lose our other moral values. If that guess is correct, he could have made the point in one simple sentence. The point is lost, partially because by the time the reader has waded through ten sentences consisting almost entirely of abstractions, clichés, repetitions, and lofty sentiments, he is too irritated to care much about the main idea.

Although the quoted paragraph represents, in my opinion, the worst kind of writing, the author has committed none of what the average student thinks of as mistakes in composition. There are no spelling, punctuation, or grammar errors; the predication error, "pleasure achieves capabilities," is a lapse, but a sophisticated one. Subjects and verbs agree, the sentences are properly constructed, words are used correctly, and on the surface at least, the writer seems to have no trouble expressing himself. The organization is poor, but all the sentences do, more or less, focus on sex, reproduction, and morality. Yet the paragraph is a disaster because it is a collection of glib and meaningless generalities and of statements so obvious they are not worth putting on paper—for example, "Reproduction is creation and creation is reproduction." Other statements look as if they are saying something but are actually incomprehensible, for example, "However, when other values are added to sex, then sex can be used to control desire and ambition." There is not a concrete word in the paragraph and not a single example to illustrate any of the concepts.

Jargon may be mistake free

Causes of Jargon

The student who wrote this theme, and several others like it, was a bright young man who liked to write and thought that the papers he was doing were not just acceptable, but really quite good. He wanted to write well, as nearly all students do. Why, then, did he write so badly? The answer has to be that he learned to write in jargon, generalities, and clichés, not because he was told to write that way, but because he got away with doing so. Earlier rewards may have caused him to make a series of assumptions about what constituted good writing, assumptions that were no longer valid.

The first such assumption is that the grade on a composition will vary in direct proportion to the length; if two pages merit a *C*, then four pages will bring an *A*. A corollary to this assumption says that the best students are those who have the most to say. If you apply this standard to writing themes, the natural result is that the ambitious student will pad his writing rather than make it concise. The common practice of requiring a minimum number of words in a theme may reinforce the idea that quantity means quality.

False assumption: quantity equals quality

The second assumption is that the grade on a paper will be based more on mechanics than content. If the paper that is the longest, is the most neatly written, and has the fewest red marks on it gets the best grade, the assumption is reinforced.

False assumption: perfect mechanics equals quality

© 1970 United Feature Syndicate, Inc.

False assumption:
complex words and
sentences equal
quality
Third, a student often assumes that big words are inherently better than little ones and that long sentences, especially if they are complex, are better than short sentences. Some of the rhetoric to which he has been exposed—debates, assembly speeches, and graduation addresses—may have given him the impression that a large vocabulary and formal style are always marks of intelligence. It is only natural for him to imitate what has been put before him as a model. The result, unfortunately, may be the kind of writing found in these sentences from some student themes.

I advocate that the whole of the residents recognize that they are existing as a single, unified community, and therefore become conscious of the entailing obligations and responsibilities that this sort of existence demands.

I feel that lowering the drinking age to eighteen would increase imbibage and satisfy none of the need for social jurisprudence.

The authors take opposite sides on the validity of the attitudes.

One of the earliest problems is the restriction placed on him regarding the standards set by dress codes. As a child, he was exposed to the enforcement of dress codes throughout his life by his parents, but since he is beginning his career as a high school student, he wants to discontinue any authority placed over him as a child.

The opinion of society sets its restrictions on abortion and forbids the divergence of opinion on the part of its individuals.

Passive verbs
contribute to jargon
Some students have also unconsciously developed a pompous style because they overload their sentences with passive verbs. This habit probably stems from three common assumptions: first, passive verbs sound more dignified and scholarly than active ones (they also take up more space); second, a writer must avoid at all costs using "I" in a paper; third, a passive verb is safer than an active one. The writer who chooses his verbs on the basis of these assumptions increases his chances of writing jargon.

False assumption:
passive verbs sound
dignified
The following example from a student theme illustrates some of the hazards of using passive verbs in order to sound dignified.

An agreement *is* also *felt* by the two dictators that people *can be made* happy if their frustrations *are stopped*. This happiness *is brought about* by the leaders. The people *are told* that sin *will be allowed* and they *are conditioned* not to feel guilty.

Although one can understand the passage, it is tedious and dull. None of the subjects acts; all are acted upon. The writing has no force, no vigor, no motion. Notice the improvement if we substitute active verbs.

> Both dictators agree that people will be happy if they have no frustrations. The leaders promote this happiness by allowing sin and eliminating guilt.

The second version is shorter, clearer, and more vigorous.

False assumption: passive verbs are needed to avoid "I"

The fear of injecting an occasional "I" into a paper may produce sentences like these.

> This experience *was obtained* by me two years ago.

> My situation *is felt* to be one of hopelessness.

> Training *will be given* me in various kinds of work.

All of these sentences are needlessly wordy and indirect. Moreover, the writer who slips into the habit of using abstract subjects in order to avoid using "I" is likely to repeat the pattern in his other sentences. For example,

> Patriotism *is brought* into question when the issue of amnesty *is raised.*

> Emotional behavior *is perceived* by society to be unstable.

Both sentences are drab and stiff.

False assumption: passive verbs make statements "safe"

A cautious student, reluctant to commit himself to a firm, direct statement on an issue, may instinctively use the passive verb form for protection. If he writes, "Marijuana is not considered habit-forming," or "IQ tests are thought to be an inadequate measure of real intelligence," he feels that he has not really endorsed what might turn out to be a controversial position. He has, however, run the risk of exasperating the alert reader who wants to know what grounds he has for making such statements. The passive voice also appeals to the lazy writer, who doesn't want to make the effort to verify his source. Writing "Claims have been made" or "Objections are being raised" is easier than taking the time to find out who claims and who objects, but a paper based on such evasive statements will be a weak one.

There is nothing wrong, of course, in using the passive construction when you do not know who the actor is or when his identity is irrelevant. "Senator Stennis was chosen to head the committee" or "Charles Jones was awarded the Medal of Honor" are good sentences that no one could reasonably criticize. Nevertheless, your writing will be stronger if you name the agent that is acting whenever possible.

Students are understandably anxious to avoid penalties for expressing what may be an unpopular or erroneous opinion. In their experience, the right answer brings rewards and the wrong one brings reprimands. Because it is hard to be completely sure that their statements are right, they try to protect themselves by hedging. In addition to using passive verbs, they weaken their writing with timid qualifiers like "It is somewhat the case that," "The author rather tends to," or "It might be said that." Phrases like these weaken your writing but do not relieve you of taking the responsibility for your statements. The ultimate form of self-protection is to fall back on some safe platitude, for example: "Man will always have anxieties and trials in his everyday affairs, and when man can challenge these trials and anxieties he is striving for the complete happiness which can only come by overcoming troublesome obstacles as he goes through life." Sentences like this make the reader wonder whether the writer is really as naive as he seems, or just cynically abiding by what he thinks are the rules of the game.

Platitudes and unneeded qualifiers contribute to jargon

In college, the goals of clarity, conciseness, simplicity, and straight thinking are more important than ever; no points are awarded for quantity, generalizations, or mere correctness. The college teacher assumes that most students know the rules of grammar and are ready to move on. Now, in order to write clear and cogent themes, term papers, and essay exams, they must concentrate on what they say and how they say it. Thus, the student finds new rules, new expectations, and the war against jargon.

How to Avoid Jargon in Your Writing

To eliminate jargon from your writing completely would be as difficult as always staying on a diet or never wasting time when you study. All of us lapse occasionally; we get careless or lazy or in a hurry and let phrases slip into our writing that we know we should revise or eliminate. So don't expect perfection of yourself or get discouraged because clichés and euphemisms keep popping into your mind as you write. Just keep crossing out the jargon and gradually your writing will become clearer and stronger.

Many jargon problems will disappear if you observe the general rules for improving your writing: try to be concrete and specific; use active verbs whenever possible; remember that writing simply is a virtue, not a defect; be as brief as you can be and still cover your topic adequately. Additional, more specific guidelines to keep in mind are these:

Six guidelines for avoiding jargon

1. Be wary of overloading your writing with abstractions; you will need some, of course, but they should be reinforced and clarified with concrete language.
2. Whenever you use the passive voice, ask yourself if it conceals the agent that is acting, slows down the sentence, or makes the sentence stiff and flat. If it does, replace it with an active verb.
3. Use straightforward (though not vulgar) diction instead of genteel expressions or euphemisms. "Under the influence of alcohol" instead of "drunk," "relieved of his position" instead of "fired," or "passed away" instead of "died" weaken your writing and irritate your reader.
4. Try to find simple substitutes for pretentious words. "Student" is better than "scholastic" and "building" is better than "edifice." There is seldom a real need for foreign words and phrases such as *vis-à-vis* or *Zeitgeist,* and business terms like "finalize" and "maximize" are not appropriate for most writing.
5. Avoid inflated expressions such as "at this point in time" instead of "now," or "it is not without a certain amount of hesitation that" instead of "I hesitate." Plain prepositions are better than stretched-out phrases; for example, use "about" instead of "in regard to" or "on the subject of."
6. Keep in mind the distinction between using needless qualifiers and making sensible reservations. Phrases such as "most students" or "many people" and words such as "often," "usually," and "frequently" put limits on what otherwise would be sweeping generalizations. "Somewhat," "to a great extent," "rather," and "to a certain degree" are phrases that usually hedge rather than clarify.

Coping with Jargon in Your Reading

Winning the war on jargon is made more difficult by the fact that students are going to encounter jargon and other forms of cumbersome, flabby writing in essays, magazines, and textbooks. What is a student to think of this paragraph by socialist Herbert Marcuse?

> A comfortable, smooth, reasonable, democratic unfreedom pre-
> vails in advanced industrial civilization, a token of technical
> progress. Indeed, what could be more rational than the suppres-
> sion of individuality in the mechanization of socially necessary
> but painful performances; the concentration of individual enter-
> prises in more effective, more productive corporation; the regula-
> tion of free competition among unequally equipped economic sub-
> jects; the curtailment of prerogatives and national sovereignties
> which impede the international organization of resources. That this
> technological order also involves a political and intellectual coordi-
> nation may be a regrettable and yet promising development.[5]

Well, one reaction the reader might have is that if Marcuse wrote all
the campaign literature for the New Left, the movement would not
be likely to get many converts. The paragraph (it is by no means the
only example in the essay) is jargon. It is almost impossible to understand not because the vocabulary is difficult—it isn't—but because it
contains few concrete words and no illustrative examples. The
individual phrases sound as if they make sense; but, when you try
to pin down the meaning, without the aid of the surrounding content,
it simply eludes you.

The average freshman may not have to read Marcuse, although
the essay from which the paragraph above was taken does appear
in a freshman anthology; it is quite possible, though, that he would
have to read an article in *Psychology Today,* a fairly popular magazine.
Here is the closing paragraph from an article:

> What all this suggests is that the religious impulse, denied the
> intermediary stage of the ethical or the demand of the transcen-
> dent, collapses back into erotic-esthetic. The result is religiosity,
> which is the esthetic masquerading as the religious (thus the coun-
> terculture's religious eclecticism that borders on the ludicrous).
> It is questionable whether what Reiff calls the "remissive" stage
> of culture can ever be the basis of satisfactory existence, since
> some form of community and commitment to persons, objects
> and endeavors seems necessary. The counterculture is, one sus-
> pects, a convulsive gasp of a culture that cries out for transcen-
> dence and meaning. The impulses it represents—the desire for
> meaning and for happiness—are not to be scorned; the ways in

[5] Herbert Marcuse, *One Dimensional Man* (Boston: Beacon Press, 1964), p. 1.

which it has so far expressed itself, however, are symptoms of the dilemma, not solutions for it.[6]

This paragraph is certainly not as bad as the former; it is comprehensible and toward the end even readable. Nevertheless, it also is too abstract and sprinkled with jargon phrases such as "demand of the transcendent," "intermediary stage of the ethical," and "the esthetic masquerading as the religious."

Here is a paragraph from the writings of John Dewey, an eminent educational philosopher whose influence on American schools has been substantial.

> The successful activities of the organism, those within which environmental assistance is incorporated, react upon the environment to bring about modifications favorable to their own future. The human being has upon his hands the problem of responding to what is going on around him so that these changes will take one turn rather than another, namely, that required by its own further functioning. While backed in part by the environment, its life is anything but a peaceful exhalation of the environment. It is obliged to struggle—that is to say, to employ the direct support given by the environment in order indirectly to effect changes that would not otherwise occur. In this sense, life goes on by controlling the environment. Its activities must change the changes going on around it; they must neutralize hostile occurrences; they must transform neutral events into cooperative factors or into an efflorescence of new features.[7]

I think the paragraph means approximately this: Although we depend for our survival on the elements around us—air, water, temperature—we cannot simply exist with them passively. We must also react to the environment, for example, by sheltering ourselves against cold. We combat our environment when we build bridges or dams to neutralize its effects; we use it to our own advantage when we do such things as produce power from water, or heat from coal.

In Dewey's paragraph too, the chief communication problem is caused by abstract language. As soon as you insert explanatory examples, the passage begins to make more sense. Phrases like "react upon

---

[6] Richard King, "The Eros Cult in the Counterculture," *Psychology Today,* August 1972, p. 70.
[7] John Dewey, *On Experience, Nature, and Freedom* (Indianapolis: The Bobbs-Merrill Co., Inc., 1960), pp. 24–25.

the environment to bring about modifications favorable to their own future" and "employ the direct support given by the environment in order indirectly to effect changes" are wordy and clumsy, and "efflorescence of new features" instead of "advantages" is pretentious. The effect of the entire paragraph is to make the eyes glaze and the mind go numb.

To say that writers like Marcuse and Dewey can get away with jargon but that you should not use it may suggest we require more from amateur writers than we do from professionals; that we have in fact a double standard. This is not so. Those philosophers and other major thinkers who write jargon do not really get away with bad writing; rather, their ideas, if they survive, survive in spite of it. Who knows how many thinkers have ruined their chances to be understood because they let their ideas be smothered by abstract, skull-cracking prose?

However maddening this kind of jargon may be, there is a lot of it around, particularly in the fields of education, philosophy, sociology, psychology, and literary criticism. What is necessary is that you learn to cope with jargon: assimilate the ideas being expressed, recognize it as bad writing, and avoid using it yourself. Every piece of writing, exposition or fiction, should be judged on its own merits; having a famous name attached to it does not automatically mean it is good. You should, however, remember that if you have difficulty with certain kinds of reading, the author is not necessarily at fault. He may be trying to express concepts that would be hard for anyone to grasp at the first reading. A dialogue by Plato or a treatise by John Stuart Mill, for example, will tax the powers of most students because the ideas in it are complex and the vocabulary unfamiliar; those qualities alone, however, do not make it bad writing.

Complex ideas and unfamiliar vocabulary alone do not make bad writing

CANT

We have been talking about a kind of writing that is fuzzy, obscure, and confusing, but not intentionally so. Jargon written by students falls into that class and so does that of writers like Marcuse and Dewey. Such writers want their audiences to understand what they are saying but they are unable to simplify their writing or unaware that they should. There are, however, two kinds of jargon that writers use to spellbind or confuse their audiences.

Definition

Stock phrases

The first of these is "cant," which is the expression or repetition of conventional, trite, or unconsidered opinions and sentiments—especially the insincere use of pious phraseology. Cant depends for its effect on piling up stock phrases calculated to reach the emotions but not the intellect of its audience. It is a kind of semantic overkill based on the premise that if you say something loud enough and often enough, you will finally force your listeners into agreement. Here is an example from Red China:

> War, this monster of mutual slaughter among men, will be finally eliminated by the progress of human society, and in the not too distant future too. But there is only one way to eliminate it and that is to oppose war with war, to oppose counter-revolutionary war with revolutionary class war. History knows only two kinds of war, just and unjust. We support just wars and oppose unjust wars. All counter-revolutionary wars are unjust, all revolutionary wars are just. Mankind's era of wars will be brought to an end by our own efforts. . . . The biggest and most ruthless of unjust counter-revolutionary wars is hanging over us, and the vast majority of mankind will be ravaged unless we raise the banner of a just war. The banner of mankind's just war is the banner of mankind's salvation. The banner of China's just war is the banner of China's salvation. A war waged by the great majority of mankind and of the Chinese people is beyond doubt a just war, a most lofty and glorious undertaking for the salvation of mankind and China, and a bridge to a new era in world history.[8]

Unsupported assertions

The paragraph is no more than a collection of platitudes; Chairman Mao does not define his terms or support any of his assertions. He simply says any war China starts is a good war, any war an enemy of China starts is a bad war. You might be tempted to dismiss such writing because you think it could not persuade anybody, but every Red Chinese soldier carries a copy of the sayings of Chairman Mao and reads it for inspiration. Political cant, repeated again and again, can become a kind of religious creed that leaders may use to justify illegal or immoral actions. Here is an example of racist cant from Nazi Germany:

> Everything we admire on this earth today—science, art, technology and inventions—is only the creative product of a few peoples and originally perhaps of *one* race. On them depends the

---

[8] Mao Tse-tung, "Problems of Strategies in China's Revolutionary War," in *Selected Works* I (Peking: Foreign Language Press, 1964), pp. 182–183.

existence of this whole culture. If they perish, the beauty of this earth will sink into the grave with them. . . .

All great cultures of the past perished only because the originally creative race died out from blood poisoning.

The ultimate cause of such a decline was their forgetting that all culture depends on men and not conversely; hence that to preserve a certain culture the man who creates it must be preserved. This preservation is bound up with the rigid law of necessity and the right to victory of the best and stronger in this world.

Those who want to live, let them fight, and those who do not want to fight in this world of eternal struggle do not deserve to live. . . .

. . . All the human culture, all the results of art, science, and technology that we see before us today, are almost exclusively the creative product of the Aryan. . . . He is the Prometheus of mankind from whose bright forehead the divine spark of genius has sprung at all times, forever kindling anew that fire of knowledge which illumined the night of silent mysteries and thus caused man to climb the path to mastery over the other beings of this earth.[9]

A purely emotional appeal

The passage repeats, almost ritualistically, certain key words and climaxes in a kind of ecstatic vision. Like all cant, it seeks not to convince so much as to hypnotize.

While it is easy enough to criticize the ways in which the exponents of alien philosophies twist language to suit their own purposes, we must be intellectually alert enough to realize that our language is as vulnerable to perversion as any other. All of us have grown up hearing *Revered platitudes* certain phrases that refer to concepts that we revere and cherish as part of our American heritage. Some of the more familiar ones are: "principles of our founding fathers," "precious freedoms," "individual liberties," "human dignity," "preservation of Constitutional rights," "freedom of speech," and "the spirit of justice." Undoubtedly, you can think of many more. The phrases are good in themselves, but, linguistically speaking, they are "the coin of the realm," available to anyone who wants to use them, whatever his purposes may be. You should be wary, then, of the speaker or writer who draws heavily on this reserve of patriotic truisms to garner the approval of his audience.

[9] Adolf Hitler, *Mein Kampf,* trans. Ralph Manheim (Boston: Houghton Mifflin Company, 1933), pp. 288–290.

In *It Can't Happen Here,* a frightening novel that describes the rise of a dictatorship in America, Sinclair Lewis shows how the vocabulary of patriotism can be transformed into cant. His demagogue, Berzelius Windrip, says,

> The Executive has got to have a freer hand and be able to move quick in an emergency, and not be tied down by a lot of dumb shyster-lawyer congressmen taking months to shoot off their mouths in debates. BUT . . . these new economic changes are only a means to an End, and that End is, and must be, fundamentally, the same principles of Liberty, Equality, and Justice that were advocated by the Founding Fathers of this great land back in 1776![10]

In another speech Windrip says,

> Love and Patriotism have been my sole guiding principle in Politics. My one ambition is to get all Americans to realize that they are, and must continue to be, the greatest Race on the face of this old Earth, and second, to realize that whatever apparent Differences there may be among us, in wealth, knowledge, skill, ancestry, or strength—though, of course, all this does not apply to people who are *racially* different from us—we are all brothers, bound together in that great and wonderful bond of National Unity, for which we should all be very glad. And I think we ought to for this be willing to sacrifice any individual gains at all. [P. 84.]

Such examples illustrate an extreme case, of course; few writers who overuse our traditional terminology to the point that rhetoric degenerates into cant are evil men. Some may fall back on stock phrases either because using them is easier than writing something fresh and concrete or simply because they can't do any better. Sometimes the stock phrases seem to be the only ones sure to communicate with a huge and diverse audience, and sometimes, it is true, such writers fall back on stock phrases because they have so little respect for their audience that they think it would prefer to hear safe sentiments rather than wrestle with issues. Whatever his motives, remember that the writer or speaker whose utterances consist largely of platitudes may forfeit serious attention or respect.

[10] Sinclair Lewis, *It Can't Happen Here* (New York: P. F. Collier & Son Corporation, 1935), pp. 38–39.

EUPHEMISMS AND "WEASEL WORDS"

The other kind of deceptive jargon employs not clichés, but what the semanticist Mario Pei calls "weasel words," the language of whitewash and evasion. Sometimes these terms are simply euphemisms coined to disguise or soften unpleasant labels: "custodian" for "janitor"; "career apparel" for "uniforms"; "budget level" for "bargain basement"; "underachiever" for "slow learner"; "cremains" for "human ashes." Such attempts to disguise reality are more amusing and pitiful than they are vicious or dangerous. There is, however, a kind of jargon that is used deliberately to conceal unpleasant facts. No one has described this kind of weaseling better than George Orwell in his famous essay "Politics and the English Language."

Purpose: deliberate evasion

> In our time, political speech and writing are largely the defense of the indefensible. Things like the continuance of British rule in India, the Russian purges . . . and the dropping of atom bombs can indeed be defended, but only by arguments which are too brutal for most people to face, and which do not square with the professed aims of political parties. Thus political language has to consist largely of euphemism, question-begging, and sheer cloudy vagueness. Defenseless villages are bombarded from the air, the inhabitants driven out into the countryside, the huts set on fire with incendiary bullets, and this is called *pacification.* Millions of peasants are robbed of their farms and sent trudging along the roads with no more than they can carry; this is called *rectification of frontiers.* People are imprisoned for years without trial, or shot in the back of the neck or sent to die of scurvy in Arctic lumber camps; this is called *elimination of unreliable elements.* Such phraseology is needed if one wants to name things without calling up mental pictures.[11]

Although Orwell wrote this essay twenty-five years ago, his comments are far from dated. Although governments may sometimes feel that war is necessary, no one seems to want to talk about it in straightforward language. Apparently, some officials feel that they must protect the general public from the harsh truth that people are being killed. Mario Pei calls the jargon such officials use "the language of annihilation."

[11] George Orwell, "Politics and the English Language," in *Shooting an Elephant and Other Essays* (New York: Harcourt, Brace, and World, 1945), p. 88.

In the field of mass destruction, [there is] a tendency to understate and minimize the implications of the concepts involved. This is natural. Total war means total annihilation and no one likes the prospect of being annihilated. Those who deal in annihilation must therefore undersell, not oversell, their commodity, which in the final analysis is death. Can death's pill be sugar coated? Apparently some think it can.[12]

Bland and abstract
words

Those in charge of the sugar-coating depersonalize their language as much as possible. In an ironic reversal of the guidelines that state that you should use vigorous and concrete language whenever possible, they deliberately use bland and abstract terms. The "language of annihilation" never mentions people; it talks of "personnel deterrents," "bisecting access routes," "consolidating territorial acquisitions," and "damage inflicted on ground forces." These phrases suggest a conflict in some unpopulated area between robots and machines—no blood ever flowing. Such weaseling should fool nobody, but, unfortunately, it probably does, perhaps even the writers who concoct the jargon.

Falling into the habit of using jargon in your writing not only confuses and annoys your reader but also has the insidious side effect of clouding your own thinking. When you fill your writing with clichés, generalities, passive constructions, and fuzzy abstractions you have probably not stopped to work out your line of reasoning and a method of supporting it. As Orwell points out in his "Politics and the English Language," it is easier to write pretentiously and tritely than it is to write clearly. "By using stale metaphors, similes, and idioms, you save much mental effort at the cost of leaving your meaning vague, not only for your reader but for yourself." Just as, in John Stuart Mill's words, society provides molds to save people the trouble of forming their own characters, every culture also provides platitudes, cant, and ready-made phrases to save people the trouble of thinking. If you rely on second- and third-hand phraseology to express yourself, you are unlikely to come up with fresh ideas or to develop your own natural writing style.

EXERCISES

1. Which of the following words are abstract, and which concrete? Notice that you may have to settle on a limited definition for some of these words before you can classify them accurately.

[12] Mario Pei, *Words in Sheep's Clothing* (New York: Hawthorn Books, Inc., 1969), p. 12.

science	expressway	tone
machine	safety	barrier
identity	recognition	son-in-law
dormitory	character	deed
condominium	treaty	abortion
duty	yellow	integrity

2. Arrange the following three lists of words into ladders of abstraction.

gasoline-propelled conveyance	three-month-old Great Dane
product of the Ford Motor Company	dog
mode of transportation	domesticated animal
two-door automobile	canine species
Mustang	mammal
Mach II fastback	puppy

the poems of T. S. Eliot

academic subjects

twentieth-century literature

English

"The Love Song of J. Alfred Prufrock"

3. Write short paragraphs that develop concretely these two opening sentences.
a. A brief tour of the campus reveals an urgent need for modernization.
b. The candidate's record on ecology issues will hurt him with young voters.

4. Bring to class a paragraph from an essay or magazine article that you think is particularly well written. What parts of the writing are concrete and what parts abstract?

5. Study the following sentences from student themes; then, rewrite them to make them more concrete and effective.
a. The behavior of the residents is also a factor of annoyance.
b. The author tends to have a negative attitude toward the values of youth.

c. Social and economic conflicts will arise if the student takes any involvement in his college affairs.

d. The author's words produce feelings of unfavorable reaction in the reader.

e. He uses phrases that negate the idea of sexual freedom in our culture.

f. The first consideration that should be taken is what particular interests the person has in the areas of job preference.

6. The following student paper was turned in to meet this assignment: "Write a short definition or description of a liberated woman. Pick out a few main points you want to emphasize; be specific and concrete and try to avoid broad generalities that do little more than repeat clichés." In your opinion, how well does the paper meet the assignment? How would you grade it? What suggestions for improvement would you make?

> Historically, women were ruled by men. Until she married, a girl was subject to her father's rule. He told her how to dress, with whom to be acquainted, when and where she could go, and whom she would marry. Her duty was to take care of his house and children, love him, and accept his decisions because her father had chosen him as her husband.
>
> American women have struggled for their liberation from these conditions for over a century. Today's woman enjoys the legal and social benefits of this work. Now a woman may choose whom to marry or if she will marry at all. She can dress how she wishes in anything from pastel frilly dresses to blue jeans. She still has commitments to her husband, but they are mutual agreements. Legally, in most states, a woman has the same right to justice as a man. Today's woman is a liberated woman, that is, she is free to choose how she will live her life.

7. Analyze the examples of student jargon on page 78. What specific faults do you find in them? How would you rewrite each one to improve it?

8. In "Politics and the English Language," George Orwell rewrote a famous passage from Ecclesiastes 9:11 as a modern author might have phrased it. Here is the original and Orwell's jargon version:

> I returned, and saw under the sun, that the race is not to the swift, nor the battle to the strong, neither yet bread to the wise, nor

yet riches to men of understanding, nor yet favor to men of skill; but time and chance happeneth to them all.

Objective consideration of contemporary phenomena compels the conclusion that success or failure in competitive activities exhibits no tendency to be commensurate with innate capacity, but that a considerable element of the unpredictable must invariably be taken into account. [P. 84.]

What particular qualities of the original passage make it good writing? What specific characteristics of jargon has Orwell incorporated into his version? The first version has more words than the second, but the second one seems much longer. Why? If you read the two versions aloud, what striking differences do you notice in the way they sound?

9. Try your hand at writing an Orwellian version of these famous lines.

We hold these truths to be self-evident: that all men are created equal, that they are endowed by their Creator with certain unalienable rights, that among these are Life, Liberty, and the Pursuit of Happiness.

10. Write down a list of standard sentiments and platitudes that you could string together to compose a paragraph of cant for one of the following occasions. Remember that all groups, liberal or conservative, have their stocks of clichés.
a. A high school athletics award banquet
b. Graduation exercises
c. A petition to abolish grades at your college
d. A meeting of the Young Socialists' Alliance

SUGGESTED
WRITING
ASSIGNMENT

Purposes: (1) To sharpen your awareness of problems created by jargon by having you write a specific criticism of a passage of jargon. (2) To give you practice in translating jargon. (3) To have you practice your own writing skills by rewriting the passage in acceptable prose.

Procedures: (1) By using the guidelines given on page 81, supplemented by what you have learned in class discussion, write a criticism of the defects in the following passage. You cannot, and should not, try to discuss all the faults in the passage. Focus your criticism on a few that seem most offensive to you, and organize your theme around those points. Give examples to support your criticism. (2) Rewrite the passage in language that is more colorful and concrete and easier to understand. You may write a free translation that makes use of your own examples and words, but it should express approximately the same idea. Your version need not be as long as the original. One tight paragraph should be enough.

High school personnel that are charged with the guidance of that portion of the student body who will go on into areas of study other than vocational should keep in mind the differentiating characteristics of the various institutions of higher learning. The multiplicity of schools that are available makes it possible to maximize learning opportunities for the individual scholastic. The most meaningful learning experiences will be encountered by those students who do not attempt to pursue their educations in an alien environment.

The following factors are to be considered. Colleges in a high density population area attract a preponderance of enrollees from socioeconomically deprived families. There will be a concentration of overachieving, work-oriented students who manifest minimal interest in nonproductive social and political activities. Fraternal and sororal associations are not made available to the student. With all these considerations in mind, the guidance person would be well advised to dissuade young people with strong social orientations from attending large urban universities.

Nevertheless, it must be kept in mind that some colleges with proportionately lower enrollments tend to exert an attraction for those young people who are apt to be avant garde in both their political inclinations and their ethical systems. The neophyte student from a middle-class background that is antipathetic to these attitudes will, it is not too unreasonable to anticipate, suffer some psychic dislocation if he attends this kind of institution in which all pretense of enforcing parietal rules has been abandoned.

The conclusion that may be hazarded from this data is this. The young person, male or female, who does not have a fully integrated personality and may show susceptibility to undergoing an identity crisis, is perhaps least apt to be traumatized if he chooses a college of medium size located in a semiurban area that minimizes opportunity for contact with individuals that exhibit characteristics dissimilar to his own.

5

Exploring the Persuasive Power of Words

In the previous chapter, we considered how the language a writer uses can affect the senses and the intellect. Well-chosen words stimulate, communicate, and clarify; poorly chosen ones may bore and confuse. We also touched briefly on some of the ways in which language affects a reader's emotions. When framing this kind of rhetorical appeal, a writer may use several techniques. One of the major ones is connotation.

CONNOTATION

Two hundred years ago Thomas Paine, in an effort to rekindle the fighting spirit of General Washington's troops, wrote his series of pamphlets called *The American Crisis.* This is the famous opening paragraph:

> These are times that try men's souls. The summer soldier and the sunshine patriot will, in this crisis, shrink from the service of his country; but he that stands it *now,* deserves the love and thanks of man and woman. Tyranny, like hell, is not easily conquered; yet we have this consolation with us, that the harder the conflict, the more glorious the triumph. What we obtain too cheap, we esteem too lightly: 'tis dearness only that gives everything its value. Heaven knows how to put a proper price upon its good; and it would be strange indeed, if so celestial an article as FREEDOM should not be highly rated. Britain, with an army to enforce her tyranny, has declared that she has a right (not only to *tax*) but "to *bind* us in *all cases whatsoever,*" and if being bound in that manner is not slavery, then is there not such a thing as slavery upon the earth. Even the expression is impious, for so unlimited a power can belong only to God.

The appeal seems to have worked; Washington's men returned to the battle.

Paine's passage is a classic example of persuasion based on emotional appeal. Its effectiveness depends on the connotative force of the words "tyranny" and "slavery," which Paine equates with hell, and the word "freedom," which he links to heaven. And the appeal works. Even today, if we put ourselves in the place of the men he is addressing, we are moved because our feelings about freedom have not changed nor has our almost instinctive revulsion toward any group associated with tyranny and slavery.

The example is an extreme one, but the principle it illustrates is sound. That principle is that in most rhetorical situations one of the most effective tools that any writer can use is connotation. It is true that he cannot use *only* connotation; some evidence is essential, and the more alert and astute the audience, the more evidence it demands. Nevertheless, without some use of connotation, some words that evoke the sympathies of the audience, an argument will fail.

Rhetoric requires
connotation

How Connotation Works

Definition

We can understand better how connotation works if we define it precisely and look at some of its sources. The connotation of a word is the emotional baggage that it carries in addition to its denotative, or strictly dictionary, definition. The term "socialism" readily illustrates the point. Denotatively, stripped of its emotional baggage, it means a system or condition of society in which the means of production are owned and controlled by the state. The definition is descriptive and neutral; it passes no judgments. The connotation of the word is quite another matter. Now, the emotional baggage added by the reader alters the word for better or worse. The average United States citizen associates socialism with Communism, Communism with totalitarianism, totalitarianism with the horrors of Orwell's *1984*. Because of this chain of associations, he distrusts and fears any proposal that has been labeled "socialist." That his view of socialism may be grossly inaccurate—there are, after all, socialist democracies such as Sweden and England—is not relevant. On the other hand, a Russian citizen, who has grown up under a socialist government and heard it praised from childhood, carries emotional baggage that predisposes him to favor any measure called "socialist." As a result of his conditioning, neither individual is likely to use the word objectively.

By the time we are young adults, all of us have added to our vocabularies an astonishing collection of emotional baggage. Those of you who studied Latin may remember that the Latin word for baggage is *impedimenta.* For our purposes, that definition is singularly appropriate because the connotative baggage we have piled on our language actually acts as an impediment to clear thinking. Obviously, we cannot purify our thought processes simply by jettisoning our emotional baggage. Nor would we really want to eliminate connotation. Language purged of all color would be fit only for conversing with a computer. What we can do, however, is minimize the extent to which we are unwittingly controlled by language by developing an acute sensitivity to connotation and by bringing the way in which it works out into the open.

Connotation functions by the process of association. At the simplest level, it does little more than trigger reactions. We hear or see the word "silky," and without actually thinking about it, we remember the sensation of feeling silk. For most people, the memory is pleasant, and the good vibrations transfer to whatever the word "silky" is describing. This is the kind of response a company depends on when it advertises, "Your hair will turn out silkier, more lustrous, glossier than it was when you started." All direct appeals to our senses work in this way. "Smooth," "soft," "shining," "shimmering" set off good reactions; "gritty," "harsh," "slimy," "mushy" set off bad ones. In the following passage, Philip Wylie depends on the reader's sensuous responses to put over his point.

Connotation appeals to the senses

> Most foods, cooked or uncooked, are destroyed in the deep freeze for all persons of sensibility. Vegetables with crisp and crackling texture emerge as mush, slippery and stringy as hair nets simmered in Vaseline. The essential oils that make peas peas—and cabbage cabbage—must undergo fission and fusion in freezers. Anyhow, they vanish. Some meats turn to leather. Others to wood pulp. Everything, pretty much, tastes like the mosses of tundra, dug up in midwinter. Even the appearance changes, oftentimes. Handsome comestibles you put down in summer come out looking very much like the corpses of wooly mammoths recovered from the last Ice Age.[1]

Wylie borrows two of the advertiser's favorite terms, "crisp" and "crackling," to get the reader's approval for fresh foods, and he condemns the frozen product by the words "slippery" and "stringy." He then reinforces his point with a series of unpleasant visual images: wood pulp, mosses, corpses of wooly mammoths.

Connotation appeals to stereotypes

Other kinds of connotation work in a more complex way by reminding us of the stereotypes that we all carry around in our heads, images that include racial types, policemen, D.A.R. matrons, small town girls, politicians, pot parties, admirals, professors, the Mafia, and dozens of others. A single reference to one of these stereotypes can evoke a mass of associations, both positive and negative. Writers are depending on this kind of nonlogical reaction when they use terms like "hippie," "hard-hat," "cop," "Communist," "bureaucrat," or other loaded labels.

[1] Philip Wylie, "Science Has Spoiled My Supper," *The Atlantic Monthly,* April 1954, pp. 45–47.

For any thoughtful reader, such a term should be a signal to stop and ask: What images does the word evoke? Are they accurate and warranted? Or, as S. I. Hayakawa puts it, do they place an imaginary map in the mind, a map that does not really describe the territory it is supposed to? Notice in the two passages that follow that the authors are setting up stereotypes even though they do not actually put labels on them.

> Tough and independent as a longhorn, [Texas Ranger Frank] Hamer stood six-feet-three-inches tall, weighed more than 200 pounds. He had oak-like arms and fists, developed by work in his father's blacksmith shop. As a youngster, he lived like the Indians he had read about, hunting and riding through the San Saba hill country, cultivating keen powers of sight, smell and hearing, and often staying out for days at a time, sleeping on the ground. When he joined the Rangers at 22, he was a superb horseman, could throw a knife with deadly accuracy, and soon won the reputation of being one of the best shots in Texas. But, despite this skill, he rarely resorted to his gun. His usual means of dealing with unruly customers was to clout them with one swipe of his open palm.
>
> A dedicated officer, he nevertheless was a loner who preferred to track down criminals by himself rather than as a part of a team. He retired from the Rangers in 1932. But when the superintendent of the Texas prison system asked 50-year-old Hamer to track down Bonnie and Clyde, he agreed.[2]

> Someone should inform the feminists that there are at least a few men who loathe their jobs—the interminable hours, the putting up with the snotty *lèse majesté* of inferiors and the bossiness of employers.
>
> This, not nirvana, is what the feminists may expect when they take over the men's jobs. . . . But what, then, of the dishes in the sink—what of the floors to be mopped, the silver to be polished, the shelves to be dusted? Who will discharge those odious little chores when the little woman is off in what was once man's world? Well, *my* apron is at the ready, and if you will just show me the way to the kitchen, what cabinet the detergents are kept in, and how to turn on the television set. . . .
>
> Naturally, it will be difficult at first to switch from making money

---

[2] John Reddy, "The Man Who Trapped Bonnie and Clyde," *Reader's Digest,* May 1968, pp. 120–121.

to home economics, but once the change-over becomes socially acceptable, the benefits should be bountiful, for where, outside Appalachia, is there dusting to do that can't be done in two hours? What I am looking forward to is the time when, with the head of the family away at the office, I can sip a beer while catching up on the soaps. Every man owes it to himself to see if *Dark Shadows* is all that the women say. And, busy though I'll be, I'm sure I'll find time to make myself presentable before the Avon lady comes calling.[3]

Connotation appeals to popular attitudes and beliefs

To attempt to track down and identify the sources of all our emotional responses to language would be an impossible task so I shall limit myself to setting up a broad and sketchy third general category of association, that of attitudes and beliefs. Because most of us believe in the traditional virtues of honesty, courage, loyalty, self-reliance, hard work, and fair play, there is little doubt about the way we will respond to words such as "indolent," "shifty," "craven," or "freeloader." We Americans conventionally believe in independence and individualism, in freedom and dignity, in progress and prosperity (all concepts we have absorbed with our education), and we nod our approval to any term that reminds us of them. We prefer—or think we do—the natural to the artificial, so "real," "genuine," "original," and "authentic" are good words; "synthetic," "imitation," "substitute," and "pseudo" are bad ones.

Connotation appeals to personal attitudes and needs

We have other attitudes that we are not quite so proud of but which influence us as much as, or more than, our traditional beliefs. We crave approval. We want to be thought of as young, sexually attractive, intelligent, and successful. No one wants to be classified as a mediocre person: dull, conventional, and timid. Notice how a magazine ad can play on these apprehensions in a positive way.

Are you the kind of man who wants *more* from life? Wants that new adventure, that special kind of vacation that others don't know about? Do you want to set the pace, not follow? If you're a leader, have that special knack for taking charge, our magazine is for you. Read *Paladin* to find out where to go for the best and the brightest. The last word in life-styles is at your nearest newsstand.

In the same way, our desire for status makes us susceptible to snob appeal ads, which encourage us to buy expensive cars that will make our neighbors envious. Brewers promote our continual pursuit of happi-

[3] George Frazier IV, "The Masculine Mystique," *Mademoiselle,* July 1970, p. 64.

ness by coining slogans such as, "You only live once—why not enjoy the finest beer brewed?"

Probably the most insidious kind of connotation is that which attempts to sway us by touching our deepest, instinctive fears. Phrases such as "Communist conspiracy" and "Fascist plot," with their innuendoes of secrecy and mysterious machinations, may immediately put us on our guard. Labels such as "outside agitators," "alien influences," and "foreign elements" appeal to the distrust and suspicion of outsiders that are difficult for even open-minded people to overcome. An inclination to panic at the prospect of injury or death assures a response to mottoes like "Insure your safety" or "Protect your loved ones," phrases that can serve equally well to sell burglar alarms, insurance, a politician's position on law and order, or an intercontinental missile system.

Using Connotation

General connotation The kinds of connotation discussed so far—and the examples are intended to be representative, not exhaustive—are broadly based and general; that is, their emotional appeal rests on warranted assumptions about the majority of the people in our society. The sum of generally shared attitudes is the conventional wisdom of our society, the prevailing opinion of that mythical man in the street. Writers at both ends of the political spectrum depend, and with good reason, on their audience's responding to words that have general connotation. The American socialist, Michael Harrington, writes in his book *The Other America*, "What is needed if poverty is to be abolished is a return of political debate, a restructuring of the party system so that there can be clear choices, a new mood of social idealism." J. Edgar Hoover, in a speech to students, said, "The real strength of our nation is the power of morality, decency, and conscience, which rights the wrong, corrects error, and works for equal opportunity under the law." Each writer seeks to promote his cause by attaching to it general words that have good associations.

The rhetorician who addresses a large, heterogeneous audience must rely on these kinds of words, but the broad, unfocused emotional appeal can have serious weaknesses. For one thing, many words and phrases have been used so often that they have lost their impact and degenerated into clichés. We are so accustomed to hearing about "good government," "individual freedom," "democratic processes," and "human rights" that the terms simply roll off our minds; at best they

Margin notes:

Advantage: expresses prevailing opinion

Disadvantages: has little persuasive impact

May alienate part
of audience

evoke mild approval and little action. Another problem is that the more alert portion of an audience refuses to be impressed by what they view as "push-button" techniques aimed at people totally governed by their emotions. The writer who tries to sway everyone may alienate rather than persuade this last group.

Selective connotation Thus, connotative language works best when it is selective, chosen with a specific audience in mind. The writer who decides to tailor his appeal to a particular group is taking a risk, of course; he must make assumptions about his audience that may be wrong. If, however, he makes a careful and rational analysis of his audience, using the methods discussed in Chapter 2, the gamble will probably pay off. For instance, a candidate who is promoting tax-supported day care centers for preschool children might speak of "more freedom for mothers" and "equal opportunity for career women" if he were addressing a group of young women. If he were advocating the same measure to a men's club, he would avoid those phrases since they have threatening implications for some men and instead talk about ways in which day care centers could improve the efficiency of women workers and about the advantages to the children of being in the care of licensed, professional people. By varying his approach,

Advantage: focuses
on audience concerns

the speaker is not compromising his principles since both his arguments are legitimate, neither contradicts the other, and both promote the same purpose. Rather, he is showing sensitivity to the concerns of his audiences and is adapting his diction to the rhetorical situations. In the same way, the astute writer senses when words like "intellectual,"

Disadvantage: may
alienate audience

"liberal," and "idealist" will antagonize his audience and finds acceptable substitutes for them. Other words with strong selective connotations are "capitalist," "businessman," "artist," "student," or "Texan"; some abstract terms that trigger mixed reactions are "law and order," "civil liberties," or "right-to-work laws." Such lists of words with controversial connotations could go on almost indefinitely, but the point should be clear. The rhetorician who is unaware of how his audience will respond to his language will fail.

Personal connotation Finally, words have personal connotations. Each of us has accumulated a store of private experiences that have had strong positive or negative effects on us. Long after the actual events have been forgotten, the associations we made at the time linger on. We may dislike the colors brown and maroon because some teacher we despised invariably wore them. Some people may find zoos depressing. Just the mention of "chemistry" could be painful to a young man who did not get into medical school because he failed the subject. On the other hand, "circus" could evoke pleasant memories from a person who remembered annual excursions with his family, or a reference to "red shoes" might recall a particularly happy experience. Such private associations can be strong, so strong that

Disadvantage: audience may not feel the same way

we are tempted to assume other people share them. We cannot, however, be sure that other people dislike maroon or that zoos repel them; thus, references of this kind have little value in most writing. Certainly it is useful to draw on your experiences to illustrate your points, but when you do, you should ask yourself whether you can be reasonably sure that your audience shares your feelings.

Don't overuse connotation

Any rhetorician risks defeating his own purpose when he overuses connotation. The writer or speaker who thinks he can persuade mainly through slanted language is assuming that his audience, like a laboratory animal, is totally conditioned and has no critical faculties. Such tactics may work when the audience is already in full agreement with the speaker; in that case he is doing little more than leading a cheering section anyway. In a genuine rhetorical situation, however, the audience is likely to be more insulted than convinced by a barrage of connotative words and phrases, whether the phrases are political slogans or advertising clichés.

Don't concentrate connotative words

The thoughtful writer husbands his value terms. Rather than concentrate all his emotional words in his first few sentences, he doles them out sparingly, saving his most dramatic ones for his conclusion. After all, if you begin a letter to the campus editor by saying, "The dormitory rules at this college are juvenile, inane, and an insult to the integrity and judgment of the students whom the administration laughingly calls adults," what else are you going to say? Since you have already thrown your conclusion at your audience, they have little reason to continue reading. Further, the logicians among your readers will immediately recognize the fallacy of "begging the question" and dismiss your argument as an amateurish effort. If, however, you start out, "The dormitory rules for this campus were set up fifty years ago when both the college and the students were different," you catch your audience's interest and establish a noncontroversial basis on which to build your case with logic and evidence. If you follow this method, your audience is not likely to quarrel with your conclusion that "The restrictive dormitory regulations at this college are unrealistic and patronizing and should be abolished if students are going to gain full maturity while they are here."

To summarize: except on those few occasions which are unabashedly emotional, such as Paine's appeal to the soldiers or Winston Churchill's Dunkirk address, connotation is most effective when it is used with restraint. Like the plaster, paint, and trimming on a building, it adds interest and appeal, but it cannot sustain much weight. The solid framework of an argument must be constructed out of evidence, logic, rational processes, and supporting examples, or it will not stand up to pressure. On the other hand, just as we would not want to live in a completely utilitarian house, stripped of all but essentials, we find it unrewarding either to construct or to read a totally logical piece of persuasion. For this reason the added ingredient, connotation, is appropriate and useful, but unless the arguer applies judgment and restraint in adding it to the main structure, it will mar rather than enhance the whole.

The Ethics of Connotation

Inevitably, the study of connotative language leaves some students with the impression that connotation is bad and should be purged from the language. The reaction is understandable. You've been warned to be sensitive to connotation, to sift through the emotional terminology and get to the facts, and to be aware of how some politicians and advertisers seek to manipulate you through language. Nevertheless, to eliminate connotation altogether would be semantic overkill; it would

Connotation has a valid place in language

leave us with a drab and sterile language fit for little but communicating data and reports. We would rob our language of much of its richness and ourselves of an indispensable tool for persuasion and expression. What we need, then, is not to do away with connotation but to find guidelines by which to evaluate the way others use it and to control it in our own writing. Such guidelines must, of course, be applied impartially; it is intellectually dishonest to endorse slanted language when we approve of its purpose but condemn it when we disagree with the writer's purpose.

Invalid use: connotation in factual writing

One area of writing in which we can say without qualification that connotation has no place is that of news stories and reports. People who read newspapers and news magazines for information have a right to a straightforward account uncolored by the opinions of the writer. An article about socialists running for office should identify the candidates as socialists, not as left-wingers or radicals. A reporter should not call an accident tragic or a victory glorious. Similarly, value terms do not belong in a report you are making for a class or a committee. If your assignment is to present evidence, you are meeting it when you say, "Thirty percent of the residents of South Chicago live in dwellings classified as substandard by the local housing commissioner"; you are not if you write, "One-third of the people exist in intolerable, subhuman conditions." The latter kind of language has its place in editorials, in persuasive feature articles, or in syndicated columns appearing beneath a writer's name but not in any writing that purports only to give facts. Thus, Rachel Carson in her book *The Silent Spring* is justified in writing, "The most *alarming* of man's *assaults* upon the environment is the *contamination* of air, earth, rivers, and sea with *dangerous* and even *lethal* materials. This *pollution* is for the most part irrecoverable; the *chain of evil* it initiates not only in the world that must support life but in living tissues is for the most part irreversible." (P. 6, italics added.) In an ecology textbook, however, the scrupulous author would avoid such biased language.

Much of what we read and write is, like Miss Carson's book, frankly persuasive. We are, after all, as interested in exchanging ideas and viewpoints as we are in learning facts. But how do we set limits on the amount and the kind of emotional language that an author may properly use to influence his audience? The answer is necessarily less than exact, but we can set a relative standard.

For example, the spokesman for a local medical association has the task of warning people against a practitioner who claims to have a cure for arthritis. For the spokesman to warn against the alleged healer by calling him a "crooked, money-grasping quack" will probably accomplish nothing. This will merely antagonize his audience and raise the suspicion that if the spokesman has to resort to name-calling, he has very little evidence to support his opinion. For the spokesman to state, however, that no cure for arthritis has been discovered (although various treatments for its symptoms are available) and that the "cure" at issue has been proved ineffective will appeal to his audience's better judgment and will be a successful warning. Trying to win an argument by clobbering your opponent with derogatory labels—whether you use "quack," "bleeding heart," "Fascist pig," or "fuzzy-minded idealist"—is both immature and foolish; that kind of excessive connotation has no place in responsible discourse. The responsible and skillful writer is one who uses connotation with judgment, good taste, and moderation, and who does not depend on it as his only, or even principal, method of persuasion.

Valid use: connotation in responsible persuasive writing

METAPHOR

Definition

As used here, the terms "metaphor" and "metaphorical language" mean figures of speech that draw comparisons between unlike things. Technically, a comparison containing "like" or "as" is a simile and one *equating* different things is a metaphor, but in practice "He plays like a demon" and "He's a regular demon on the basketball court" say the same thing. (Remember, though, that not all comparisons are metaphors. When you say "She is just like her mother" or "Washington is a cleaner city than Chicago," you are making comparisons, but you are not using metaphorical language.)

The inclination to express ourselves in metaphor must be as old as speech itself. Our desire to communicate with others makes us instinctively draw comparisons, search for a reference to the familiar to explain the unknown. Imagine, for instance, an Indian who has been scouting new hunting grounds for the tribe. He comes back to tell them of the vast herds of buffalo he has seen beyond the river. How can he best convey his information graphically and impressively? Rather than talk of dozens or hundreds, he says, "There are as many animals as there are trees in the forest around us" or "The buffalo are as thick as ants swarming on the carcass of a dead dog." He would get his point across, particularly if the metaphor he chose were new to his audience.

Our own everyday language abounds in metaphorical expressions, but too often we do not get our point across because our figures of speech are so familiar they have lost their impact on people. Expressions such as "sleep like a log," "eat like a horse," "cry like a baby," "feel fit as a fiddle," and "work like a trooper" have lost the power to enlighten or impress. We have an inexhaustible supply of worn-out metaphors that make casual conversation almost effortless. Without thinking we refer to "being caught in the rat race," "fighting tooth and nail," "blowing a fuse," "playing the game," or "being driven up the wall." Certainly no real harm is done by our resorting to such clichés when we are only making small talk with friends. If we had to think constantly of new and vigorous ways to express ourselves in everyday talk, conversation would become a terrible chore. But when we are speaking or writing seriously with the desire to explain, to clarify, or to persuade, it is essential that we get rid of metaphors that anesthetize rather than stimulate the audience. In those situations, if you cannot find a fresh metaphor that will serve your purposes, it is probably better not to use one at all.

Metaphors in everyday language: clichés

How Metaphor Works

We can understand the benefits of figurative language as a rhetorical tool if we examine how it works and what some of its uses are. Like connotation, metaphor works by setting up associations, but it operates more directly and specifically. For example, a book written in 1893 by the American novelist Frank Norris has as its theme the railroad's exploitation of the people and lands of the western United States in the late nineteenth century; the title of the book is *The Octopus*. For most readers the word "octopus" raises an unpleasant image; they see a frightening creature with tentacles that stretch out to grab anything within its reach and strangle it to death. Because Norris has equated the railroad with the octopus, the reader transfers his impressions of the creature to the railroad and thinks of it as a grasping and destructive live thing that preys upon people.

A passage from the literary critic Alfred Kazin's autobiography, *A Walker in the City,* provides another example. He writes, "When I passed the school, I went sick with all my old fear of it. . . . It looks like a factory over which has been imposed the facade of a castle." Here Kazin wants the reader to attribute the characteristics of a factory to the school. Our picture of a factory is that of a place in which a uniform product is turned out by assembly line techniques. The atmosphere seems mechanized, regimented, and impersonal; any item that does not meet the specifications set by the management is rejected. When the reader envisions a school that operates this way, he reacts in a surge of pity for students caught in such a system. Notice too the phrase "the facade of a castle," another metaphor that illustrates the school administration's pretensions about the insti-

The metaphorical equation

tution. The method employed by Norris and Kazin is simple: A = B; therefore, B has the characteristics of A. The effect is illumination; the reader sees a thing that is ordinary and familiar to him in a new light. For convenience, we shall call this kind of comparison straight metaphor, a simple equation of unlike objects. We need also to consider three other categories, the submerged metaphor, the extended metaphor, and allusion.

Submerged Metaphor

Definition

The submerged metaphor is the simplest, commonest, and the easiest to incorporate into your writing. It consists of implied comparisons made in one or two words, usually verbs, nouns, or adjectives. Take the sentence "The vice-president of the firm had clawed his way to the top." The word "clawed" is metaphorical, not literal; people do not have claws. The verb implies the ruthlessness and ferocity associated with a wild animal; the writer has gotten a lot of mileage (notice the submerged metaphor in the noun "mileage") out of a single word. The phrases "He cut down the opposition's case" and "She tortured her hair into the latest style" use the same verbal technique. Although this kind of metaphor is sometimes deliberatively connotative, frequently a writer uses submerged comparisons to give his

Purpose: to provide
vigor and color

language vigor and color. For example, "The speech triggered immediate repercussions"; "Jim erupted into a stream of profanity"; "The author was deluged with requests for interviews." Reading just a few pages of a newspaper or a magazine like *Time* or *Newsweek* reveals how heavily reporters depend on figurative language. "The company recently launched a new advertising campaign"; "The movie has spawned a host of imitations"; "Today the police chief said they had dealt a knock-out blow to drug pushers in the city." Of course, the device can get out of hand. Tabloid writers' efforts to find a sensational adjective become comic at times, and many authors of mystery and adventure stories overload their fiction with fast-action verbs and shocking metaphors.

Most student writing, however, is not likely to be marred by too much flashy language. More often, the desire to play it safe, to be correct, and to sound weighty overcomes natural speech habits. The color fades from writing as the proportion of abstractions, passive constructions, and linking verbs increases. The result is dull to write and dull to read. If you are adventuresome enough to try a metaphor now and then, either straight or submerged, you can put some life into your prose. Instead of writing "It is my opinion that drastic changes must be made if we are to solve this problem," try "The problem calls for a full-scale overhaul of the system." Whenever possible use verbs that call to mind some kind of physical action. Occasionally, your imaginative efforts may misfire, but with practice you will learn to write with a livelier style. The gamble is worth it.

Extended Metaphor

Definition

Working with extended metaphor, one that expands a comparison through several sentences or even paragraphs, is more complex although not necessarily beyond the abilities of an inexperienced writer. Let us look at a specimen written by an expert.

> The wrath of God is like great waters that are dammed for the present; they increase more and more and rise higher and higher, till an outlet is given; and the longer the stream is stopped, the more rapid and mighty is its course when once it is let loose.

It is true that judgment against your evil works has not been executed hitherto; the floods of God's vengeance have been withheld; but your guilt in the meantime is constantly increasing, and you are every day treasuring up more wrath; the waters are constantly rising . . . and there is nothing but mere pleasure of God that holds the waters back. . . . If God should only withdraw his hand from the flood-gate, it would immediately fly open, and the fiery floods of the fierceness and wrath of God would rush forth with inconceivable fury.

The passage is from the Puritan minister Jonathan Edwards' famous sermon, "Sinners in the Hands of An Angry God." Edwards' stated purpose in the sermon is "to awaken the unconverted"; there is no better way to do it than with a visual image that transfers the characteristics of a known, flood waters, to an unknown, God's wrath.

Purpose: to emphasize and explain

He extends the comparison simply for emphasis, to make his audience shiver at the thought of the awful fury that hangs over them.

Other writers employ the extended metaphor for different kinds of illustrative purposes. The anthropologist Loren Eiseley, in his book *The Immense Journey*, compares his descent into a deep crevice to a journey back into time. As he goes down, he reconstructs history from the bits of fossil in the geological strata. In order to explain the anguish of learning to handle his hatred of white men, the black writer James Baldwin builds an extended metaphor around disease.

One is always in the position of having to decide between amputation and gangrene. Amputation is swift but time may prove that amputation was not necessary—or one may delay the amputation too long. Gangrene is slow, but it is impossible to be sure that one is reading one's symptoms right. The idea of going through life as a cripple is more than one can bear, and equally unbearable is the risk of swelling up slowly in agony, with poison.[4]

The passage, which comes near the end of the essay "Notes of a Native Son," is an expansion and reinforcement of two metaphors that Baldwin uses throughout the piece: racism is a disease and hatred is poison.

Allusion

Definition

A final kind of metaphor is allusion, a reference to events or characters from an outside source, usually literary or historical. The device acts

[4] James Baldwin, *Notes of a Native Son* (Boston: Beacon Press, 1955), p. 112.

Purposes: 1. to add
extra meaning

as a rhetorical shorthand, which enables a writer to compress extra meaning into a few words when he uses a short phrase that brings associations to mind. For example, the phrases "sour grapes" and "cry wolf" describe certain kinds of human behavior with a minimum of words because we know the Aesop's fables to which the writer refers. The terms "Good Samaritan" and "kiss of death" describe by evoking our memories of Bible stories, and references like "Achilles' heel" and "Trojan horse" say a great deal in a few words if we have read *The Iliad*. Although myth, legend, classical literature, and the Bible are the commonest sources of allusion, a writer can also use contemporary references with good effect. You might characterize a prejudiced but likable person by calling him "an Archie Bunker"; a quick and effective way to describe a reformer would be to compare him

2. to add vigor and
increase rapport
with audience

to Ralph Nader. Such references not only add vigor and concreteness to your writing but also increase your rapport with your audience by drawing on a stock of shared experiences and common knowledge. Emphasizing the need for a traffic light at a busy corner by comparing the street to the Indianapolis 500 would enliven a report based mainly on statistics; describing a girl's figure by comparing her to the Playmate of the Month does away with the need for further details. Sports, television, movies, popular songs, books, current events, magazines—almost everything around us can furnish material for allusions that will help us to communicate.

The use of allusion, however, carries with it built-in problems that we do not encounter with other kinds of metaphor. Imagine, for instance, writing for a Japanese audience that had an excellent text-

Effectiveness of
allusions depends on
audience

book command of English but knew nothing about American history, Greek mythology, the Bible, or contemporary life in the United States. You could not use allusions with such an audience because there is virtually no shared experience or common knowledge from which to draw them. The example is extreme, of course; you will have an abundance of information in common with most audiences that you are trying to reach. Nevertheless, when you are using allusions, you should stop to ask yourself if they are general enough for an educated reader to grasp; if not, you should omit them. On the other hand, part of your own educational responsibility is to increase your stock of general information so that you can learn from the writings of others. The student who knows nothing of Greek myths, Arthurian legend, Shakespeare, or Biblical history is handicapped whether he is reading *The Great Books* or *Newsweek* magazine. Serious authors assume they are writing for educated audiences; your obligation is to rise to their expectations by looking up allusions in a dictionary or encyclopedia.

Using Metaphor

Understandably, the student writer may despair of achieving this kind of eloquence in his own writing, but actually he may be able to do something comparable on a modest scale. The key is to find a well-known process or object to use as one part of your metaphorical equation, then to show how the concept you want to clarify resembles what is already familiar. For example, one student compared the frustration of trying to decipher a passage of jargon to the frustration of trying to see through frosted glass. A football player on scholarship equated his way of life with that of a prize fighter, who entertains the public for a living.

Equate a "known" to what you want to clarify

The varieties of metaphor serve several rhetorical purposes. First, as already discussed, they give color and vigor to writing, bring it to life, make it move. That result alone helps to win your audience. Secondly, using metaphor is one way to make the abstract concrete. Philosophers and psychologists frequently employ metaphor to help their readers grasp difficult concepts. In one of the most dramatic passages in philosophy, Plato illustrates the function of the soul by saying that it is like a team of two horses with its charioteer; the charioteer is the guiding force for the horses, one of which represents good instincts and the other, bad instincts.

Use metaphors: 1. to add vigor

2. to make the abstract concrete

> The horse that holds the nobler position is upright and clean-limbed; it carries its head high, its nose is aquiline, its color white, its eyes dark; it is a lover of honor . . . temperance, and decency. . . . It needs no whip, but is driven by word of command alone. The other horse, however, is huge, but crooked, a great jumble of a creature with a short, thick neck, a flat nose, dark color, grey bloodshot eyes, the mate of insolence and knavery, shaggy-eared and deaf, hardly heeding whip or spur.[5]

Plato extends the figure of speech for several paragraphs, vividly dramatizing the struggle that reason, the charioteer, has in finally bringing the black horse, or the soul's sensual desires, under control.

The Englishman C. S. Lewis has a more complicated theory about the instincts which he also makes concrete by extended metaphor. Lewis maintains that no instinct is in itself good or bad since what may be a bad instinct at one time, for example, the impulse to kill, may at another time be a good and valuable instinct. He prefers to say that our instincts are like the notes on the piano; we have a range

[5] Plato, *Phaedrus,* trans. W. C. Helmbold and W. B. Rabinowitz (Indianapolis: The Bobbs-Merrill Co., Inc., 1956), p. 38.

of them, each one different. What guides us in making the proper use of them is Moral Law, which he likens to the sheet of music that tells us what tune to play. The nineteenth century social philosopher John Stuart Mill in his essay *On Liberty* repeatedly emphasizes his main idea by comparing individuals to plants or trees that must "breathe in an atmosphere of freedom" if they are to develop fully their potential. For example, he says, "Human nature is not a machine to be built after a model, and set to do exactly the work prescribed for it, but a tree, which requires to grow and develop itself on all sides, according to the tendency of the inward forces that make it a living thing."

3. to explain a theory

Similarly, writers often use metaphor to clarify or explain a theory. The sociologist David Riesman elucidates his classification of people as "inner-directed" and "other-directed" by saying that inner-directed people have what he calls a "psychological gyroscope." "This instrument, once it is set by the parents and other authorities, keeps the inner-directed person . . . 'on course' even when tradition . . . no longer dictates his moves." In contrast, other-directed people pattern their behavior according to the responses they receive from those around them. "What [is] internalized is not a code of behavior but the elaborate equipment needed to attend to . . . messages. . . . This control equipment, instead of being like a gyroscope, is like a radar."[6] This kind of vivid clarification we find too seldom in the writing of social scientists, many of whom seem addicted to writing in wordy and weighty abstractions. When we do encounter such striking figures,

4. to explain the unknown

they stick in our memories. Another example of a metaphorical explanation is one used by a psychologist to make a normal person comprehend the agony felt by a person who is the victim of irrational fears. He dramatized the psychotic's fears of the most routine things, such as sleep, by comparing the psychotic's feelings to those a normal person would have if he had to sleep with his bed at the edge of a precipice.

5. to persuade

A final rhetorical function of metaphor is that of persuasion. By drawing a comparison, not only can a writer make you see something more clearly but also very often he can influence you to see it his way. Some persuasive metaphors are obvious, of course: "Television is a giant wasteland" or "Lake Michigan is the sewer of Chicago." Others, however, are so subtle that the reader may not realize he is being influenced. Let us take another example from James Baldwin's *Notes of a Native Son*.

[6] David Riesman, *The Lonely Crowd* (New Haven, Conn.: Yale University Press, 1950), pp. 31–32, 37.

That year in New Jersey lives in my mind as though it were the year during which, having an unsuspected predilection for it, I first contracted some dread, chronic disease, the unfailing symptom of which is a kind of blind fever, a pounding in the skull, a fire in the bowels. Once this disease is contracted, one can never be really carefree again, for the fever, without an instant's warning, can recur at any moment. It can wreck more important things than race relations. There is not a Negro alive who does not have this rage in his blood—one has the choice, merely, of living with it consciously or surrendering to it. As for me this fever has recurred in me, and does, and will until the day I die. [P. 94.]

Baldwin equates his resentment and anger and hatred—his rage in the blood—with a disease. Think for a minute of the characteristics of a disease. First, it infects a person without his knowing it; one does not deliberately choose to have a disease. Thus, Baldwin cannot be held responsible for his "rage in the blood." Second, a disease, and particularly a fever (notice that he repeats the word three times) affects a person's ability to act rationally. Again, we cannot hold Baldwin responsible for what he does while he is in its grip. Third, a disease is painful ("a pounding in the skull, a fire in the bowels") so we feel sympathy, not anger, for the person afflicted with it. If we make the transfer of characteristics that Baldwin wants us to make, we will view some of the black man's problems from a new perspective.

In this passage, written a hundred years earlier, John Stuart Mill also used persuasive metaphors to make a plea for understanding.

Persons of genius are more individual than any other people—less capable, consequently, of fitting themselves, without hurtful compression, into any of the small number of molds which society provides them in order to save its members the trouble of forming their own character. If from timidity they consent to be forced into one of these molds, and to let all that part of themselves which cannot expand under the pressure remain unexpanded, society will be the little better for their genius. If they are of strong character, and break their fetters, they become a mark for the society, which has not succeeded in reducing them to commonplace, to point at with solemn warning as "wild," "erratic," and the like; much as if one should complain of the Niagara River for not flowing smoothly between its banks like a Dutch canal.[7]

[7] John Stuart Mill, *On Liberty* (Indianapolis: The Bobbs-Merrill Co., 1956), pp. 77–78.

The imagery of people being forced into molds is worth noting here, but more interesting and subtle is the comparison of persons of genius to the Niagara River. We associate the Niagara with energy and power; we are awed by its magnificence and repelled by the thought that someone might want to tame and subdue it. By getting the reader to transfer his attitudes toward the river to people of genius, Mill succeeds in persuading him that genius is not only necessary to society but also an actual asset.

You may protest that the power of metaphor is exaggerated, that you do not make all these associations when you read and therefore are not particularly affected by an author's clever comparisons. It is true, of course, that because few of us pause in our reading to make a close analysis of figurative language, many of the author's nuances escape us; nevertheless, if we accept the metaphors he creates, we also, without really thinking about it, are inclined to accept his point of view. A particularly apt comparison, such as Kazin's identification of his elementary school with a factory, can be more persuasive than an elaborate explanation.

TONE

Definition

The tone of a piece of writing is the emotion that it conveys to the reader. Analogous to a speaker's tone of voice, it reveals the attitude of the writer toward his audience and his material. It is an extension of his persona, an essential part of the image of himself that he projects to his audience. For this reason, the rhetorician who wants to make a favorable impression will use great care in choosing his words. A passage from Benjamin Franklin's *Autobiography* illustrates how important one's manner of speaking is. As a young man, Franklin worked out a program for self-improvement; he made a list of twelve character traits he wanted to acquire and outlined a plan for achieving them. In writing about his program, he comments:

> My list of virtues contain'd at first but twelve; but a Quaker friend having kindly informed me that I was generally thought proud; that my pride show'd itself frequently in conversation; that I was not content with being in the right when discussing any point, but was overbearing, and rather insolent, of which he convinc'd me by mentioning several instances; I determined endeavouring to cure myself, if I could, of this vice or folly among the rest, and I added *Humility* to my list, . . .

I cannot boast of much success in acquiring the *reality* of this virtue, but I had a good deal with regard to the *appearance* of it. I made it a rule to forbear all direct contradiction to the sentiments of others, and all positive assertion of my own. I even forbid myself . . . the use of every word or expression in the language that imported a fix'd opinion; such as *certainly, undoubtedly,* etc., and I adopted, instead of them, *I conceive, I apprehend,* or *I imagine* a thing to be so or so; it so *appears to me at the present.* When another asserted something that I thought an error, I deny'd myself the pleasure of contradicting him abruptly, and of showing him immediately some absurdity in his proposition; and in answering I began by observing that in certain cases or circumstances his opinion would be right, but in the present case there *appear'd* or *seem'd* to me some difference, etc. I soon found the advantage of this change in my manner; the conversations I engag'd in went on more pleasantly. The modest way in which I propos'd my opinions procur'd them a readier reception and less contradiction; I had less mortification when I was found to be in the wrong, and I more easily prevail'd with others to give up their mistakes and join me when I happened to be in the right.

And this mode, which I first put on with some violence to natural inclination, became at length easy, and so habitual to me, that perhaps for fifty years past no one has ever heard a dogmatical expression escape me. And to this habit (after my character of integrity) I think it principally owing that I had early so much weight with my fellow—citizens when I proposed new institutions, or alterations in the old, and so much influence in public councils when I became a member; for I was but a bad speaker, never eloquent, subject to much hesitation in my choice of words, hardly correct in language, and yet I generally carried my points.[8]

What Franklin changed, of course, was his tone. By doing so he induced his audience to accept him as a reasonable and moderate man. Hypocritical? Not at all. He gave up no principles and did nothing dishonest. He simply adjusted his diction and delivery to show respect rather than contempt for his audience.

There is, of course, much writing that is essentially "toneless" because the author has no purpose other than to convey information as accurately and objectively as possible. For example, in the following passage Isaac Asimov explains acceleration to the layman.

[8] Benjamin Franklin, *The Works of Benjamin Franklin*, ed. and comp. John Bigelow (New York: G. P. Putnam's, 1904).

When something moves, it has kinetic energy. The quantity of kinetic energy possessed by a moving object depends upon its velocity and its mass. Velocity is a straightforward property that is easy to grasp. To be told something is moving at a high or low velocity brings a clear picture to mind. Mass, however, is a little more subtle.[9]

Informational writing should be "toneless"

You are no more aware of tone in this writing than you would be of tone of voice in a weather report or the stock market quotations. Writing that is strictly informational—and that includes newspaper reports—should have a neutral and unemotional tone; if the writer allows his bias to show, he is violating his persona of the objective and impersonal observer.

Rhetorical writing has tone
Tone shows writer's attitude toward subject

Tone sets distance between writer and audience

Most of the kinds of writing we are concerned with, however, are frankly rhetorical. The writer seeks to persuade, and, consciously or not, he chooses a tone that reflects his feelings about his material and establishes a relationship with his audience. Usually the relationship with the audience can be described in one of three ways: casual, informal, and formal. One important way to determine which of these tones a writer is using is to imagine the distance he is putting between himself and his readers.

The other element besides distance that controls the tone of a piece of writing is the author's attitude toward his subject matter. The list of terms for describing that attitude include almost all of the words we use to characterize emotions: angry, proud, sorrowful, disgusted, indignant, pitying, indifferent, bitter, arrogant, ironic, amused—the list could go on for half a page. We also need to keep in mind the kind of words that describe the writer's presentation of himself. Is he being flattering, critical, judgmental, patronizing, dogmatic, maudlin? Again, there are dozens of terms that could apply.

Casual Tone

Characteristics:
1. contractions, slang, nonstandard usage

2. personal pronouns

Writers achieve a casual, easygoing, conversational tone by using language suited to talking intimately with a few people. They make free use of contractions such as "it's," "don't," "wouldn't," and "can't." They may inject a few slang words and phrases such as "swinging" or "cool" and occasionally lapse into one of the minor grammatical errors that people often make in conversation: "It's me" or "It runs good." The pronouns "I," "you," "we," and "our" appear frequently,

[9] Isaac Asimov, "The Ultimate Speed Limit," *Saturday Review of Science,* July 8, 1972, p. 53.

and bits of conversations are quoted directly. Most of the words are concrete rather than abstract, and the sentences are comparatively short and simple. In writing with this kind of tone there is virtually no distance between writer and reader; it is as if two or three people were chatting over a cup of coffee or a beer.

Some writing assignments may warrant your using this casual, colloquial tone, but they are apt to be few. Unless you are writing a personal narrative or doing a satiric description of a person or a group, extreme casualness is inappropriate. One problem is that advertisers have so overused the casual tone that it often sounds insincere. The fake friendliness of The First Metropolitan National Bank ads that say "We're hankerin' to do something really nice for *you!*" and the false concern of deodorant ads that whisper "We want to help you with your most personal problem" have made it difficult for the amateur writer to write in a colloquial tone without running the risk of sounding cute, coy, and phony.

Informal Tone

The tone that will best meet most of your writing needs is that of informality. The term "informal tone" is about as broad and inclusive as the phrase "informal clothing," and there are parallels between the two classifications. The notation "informal attire" on an invitation, loosely interpreted, means "Don't wear a nightgown or a swim suit, and don't wear a tuxedo or white tie and tails, but almost anything else will do." Similarly, informal tone excludes the intimate or the formal, but almost any other kind of writing qualifies. When a writer uses an informal tone he establishes a comfortable distance between him and the reader, a distance at which he would not have to raise his voice or use a public address system, one that would allow him to see the faces of his audience and feel their interest. The writer's imaginary setting might be a classroom, a club meeting, or a gathering of colleagues at a dinner. An author who is writing for this kind of situation probably makes free use of the personal pronouns "I" and "you," assuming that he and the audience have mutual concerns and interests. He writes carefully and employs standard English usage although he might use a few contractions; if he brings in a slang term, he probably puts it in quotation marks. His vocabulary is that of an educated though not erudite person, and his language a mixture of the abstract and concrete.

You may say that the description of informal tone is so general

3. concrete words and simple sentences

4. no distance between writer and reader

5. few uses

Characteristics:
1. comfortable distance between writer and reader

2. personal pronouns

3. some contractions, standard usage
4. educated vocabulary, both abstract and concrete words

5. many uses

it fits almost everything you read. And you would be right. The label is as applicable to James Thurber's essay "How to Name a Dog," which begins "Every few months somebody writes me and asks if I will give him a name for his dog," as it is to an essay on ethics that starts "Man is the animal who can reflect." The advantage of choosing the informal tone is that within it you can develop topics ranging from the humorous to the serious, the simple to the complex. Furthermore, it will stretch to accommodate a wide range of emotions: sympathy, amusement, outrage, cynicism—almost any feeling a writer wants to express.

Formal Tone

Characteristics:
1. a great distance between writer and audience

2. elevated vocabulary, abstract words
3. long, complex sentences
4. few personal pronouns
5. correct usage, no slang or popular idioms

6. few uses

The uses of formal tone, on the other hand, are limited, mainly because of the distance the writer puts between himself and his readers. The person who writes in a consistently formal tone gives the impression that he is addressing a large audience whom he does not know. The imaginary scene could be one in which he is addressing a crowd from a speaker's podium; the occasion would be dignified, the topic serious. In formal writing the writer uses an elevated vocabulary and an abundance of abstract terms; his sentences are relatively long, probably complex. He may use the pronoun "I" but does not address his audience as "you." The grammar is meticulously correct and there is no slang or use of popular idiom. The uses for formal tone are almost as limited as those for a cutaway coat; after all, you do not joke or get angry or show deep emotion when you have put yourself at such a distance that there is little sense of identity between you and your audience.

In our time, so few people speak or write formally that it is almost impossible to find examples. President Kennedy's inaugural address comes close to it.

We dare not forget today that we are the heirs of that first revolution. Let the word go forth from this time and place, to friend and foe alike, that the torch has been passed to a new generation of Americans—born in this century, tempered by war, disciplined by a hard and bitter peace, proud of our ancient heritage—and unwilling to witness or permit the slow undoing of those human rights to which this nation has always been committed, and to which we are committed today at home and around the world.

The balanced and complex sentence structure, the abstract language, and the lofty sentiments expressed qualify the passage as formal writing, although Kennedy does not seem completely remote from his audience. A brief excerpt from an address given by Dr. J. Robert Oppenheimer at Columbia University in 1954 is another example. Notice the abstract diction, the long complicated sentences, and the broad and elevated nature of his topic.

> In an important sense this world of ours is a new world, in which the unity of knowledge, the nature of human communities, the order of society, the order of ideas, the very notions of society and culture have changed and will not return to what they have been in the past. What is new is new not because it has never been there before, but because it has changed in quality. One thing that is new is the prevalence of newness, the changing scale and scope of change itself, so that the world alters as we walk in it, so that the years of man's life measure not some small growth or rearrangement or moderation of what he learned in childhood, but a great upheaval.[10]

In earlier, less hurried times, there was an abundance of formal writing. You will encounter it now mainly in reading nineteenth century writers like Matthew Arnold or John Stuart Mill or in our own Federalist papers. It can be eloquent and elegant, but neither statesmen nor the public seem any longer to have the temperament or the patience for it.

Although students should learn to read formal writing and to appreciate its dignity, they should avoid it in their own writing. On the few occasions when your topic might seem weighty and lofty enough to call for it, it would be better to stay with serious informal writing. If not handled with great skill, formal writing can be dull, pretentious, and difficult to follow. At its worst, it degenerates into jargon.

How Tone Works

By now you may be thoroughly confused and asking, "How am I supposed to be able to discover all these fine points about tone?" The process is not really difficult; it is a matter of deciding how you react to what you read. At this point, analyzing examples will be more helpful than theorizing.

What are your reactions?

> The mass of men serve the state thus, not as men mainly, but as machines, with their bodies. They are the standing army, and

[10] J. Robert Oppenheimer, "Address Delivered at Columbia University's Bicentennial, 1954," in *Fifty Great Essays* (New York: Bantam Books, Inc., 1964), p. 277.

the militia, jailers, constables, *posse comitatus*,[11] etc. In most cases there is no free exercise whatever of the judgment or of the moral sense; but they put themselves on a level with wood and earth and stones; and wooden men can perhaps be manufactured that will serve the purpose as well. Such command no more respect than men of straw or a lump of dirt. They have the same sort of worth only as horses and dogs. Yet such as these even are commonly esteemed good citizens. Others—as most legislators, politicians, lawyers, ministers, and office-holders—serve the state chiefly with their heads; and, as they rarely make any moral distinctions, they are as likely to serve the devil, without *intending* it, as God.

Thoreau's tone is informal and direct. He is disgusted and angry with his fellow men for their unquestioning loyalty to the state. His description of them as straw or a lump of dirt and the comparison to horses and dogs reveal his harsh opinion. He is not at all sympathetic with their low state but suggests that it is their own fault. Notice, however, that his tone tells as much about himself as it does others; he is arrogant and judgmental. His comments make it evident that he thinks he is superior to "the mass of men."

The tone is sharply different in this selection from Harvey Swados' *On the Line.*

His surroundings meant nothing to Walter, who had not expected that the factory would look like an art gallery; but the work, and the conditions under which he had to do it, were a nightmare of endless horror from which Walter sometimes thought, stumbling wearily out of the plant after ten hours of unremitting anguish, he would one day awaken with a scream. It was not simply that the idea of working on an endless succession of auto bodies as they came slowly but ineluctably rolling down the assembly line like so many faceless steel robots was both monotonous and stupefying, or that the heavy work of finding bumps and dents in them, knocking them out and filing them down, was in itself too exhausting.[12]

Swados' tone is that of a sympathetic observer. The words "stumbling wearily," "unremitting anguish," "awaken with a scream," and "exhausting" show his compassion and concern for the man he is

[11] Power or authority of the county.
[12] Harvey Swados, *On the Line* (Boston: Little, Brown and Company, 1957), p. 46.

describing; the phrases "nightmare of endless horror," "rolling down the assembly line like so many faceless steel robots," and "monotonous and stupefying" reveal the author's anger over an industrial system that is so dehumanizing. There is no hint of superiority in his tone.

Although Swados may be angry, his tone is restrained compared to that of Malcolm X in a speech he quotes in his *Autobiography*.

> Not even in the *Bible* is there such a crime! God in His wrath struck down with *fire* the perpetrators of *lesser* crimes! *One hundred million* of us black people! Your grandparents! Mine! *Murdered* by this white man. To get fifteen million of us here to make us his slaves, on the way he murdered one hundred million! I wish it was possible for me to show you the sea bottom in those days—the black bodies, the blood, the bones broken by boots and clubs! The pregnant black women who were thrown overboard if they got too sick! Thrown overboard to the sharks that had learned that following the slave ships was the way to grow fat!
>
> Why the white man's raping of the black race's women began right on those slave ships! The blue-eyed devil could not even wait until he got them here! Why, brothers and sisters, civilized mankind has never known such an orgy of greed and lust and murder.[13]

Malcolm X is very close to his audience, blacks he is trying to convert to the Muslim faith. Someone who reads the speech senses his tone of furious outrage and his impassioned hatred of the white man partly because of the italics and exclamation points, which indicate the speaker's stress and his raised voice. His most effective tool, though, is the shocking imagery of "black bodies, the blood, the bones broken by boots and clubs" and the slaves thrown overboard to the sharks. He underscores his fury with the repetition of the words "crime" and "murder" and the phrase "orgy of greed and lust." The tone is so strong that the reader can almost feel Malcolm X's presence.

In radical contrast is the following passage by James Thurber, whose tone of gentle humor is a rarity these days.

> Dr. Bisch, the Be-Glad-You're-Neurotic man, has a remarkable chapter which deals, in part, with man, sex, and the machine. He

[13] Malcolm X and Alex Haley, *The Autobiography of Malcolm X* (New York: Grove Press, Inc., 1964), p. 202. Reprinted by permission of Grove Press, Inc. Copyright © 1964 by Alex Haley and Malcolm X. Copyright © 1965 by Alex Haley and Betty Shabazz.

examines the case of three hypothetical men who start across a street on a red light and get in the way of an oncoming automobile. A dodges successfully; B stands still, "accepting the situation with calm and resignation," thus becoming one of my favorite heroes in modern belles-lettres; and C hesitates, wavers, jumps backward and forward, and finally runs head on into the car. To lead you through Dr. Bisch's complete analysis of what was wrong with B and C would occupy your whole day. He mentions what the McDougallians would say ("Instinct!"), what the Freudians would retort ("Complexes!"), and what the behaviorists would shout ("Conditioned reflexes!"). He also brings in what the physiologists would say—deficient thyroid, hypoadrenal functioning, and so on. The average sedentary man of our time who is at all suggestible must emerge from the chapter believing that his chances of surviving a combination of instinct, complexes, reflexes, glands, sex, and present-day traffic conditions are about equal to those of a one-legged blind man trying to get out of a labyrinth. . . .

. . . Dr. Bisch himself leans toward the Freudian analysis of Mr. C, for he says in this same chapter, "An automobile bearing down on you may be a sex symbol at that, you know, especially if you dream it." It is my contention, of course, that even if you dream it, it is probably not a sex symbol, but merely an automobile bearing down on you. And if it bears down upon you in real life, I am sure it is an automobile. I have seen the same behavior that characterizes Mr. C displayed by a squirrel (Mr. S) that lives in the grounds of my house in the country. He is a fairly tame squirrel, happily mated and not sex-hungry, if I am any judge, but nevertheless he frequently runs out toward my automobile when I start down the driveway, and then hesitates, wavers, jumps forward and backward, and occasionally would run right into the car except that he is awfully fast on his feet and that I always hurriedly put on the brakes of the 1935 V-8 Sex Symbol that I drive.[14]

The mild, whimsical tone suits the persona that Thurber frequently adopted: the good-natured observer, slightly baffled by the frenzied activity he sees going on around him. He is kidding psychiatrists, their

[14] James Thurber, *Let Your Mind Alone* (New York: Harper & Row, Publishers, 1937), pp. 75-77. Copyright © 1937 James Thurber. Copyright © 1965 Helen W. Thurber and Rosemary Thurber Sauers. From *Sex Ex Machina* in *Let Your Mind Alone*, published by Harper and Row. Originally printed in *The New Yorker*.

jargon, and their insistence on seeing sexual overtones in every action, but he is not sarcastic about it. Instead, he achieves his effect by an exaggeration that spoofs the tendency to attribute dark and complex motives to simple actions, and he makes fun of the case study method by bringing in Mr. S, the squirrel. There is not an angry word in the passage nor does Thurber suggest that he is disgusted with Freudian analysis; he is just an ordinary man who is amused.

Avoid invective

Avoid being "nice"

Use a tone appropriate
to the situation

In practice, you probably do not have to worry a great deal about the tone of your writing if you write naturally and observe the rules dictated by ordinary good sense. One rule is to avoid invective and name-calling that will antagonize your audience and brand you as ill tempered and irrational. Another is to eliminate from your writing the standard kinds of "nice" sentiments, those routine moralistic comments (such as "Learning to meet and overcome obstacles is part of growing up") that, unfortunately, often bring approval in civic essay contests but which strike most college teachers as superficial. Finally, take care to see that your tone is appropriate to your writing situation. Comparatively minor issues such as campus parking problems do not warrant the same seriousness of tone as do crucial ones like poverty programs or drug addiction. Similarly, you should avoid a witty or casual tone when the occasion calls for straight, serious writing, as a petition, a report, or an application for a scholarship does. If you approach your writing assignments with responsibility and honesty, your tone will reflect those qualities. The sympathetic reader expects no more than that.

IRONY

Function of irony: to
reveal discrepancy

Ironic tone often causes problems for students and so deserves special attention. The ironist points out the discrepancy between the way things are and the way he thinks they ought to be; he emphasizes the inconsistencies between word and deed, between the ideal and the real, and between myth and fact. Of course, other writers also perform this function when they criticize existing conditions and institutions; Harvey Swados and Malcolm X certainly wrote as social critics. Their attacks, however, were direct, and their tones showed that they were emotionally involved with their topics. The writer who employs irony as a rhetorical device attacks indirectly and assumes an air of detachment toward his subject. The most famous example of this kind of prose is Jonathan Swift's "A Modest Proposal," in which the author made the apparently calm and objective suggestion that the Irish solve their problems of starvation, poverty, and overpopulation by allowing the poor to sell their babies for food. Although he was actually outraged, he achieved more shock value by pretending to be callous and indifferent.

Irony may confuse

This straight-faced "put-on" by a writer may sometimes confuse readers because many people are inclined to assume that any article that appears in a newspaper, magazine, or book of essays is serious. An article that deals ironically with a major political or social issue is especially apt to be misjudged because we approach it expecting a straightforward discussion. Occasionally, we realize immediately that a writer is being heavily sarcastic, saying precisely the opposite of what he means. We may, however, fail to grasp the purpose of a writer who slips in an occasional ironic phrase, or we may miss the subtle innuendoes of a writer who is treating his material with tongue in cheek. Unfortunately, the reader who is consistently insensitive to irony not only deprives himself of much pleasure in his reading but also runs the risk of being thought naive because, as Thrall and Hibbard, the authors of *A Handbook to Literature,* point out, "The ability to recognize irony is one of the surest tests of intelligence and sophistication."

Exaggeration

Obviously, an ability to recognize irony cannot be developed overnight with the help of Five Easy Rules for Recognizing Irony; even the practiced and perceptive reader occasionally has to ask himself, "Is this writer really serious, or is he kidding me?" Nevertheless, authors writing in an ironic tone employ certain techniques often enough for us to come up with some guidelines. One such device is exaggeration, which is Art Buchwald's method of making an ironic comment on political commercials in the following column (quoted in part):

> I sat in on a session where the top advertising men were brainstorming a TV commercial for their candidate, Philbus Wurm, who was running for the U.S. Senate against the incumbent senator, Senator Allegro Symphony.
>
> This is how it went:

"As I see it," said the copy writer, "we have to sell the people on Symphony's softness on pornography. Now what I suggest we do is have a woman sleeping in bed, and a guy comes in and rapes her, and the voice says, 'These are the people Sen. Symphony wants to let into your bedroom.'"

"Not enough shock value," the art director says. "How about this? A group of dirty, hairy students sneaks up to a building and plants a bomb. The bomb goes off and the voice-over says, 'Symphony voted for the last education bill.'"

"That's not bad," said a vice-president. "I thought we might use a lot of footage from the California brush fires. You know, homes burning and stuff like that, and then a short of Symphony playing the violin, which he does. The voice-over could say, 'Nero wasn't the only one who fiddled.'"

. . . .

The art director said, "I think you'll like this one. It portrays Washington going up in a mushroom cloud and then a bunch of Soviet officers laughing. The voice-over says, 'Senator Symphony voted against the ABM.'"

"It's dirty, but it will sell," the campaign manager laughed.

"But what about our own candidate, Philbus Wurm?" someone asked. "Don't you think we ought to make one commercial with him in it?"

"Hell, no! If anyone sees that idiot on TV, we'll lose all our votes."[15]

Through exaggeration Buchwald is making an ironic comment on the standard propaganda device of establishing guilt by association. The piece has some nice touches such as the suggestion that rape would not shock a TV audience and the idea that the worst thing the party could do would be to show its own candidate. Some students, however, in spite of the obvious clues in the names "Philbus Wurm" and "Senator Allegro Symphony," took the article seriously and thought Buchwald was making a straight condemnation of television shows. One wrote, "I would never allow a son or daughter of mine to witness a rape scene on TV. Likewise I would never support a TV station that showed such things." That student was taken in because

[15] Art Buchwald, "Buy Our Senator," *Austin (Texas) American & Statesman,* October 11, 1970.

he did not consider the toal content of the article and did not realize Buchwald's examples were too outrageous to be factual.

Tom Wolfe uses a variation of the exaggeration technique to make an ironic comment about articles on celebrities.

> Thirty-nine years old! A recluse! Bonafide! Doesn't go out, doesn't see the light of day, doesn't put his hide out in God's own uncon-ditioned Chicago air for months on end; *years.* Right this minute, one supposes, he is somewhere there in the innards of those forty-eight rooms, under layers and layers of white wall-to-wall, crimson wall-to-wall, Count Basie-lounge leather, muffled, baffled, swad-dled, shrouded, closed in, blacked out, shielded by curtains, drapes, wall-to-wall, blond wood, screens, cords, doors, buzzers, dials, Nubians—he's down in there, the living Hugh Hefner, 150 pounds, like the tender-tympany green heart of an artichoke.[16]

Through his accumulation of adjectives describing Hefner's apartment, Wolfe satirizes not only effusive articles in fan magazines but also Hefner himself and those *Playboy* articles that feature erotic bachelor "pads."

Understatement

A very different kind of ironic technique is understatement. Jonathan Swift was responsible for one of the classics in that category when he said, "Last week I saw a woman flayed [skinned], and you will hardly believe how much it altered her person for the worse." John Stuart Mill was also using this device when he said, "Persons of genius are more individual than any other people—less capable, therefore, of fitting themselves into any of the *small number of molds which society provides in order to save its members the trouble of forming their own character.*" (Italics added.) Such a restrained, low-key jibe at conformity impresses the perceptive reader more than a tirade would. Mark Twain often expressed his deep loathing for slavery and slave holders by the same method, which shocks the reader into aware-ness by treating abuses in an apparently indifferent manner. In *The Adventures of Huckleberry Finn,* he has Huck telling his hostess about a steamboat explosion:

[16] Tom Wolfe, "King of the Status Drop-outs," in *The Pump House Gang* (New York: Farrar, Straus & Giroux, Inc., 1968), p. 49.

"We blowed out a cylinder head."
"Good gracious! Anybody hurt?"
"No'm. Killed a nigger."
"Well, it's lucky; because sometimes people do get hurt."

This shocking understatement is much like the modern technique of black humor.

Unexpected Juxtaposition

Another favorite method of the ironist is to point up human inconsistencies by showing totally contradictory ideas existing side by side; this is called unexpected juxtaposition. Here is an example from the September, 1972, *Playboy*: "On Los Angeles' Channel 4, a recent special called *The Bombing of Haiphong* pre-empted a documentary called *Thou Shalt Not Kill*." George Orwell, in his book *Down and Out in Paris and London,* remarks on the French custom of inscribing their national motto, "Liberty, Equality, Fraternity," not only over the pawnshops but also over the doors of the jails. The technique is also one of Twain's favorite devices. In *A Connecticut Yankee in King Arthur's Court,* he has a scene in which Queen Morgan le Fay is interrupted in her torturing and killing of prisoners by the call to prayers. The narrator's comment is, "I will say this much for the nobility: that, tyrannical, murderous, rapacious and morally rotten as they were, they were deeply and enthusiastically religious."

The Irreverent Twist

Catching the reader's attention by emphasizing the unexpected and incongruous is also the basis of a form of irony called the "irreverent twist" or "deflating anticlimax." Here the writer begins with what promises to be a routine comment then suddenly changes direction. An example from the Victorian era is Clough's poem, "The Latest Decalogue":

Thou shalt have one God only; who
Would be at the expense of two?
No graven images may be
Worshipped, except the currency.
Swear not at all; for, for thy curse
Thine enemy is none the worse.

At church on Sunday to attend
Will serve to keep the world thy friend.
Honor thy parents; that is, all
From whom advancement may befall.
Thou shalt not kill; but need'st not strive
Officiously to keep alive.
Do not adultery commit;
Advantage rarely comes of it.
Thou shalt not steal; an empty feat
When it's so lucrative to cheat.
Bear not false witness; let the lie
Have time on its own wings to fly.
Thou shalt not covet, but tradition
Approves all forms of competition.

Mark Twain, who always enjoyed deflating pretension, frequently used this form of ironic comment. One of the most famous appears in his *Pudd'nhead Wilson's Calendar*: "The holy passion of Friendship is of so sweet and steady and loyal and enduring a nature that it will last through a whole lifetime, if not asked to lend money." The black comedian Dick Gregory employed the same device when he remarked that he sat in at a lunch counter for a week, and when they finally agreed to serve him, there wasn't anything on the menu that he liked.

Inverted Meaning

Finally, there is the standard ironic device of flatly saying the opposite of what is actually meant. When John Stuart Mill talks about people being upset by "dissentients afflicted with the malady of thought," he certainly does not mean that thought is an illness or an affliction; by inversion, he is criticizing those who do not think. When a magazine refers to a man's mistress as his "great and good friend" or to a congressman who has been convicted of fraud as "that distinguished representative of the people," the editors expect the reader to infer their real meaning. The campus newspaper could characterize an authoritarian dean as "that great defender of student freedom" or a television reviewer could call *Laugh-In* "an outstanding example of American cultural achievements." Used sparingly, this kind of irony is effective, but the writer who overdoes it runs the risk of letting his criticism deteriorate into heavy-handed sarcasm.

Using Irony

Although few of us will ever be able to handle irony with the deft touch of Buchwald or Twain, the technique is still within the abilities of a student writer. You may not be able to sustain an ironic tone throughout an entire paper, but a touch of it here and there can make your writing more interesting for both you and your reader. For example, one student used exaggeration to satirize the ritual of his initiation into a fraternity. Others have made good use of the unexpected juxtaposition technique to highlight discrepancies between the chamber of commerce brochures about their home towns and their own views of those communities; you could use the same technique when comparing the promises made by your college's promotion material and your experience on campus. Straight-faced understatement might give you a new approach for attacking chronic problems like traffic congestion, pollution, or sexual discrimination. The advantage of treating such topics ironically is that you can make your point without seeming to preach. If, however, you think that irony is not your thing, you will probably do better to avoid it.

Irony avoids
the disadvantages
of preaching

EXERCISES ON
CONNOTATION

1. Analyze the connotations of the terms in each of these groups.

club woman, joiner, civic leader	playboy, hedonist, good-time Charlie
moralistic, straight-laced, ethical	do-gooder, crusader, volunteer worker
athlete, sportsman, jock	pious, sanctimonious, devout
nonconformist, individualist, eccentric	reactionary, conservative, prudent

2. What associations do you think automobile manufacturers wanted to establish when they chose these names for their cars?

Cougar	Imperial
Skylark	Toronado
Cutlass	Tempest
Mustang	Jaguar
Charger	Firebird

3. What stereotypes do these labels evoke?

red neck	cowboy
freak	quack
brass hat	egghead
bleeding heart	banker
frat rat	homemaker
bureaucrat	women's libber

4. Rewrite the following paragraph, first with unfavorable connotation, then with favorable connotation. Which rewriting do you find easier to do? Why?

In 1970 the President's Commission on Obscenity and Pornography concluded that the sale and distribution of pornographic material to adults in the United States should not be restricted. The report asserts that no one has established a connection between exposure to pornography and sexual offenses, that legislation to ban pornography is ambiguous, unenforceable, and potentially repressive, and that a nation-wide sex education program would do more to solve sex-related problems than the banning of pornography.

5. Identify the connotative words in the following passage, then rewrite the passage without them. Is the meaning of the rewritten passage substantially different from the original?

The amiable dumbbell has for decades been a part of campus folklore, like the absentminded professor. It is when you multiply him by a million that he grows ominous, swamping the campus as with creeping molasses. His uncle of 40 years ago, Joe College, had no more interest in learning than Johnny does, but none of Johnny's baleful power. With a certain talent for grotesque stylization, he conducted his ballet of raccoon coats, hip flasks, and whiffenpoofery, while the business of the academy . . . went on.

What has created the Johnny problem isn't some freakish metamorphosis of Joe College into numberless protozoa, but rather the nearly universal conviction that everybody ought to spend four years at college if it can possibly be managed.[17]

[17] Hugh Kenner, "Don't Send Johnny to College," *Saturday Evening Post,* November 14, 1964, pp. 12–16.

Theme 1

Purpose: To have you evaluate the effects that a political writer can achieve through the use of connotation.

Procedure: Read the Goldwater passage carefully two or three times and decide what his specific persuasive purposes are, both positive and negative. Jot these down as part of your prewriting process. Then, go through the passage and underline the connotative words. At the same time set up two lists, positive and negative, of these words. For example, "dependent" is a negative word, "spiritual" is a positive one. Although not all the words can be that easily classified, you can select the strongest ones in each category for your paper.

Begin your paper with a short paragraph in which you summarize Goldwater's persuasive purposes in your words. Do not try to include all his points; mainly, just answer the question "What does Goldwater want the reader to believe after he reads this passage?" Then, using as many paragraphs as you need, analyze the way in which Goldwater has used connotation to achieve his purpose. Illustrate your analysis with specific examples from the passage and show *how* the connotative words and phrases work; that is, if you use the word "spiritual" as an example of favorable connotation, say why it is favorable. You will have a better and more concise theme if you analyze the passage as a whole rather than discuss it paragraph by paragraph.

Conclude your paper by evaluating the effect of the passage on a reasonably well-informed and educated audience. Review the standards for proper use of connotation given in the text (page 103) before you do your evaluation and support your opinion with concrete reasons for thinking the passage is or is not effective.

Be careful to avoid the two commonest mistakes in rhetorical analysis. Do not make your theme primarily a summary of the passage, and do not either argue or agree with the author's ideas.

Consider the consequences to the recipient of Welfarism. For one thing, he mortgages himself to the federal government. In return for benefits, which in the majority of cases he pays for, he concedes to the government the ultimate in political power—the power to withhold from or grant him the necessities of life as the government sees fit. Even more important, however, is the effect on him—the elimination of any feeling of responsibility for his own welfare and that of his family and neighbors. A man may not immediately, or ever, comprehend the harm thus done to his character. Indeed, this is one of the great evils of Welfarism—that it transforms the individual from a dignified, industrious, self-reliant *spiritual* being into a dependent animal creature without his knowing it. There is no avoiding this damage to the character under the Welfare State. Welfare programs cannot help but promote the idea that the government *owes* the benefits it confers on the individual, and that the individual is entitled, by right, to receive them. . . . How different it is with private charity where both the giver and the receiver understand that charity is the product of the humanitarian impulses of the giver, not the due of the receiver.

Let us, then, not blunt the noble impulses of mankind by reducing charity to a mechanical operation of the federal government. Let us, by all means, encourage those who are fortunate and able to care for the needs of those who are unfortunate and disabled. But let us do this in a way that is conducive to the spiritual as well as the material well-being of our citizens—and in a way that will preserve their freedom. Let welfare be a private concern. Let it be promoted by individuals and families, by churches, private hospitals, religious service organizations, community charities and other institutions that have been established for this purpose. . . .

We can shatter the collectivists' designs on individual freedom if we will impress upon the men who conduct our affairs this one truth: that the material and spiritual sides of man are intertwined; that it is impossible for the State to assume responsibility for one without intruding on the other; that if we take from a man the personal responsibility for caring for his material needs, we take from him also the will and the opportunity to be free.[18]

Theme 2

Purpose: To make you aware of the ways in which critics of contemporary culture use connotation as a persuasive tool.

Procedure: Begin with a short paragraph in which you summarize in your own words the author's main purpose in the passage;

[18] Barry Goldwater, *The Conscience of a Conservative* (Shepherdsville, Ky.: Victor Publishing Co., Inc., 1960) pp. 75–77.

answer the question "What specific attitude does Keats want the reader to have toward the Baxters and their suburban life?" Then, discuss, giving examples, the connotative words and phrases he uses to achieve his purposes. Naturally, you cannot include them all; pick out the ones that seem the strongest to you and show *how* they work. Conclude by stating what you think the rhetorical effect of the passage would be on a fairly intelligent and perceptive reader and support your evaluation with reasons. Be specific in your conclusion; such comments as "The passage is easy to read" and "He holds the reader's attention" do not constitute specific judgments.

Again, be sure to avoid the two common errors in rhetorical analysis. Do not simply summarize the content of the passage, and do not waste your time either agreeing or disagreeing with Keats' viewpoint.

Nick and Fran Baxter live, so to speak, with their three children in one of the five hundred three-bedroom houses of a real-estate nightmare we shall call Apple Drive. Neat, clean, wholesome, slightly vacuous, the Baxters look like one of those idealized suburban families you see in the full-color advertisements of the women's magazines. They bought their house because a) they were told that a family should own one, and b) they imagined it would be cheaper to buy a house in the suburbs than to rent in the city. This was thoughtless of them, and they are now beginning to discover the hidden prices: the years wasted in commuting, the rising assessments. Together with all others trapped in this development miles from nowhere, the Baxters are the prey of pressures less readily apparent to them, but which conspire to make suburban life somewhat disappointing. For one thing, Apple Drive, like most developments, is a jail of the soul, a wasteland of look-alike boxes stuffed with look-alike neighbors.

Here are no facilities for human life, other than bedrooms and bathrooms. Here is a place that lacks the advantages of both city and country but retains the disadvantages of each. Each suburban family is somehow a broken home, consisting of a father who appears as an overnight guest, a put-upon housewife with too much to do, and children necessarily brought up in a kind of communism. For Apple Drive children, life is play school at age three, preschool at age four, kindergarten at age five. Thus do suburban mothers force their primary responsibilities upon someone else as soon as they can, in order to cope with the lesser but insistent needs to drive to the supermarket, clean the house, gabble on the telephone, and attend the *Kaffeeklatsch*. So, suburban children learn the dreary steaminess of group life as soon as they can walk, and after school they are plunked down before the television set to watch the slaughter in the late afternoon while mom thaws supper. In the evening the baby sitters arrive.

In addition, the families who live in our nation's Apple Drives are divided by the rifts in interest between mothers and fathers; they encounter the schizoid experience of the boring workday and the glittery weekend, the problems of shopping in person by automobile at the low-quality stores of the shopping centers, the eternal chauffeuring of the children, the pressure of having to be friends with the folks next door simply because they live next door. They try to reconcile the fact that this is a man's world with the obvious fact that suburbia is a world of women without men, a matriarchy by default. Uneasily, some suburbanites suspect— along with many psychiatrists—that a matriarchy is no fit place to raise a child.[19]

**EXERCISES ON
METAPHOR**

1. Analyze the persuasive purpose of the following metaphors:
   a. "Television is the opiate of the white middle classes and the agent provacateur of the black masses." (John Hersey, *The Algiers Motel Incident*)
   b. "The socialists and the Communists strive with all their might to strap humanity to an operating table, and the truth is now abroad that these social surgeons are maniacal quacks who would operate on us with an ax." (Eric Hoffer, "No Redemption via Socialism")
   c. "And if a beachhead of cooperation may push back the jungles of suspicion, let both sides join in creating a new endeavor. (John F. Kennedy's inaugural address)

2. Identify the submerged metaphors in the following sentences:
   a. The lobbyists carefully cultivate the congressmen with favors and reap their rewards when the votes are taken.
   b. Trapped in a white-dominated world, the black man has learned to live with trouble.

[19] John Keats, "Compulsive Suburbia," *The Atlantic Monthly,* April 1960, pp. 47–50. Copyright © 1960 by John Keats. Reprinted by permission of The Sterling Lord Agency, Inc.

c. The methods of psychoanalysis remain shrouded in half truths.
d. Professionals steeped in jargon are bound to ooze it out in their writing.
e. Contemporary man is free, but often rudderless.
f. Office holders are besieged by requests for special favors.
g. He is a hard-boiled character.
h. Marxism carries the seeds of its own destruction.
i. One of the main planks of their platform is a pledge to close tax loopholes.
j. The program has too many strings attached to it.

3. Study the front-page stories and the editorials in your daily newspaper to find examples of metaphorical language. Which ones seem to be chosen deliberately and which are little more than clichés? In your opinion, do those that appear to be chosen deliberately help the writer's persuasive purpose? How?

4. Analyze the rhetorical implications of the following metaphorical passage. Then try to rewrite the passage using no figurative language. Does it take more or fewer words? Which version do you judge to be more effective?

> What happened here [in America] on this enormous expanse of intact wilderness is that mankind got out from under and spread out. From under what? From under the lid—everybody, from under all the lids—kings, churches, aristocracies, landlords, the military caste, the burgher class, the lawyers, the lesser nobility, the petty bourgeoisie—the piles of subclasses on top of subclasses that formed the structure of old Europe. They left an old world to stretch their limbs and spread out flat, with only the sky above them. Their goal was space. When the Eastern end thickened into layers for a new social pyramid, the underlayers slid out again to the West.[20]

5. Write out the meaning suggested by each of the following allusions. For example, you might explain the phrase "the Midas touch" as the ability to make money from any business venture. If necessary, consult an unabridged dictionary or a desk encyclopedia.

[20] Jacques Barzun, *God's Country and Mine* (New York: Vintage Books, Inc., 1954), p. 8.

Procrustean bed	Pyrrhic victory
Achilles' heel	Gordian knot
Socratic method	Rabelaisian humor
Machiavellian tactics	Panglossian optimism

6. Think of ways in which these contemporary references could be used as allusions in your writing.

Ralph Nader	Disneyland
Hugh Hefner	Joe Namath
Marshall McLuhan	Li'l Abner

SUGGESTED
WRITING
ASSIGNMENT

Purpose: To sharpen your awareness of the rhetorical function of figurative language by having you do a careful analysis and evaluation of an extended metaphor.

Procedure: Read the following passage carefully at least twice. Decide what the author's persuasive purpose is and what associations he wants his reader to draw from the extended metaphor he creates. Begin your paper with a short paragraph that states specifically the main idea that Bellamy is trying to convey to his audience. Then, using as many paragraphs as you need, analyze the important parts of the metaphor and show how they work to achieve the desired effects. Conclude your theme with a short evaluation of the author's rhetoric: does he, through the use of his figurative language, succeed in convincing his reader of his point of view? why or why not?

By way of attempting to give the reader some general impression of the way people lived together in those days, and especially of the relations of the rich and poor to one another, perhaps I cannot do better than to compare society as it then was to a prodigious coach which the masses of humanity were harnessed to and dragged toilsomely along a very hilly and sandy road. The driver was hunger and permitted no lagging, though the pace was necessarily very slow. Despite the difficulties of drawing the coach at all along so hard a road, the top was covered with passengers who never got down, even at the steepest ascents. These seats on top were very breezy and comfortable. Well up out of the dust, their occupants could enjoy the scenery at their leisure, or critically discuss the merits of the straining team. Naturally such places were in great demand and the competition for them was keen, everyone seeking as the first end in life to secure a seat on the coach for himself and to leave it to his child after him. By the rule of the coach a man could leave his seat to whom he wished, but on the other hand there were so many accidents by which it might at any time be lost. For all that they were so easy, the seats were very insecure, and at every sudden jolt of the coach persons were slipping out of them and falling to the ground, where they were instantly compelled to take hold of the rope and help to drag the coach on which they had before ridden so pleasantly.

. . . had they no compassion for fellow beings from whom fortune alone distinguished them? Oh, yes, commiseration was frequently expressed by those who rode for those who had to pull the coach, especially when the vehicle came to a bad place in the road, or to a particularly steep hill. . . . At such times the passengers would call down encouragingly to the toilers of the rope, exhorting them to patience, and holding out hopes of possible compensation in another world for the hardness of their lot, while others contributed to buy slaves and liniments for the crippled and injured. It was agreed that it was a great pity that the coach should be so hard to pull, and there was a sense of general relief when the specially bad piece of road was gotten over. This relief was not, indeed, wholly on account of the team, for there was always some danger at these bad places of a general overturn in which all would lose their seats.[21]

EXERCISES
ON TONE

1. Analyze the tone of the following passages. Ask yourself these questions: What reaction does the author seek to evoke from his audience? How does the author present himself? What word or words describe the tone? What specific elements in the passage contribute to that tone?

a. Main Street is the climax of civilization. That this Ford car might stand in front of the Bon Ton Store, Hannibal invaded Rome and Erasmus wrote in Oxford cloisters. What Ole Jenson the grocer says to Ezra Stowbody the banker is the new law for London, Prague, and the unprofitable isles of the sea; whatsoever Ezra does not know and sanction, that thing is heresy, worthless for knowing and wicked to consider.

[21] Edward Bellamy, *Looking Backward* (Boston: Houghton Mifflin Company, 1966; originally published in 1888), pp. 6–8.

Our railway station is the final aspiration of architecture. Sam Clark's annual hardware turnover is the envy of the four counties which constitute God's Country. In the sensitive art of the Rosebud Movie Palace there is a Message, and humor strictly moral.

Such is our comfortable tradition and sure faith. Would he not betray himself an alien cynic who should otherwise portray Main Street, or distress the citizens by speculating whether there may not be other faiths?[22]

b. There is in James Baldwin's work the most grueling, agonizing, total hatred of the blacks, particularly of himself, and the most shameful, fanatical, fawning, sycophantic love of the whites that one can find in the writing of any black American writer of note in our time. . . .

A reading of *Nobody Knows My Name* cannot help but convince the most avid of Baldwin's admirers of the hatred for blacks permeating his writings. . . . The portrait of Baldwin which comes through his words is that of a mind in unrelenting opposition to the efforts of solemn, dedicated black men who have undertaken the enormous task of rejuvenating and reclaiming the shattered psyches and culture of the black people, a people scattered over the continents of the world and the islands of the seas, where they exist in the mud of the floor of the foul dungeon into which the world has been transformed by the whites.[23]

c. These are the antibiotic days, when even newborn pigs are removed to sanitary surroundings, to be raised on laboratory milk, innocent of any connection with the sow. Pigs are "hatched" nowadays, rather than farrowed. After a few brief swigs of colostrum, they are transferred to the brooder, where an electric heat lamp comforts them, and where they are soon nuzzling the great, many-teated breasts of science and drinking an elixir of terramycin, skim milk, and concentrated vim. (How much of the terramycin finds its way to the consumer in ham and pork, to plague those who have an allergy to that drug and to lower everyone's resistance to Virus X, has not yet been demonstrated.)

Farmers who have experimented with the artificial method of rais-

---

[22] Sinclair Lewis, *Main Street* (New York: Harcourt, Brace, and World, Inc., 1920), Preface.
[23] Eldridge Cleaver, "Notes on a Native Son," in *Soul on Ice* (New York: McGraw-Hill Book Company, 1968), pp. 97–98.

ing pigs have discovered that it is advisable to retain one link with nature—one remembrance of things past. So the modern pig nursery is equipped with a record-player, and at proper intervals the infants hear the victrola give forth the sounds of suckling—the blissful grunting of sows as they let down their milk. The little pigs respond. A chord is touched. They awake and feed.[24]

d. The revival of the forties and fifties is upon us. That Middle-American time of my youth is gaining its place in our historical imagination. Movies, essays, stories, novels, and the sheer passage of time have already begun transforming that era from banal to exotic. The record is being filled not only with nostalgia but with critical insight, as writing men of wit try to pin down those days. Nevertheless, something crucial is missing, for the reality being recorded about that era is essentially a male reality, the experience male experience. And until the female side is acknowledged and recorded, the era cannot even begin to emerge in perspective. . . .

. . . Girls sat in the same movie theaters, attended the same football games, struggled in the back seats of the same parked cars. But the view from the bleachers is very different from the one on the field; and whether we gave in or held out in the parked cars, we had more fearsome concerns than simply making out. We were concerned with survival.

Our experience was no less important, our feelings no less urgent. Yet for some reason, only male versions have been recorded. Well, it certainly won't be the first time we were left out of the chronicles. Even back then it was the boys who delivered the graduation speeches; boys who got their pictures in the paper for football, win or lose; boys who, claiming the American privilege of free speech, spread slanderous things about us to boost their ratings. And the girls? The girls, when we were not simply ignored, were too often driven against our will to some dark lonely street where we were badgered or sweet-talked into going one step further than intended, and afterwards were frightened into silence. Only now are we beginning to speak.[25]

[24] E. B. White, *The Second Tree from the Corner* (New York: Harper and Brothers, 1954), pp. 125–129.
[25] Alix Kates Shulman, "The War in the Back Seat," *The Atlantic Monthly*, July 1972, p. 50. Reprinted by permission of Curtis Brown, Ltd. Copyright © 1972 by The Atlantic Monthly Company.

2. After you read "The Body of an American" by John Dos Passos (below), answer the following questions:

a. What effect is Dos Passos trying to achieve by running together the words in the first paragraph?

b. What is the effect of Dos Passos' sandwiching the second paragraph between the first and the third?

c. What is the tone of the indented paragraphs? How does it contrast with the tone of the other paragraphs? What kind of words does Dos Passos use to achieve his effect in the paragraphs that are not indented?

d. What is the effect of the words attributed to President Harding?

e. What is the effect of the sentence "Where his chest ought to have been they pinned"? What impression is Dos Passos trying to achieve by the list of medals and honors that follows?

f. What do you think is Dos Passos' overall purpose in the passage? What is the predominant tone? What techniques does he use to give that tone to the passage?

Whereasthe Congressoftheunitedstates
byaconcurrentresolutionadoptedon the4thday ofmarch
lastauthorizedthe Secretaryofwar to cause to be
brought to theunitedstatesthe body of an Americanwho
wasamemberoftheamericanexpeditionaryforcesineurope
wholosthislifeduringtheworldwarandwhoseidentityhas
notbeenestablished for burial inthememorialamphitheatre
ofthe nationalcemeteryatarlingtonvirginia

In the tarpaper morgue at Chalons-sur-Marne in the reek of chloride of lime and the dead, they picked out the pine box that held all that was left of

enie menie minie moe plenty other pine boxes stacked up there containing what they'd scraped up of Richard Roe

and other person or persons unknown. Only one can go. How did they pick John Doe?

Make sure he aint a dinge, boys,

make sure he aint a guinea or a kike,

how can you tell a guy's a hundredpercent when all you've got's a gunnysack full of bones, bronze buttons stamped with the screaming eagle and a pair of roll puttees?

. . . and the gagging chloride and the puky dirtstench of the yearold dead . . .

The day withal was too meaningful and tragic for applause. Silence, tears, songs and prayer, muffled drums and soft music were the instrumentalities today of national approbation.

. . . .

—busboy harveststiff hogcaller boyscout champeen cornshucker of Western Kansas bellhop at the United States Hotel at Saratoga Springs office boy callboy fruiter telephone lineman longshoreman lumberjack plumber's helper,

worked for an exterminating company in Union City, filled pipes in an opium joint in Trenton, N.J.

Y.M.C.A. secretary, express agent, truckdriver, fordmechanic, sold books in Denver Colorado: Madam would you be willing to help a young man work his way through college?

President Harding, with a reverence seemingly more significant because of his high temporal station, concluded his speech:

> We are met today to pay the impersonal tribute;
>   the name of him whose body lies before us took flight with his imperishable soul . . .
>   As a typical soldier of this representative democracy he fought and died believing in the indisputable justice of his country's cause . . .

by raising his right hand and asking the thousands within the sound of his voice to join in the prayer:

> Our Father which art in heaven hallowed be thy name . . .

. . . .

The shell had his number on it.

The blood ran into the ground.

The service record dropped out of the filing cabinet when the quartermaster sergeant got blotto that time they had to pack up and leave the billets in a hurry.

The identification tag was in the bottom of the Marne.

The blood ran into the ground, the brains oozed out of the cracked skull and were licked up by the trenchrats, the belly swelled and raised a generation of bluebottle flies.

and the incorruptible skeleton,

and the scraps of dried viscera and skin bundled in khaki
they took to Chalons-sur-Marne
and laid it out neat in a pine coffin
and took it home to God's Country on a battleship
and buried it in a sarcophagus in the Memorial Amphitheatre
in the Arlington National Cemetry
and draped the Old Glory over it
and the bugler played taps
and Mr. Harding prayed to God and the diplomats and the gener-
als and the admirals and the brasshats and the politicians and
the handsomely dressed ladies out of the society column of the
Washington Post stood up solemn
and thought how beautiful sad Old Glory God's Country it was
to have the bugler play taps and the three volleys made their ears
ring.
Where his chest ought to have been they pinned
the Congressional Medal, the D.S.C., the Medaille Militaire, the
Belgian Croix de Guerre, the Italian gold medal, the Vitutea Militara
sent by Queen Marie of Rumania, the Czechoslovak war cross,
the Virtuti Militari of the Poles, a wreath sent by Hamilton Fish,
Jr., of New York, and a little wampum presented by a deputation
of Arizona redskins in warpaint and feathers. All the Washing-
tonians brought flowers.
Woodrow Wilson brought a bouquet of poppies.[26]

3. Bring to class two advertisements with contrasting tone. Some pairs
of magazines that could be useful are *Saturday Review* and *Seventeen,*
Playboy and *Ebony, Cosmopolitan* and *Reader's Digest,* or *Psychology
Today* and *Ladies' Home Journal.*

4. Opening paragraphs are particularly important in setting the tone
of a piece of writing. Write an introductory paragraph of about 100
words that you think would set an appropriate tone for each of these
writing assignments.
a. An autobiographical sketch of about 500 words that you must submit as part of your application for medical school or for a job in
   your congressman's Washington office next summer.
b. An advertisement soliciting members for either the Young Socialists' Alliance or the Young Conservative League on campus.

---

[26] John Dos Passos, *U.S.A.:1919* (Boston: Houghton Mifflin Company, 1946), pp. 539–545.

c. A petition to the head of the English department requesting that the department add a course in black literature, one on women writers in America, or one on the literature of the South or West.

SUGGESTED
WRITING
ASSIGNMENTS

Theme 1

Purpose: To give you practice in writing a short talk and establishing a tone that will be effective for the particular audience.

Procedure: Imagine that you have been asked to come back to the homecoming assembly in your small high school and give a talk entitled "Things I Wish I Had Known Before I Went to College." The invitation makes you nervous, of course, but you are willing to do it because you think that your high school promotes some attitudes that can cause a college freshman problems. Remember that your real audience is the students although it may be that the teachers need enlightenment too. The first step in your prewriting should be to narrow your topic to a manageable size by choosing some particular area in which false ideas are common. Possibilities could be grading standards, study habits, clothes, relative importance of athletics and other activities, or anything else you have found caused you problems. Decide on the main points you want to make and what examples you will use to illustrate them. Your tone could be serious, humorous, ironic, or, if you think the situation warrants it, even bitter, but decide ahead of time what tone you think will best suit your purpose and try to be consistent throughout your paper.

Theme 2

Purpose: To give you practice in developing a method and tone that could be useful for writing a paper in sociology, government, history, or a general studies course.

Procedure: One of the rhetorical techniques used by social critics who want to illustrate the need for change is to show the difference between commonly held beliefs, or conventional wisdom, and the actual situation. Choose one of the beliefs listed below and refute it using the comparison/contrast method; that is, give an example or examples that illustrate the myth and one that illustrates the reality as you see it. Remember that you should be as specific as possible; a few concrete cases or situations are more impressive than generalities. Again, be sure to narrow your topic to a manageable size.

Topics

a. Thrift is a trait that is highly valued in our culture.

b. Anyone who has ability and persistence can go to college if he really wants to.

c. You can achieve anything you set your mind on if you work hard enough.

d. A good education is essential for success in our society.

e. Write and then refute a similar topic suggested to you by your own experience. (It would be prudent to check it out with your instructor ahead of time.)

6

Modes
of
Argument

Developing a sensitivity to and control over the language of rhetoric is the first essential step in learning to read critically, write well, and argue effectively. By itself, however, language cannot sustain the weight of persuasion and exposition. Like food or gasoline, it functions only when it has a mechanism within which to operate. The various modes of argument provide those mechanisms.

WHAT ARE ARGUMENTS?

Before going any further, it would be good to stop and define the term "argument." In the following passage from *The Art of Making Sense,* Lionel Ruby defines the term as it is used here and in subsequent chapters.

Definition

By "argument" we shall mean the *basic unit of reasoning.* The proof of any statement or belief is always presented in the form of an argument, defined as "a unit of discourse in which beliefs are supported by reasons." Our interest henceforth is in argument not for the purposes of contention, but insofar as arguments are an indispensable element in the quest of truth. Argument in this sense is the heart and soul of the rational enterprise.[1]

Purposes: to enlighten and to convince

Ruby goes on to say that arguments are not things that are won or lost; their purpose is as much to enlighten as it is to convince. By this definition, the term "argument" encompasses expository writing as well as straight persuasion.

The starting point of any argument is an assertion, which states the belief, position, or point of view that the arguer is going to expand and support. As pointed out in Chapter 3, the proposition that you undertake to support should be a moderate one, limited by reasonable qualifications that keep you from committing yourself to more than you can handle. For when you state the proposition, you take on an obligation, the obligation to develop that proposition by rational and logical methods. You have said, in effect, "Here is what I believe and

[1] Lionel Ruby, *The Art of Making Sense* (New York: J. B. Lippincott Company, 1954), pp. 104–105. In his *Rhetoric,* Aristotle described several different kinds of arguments and called them "the topics," a term he derived from the Greek word *topoi* meaning "places or regions." His intent was to show that there are specific areas of experience or knowledge in which a person can find arguments to support his assertions. Thus, the term "rhetorical topics" designates various kinds of arguments. Since we are accustomed, however, to using the word "topic" in other contexts, the modes of argument will be discussed here in terms that are simply descriptive.

Use: arguments support
assertions

I shall show why I believe it." You have made a commitment and you are responsible for following it up with supporting arguments. The purpose of this chapter is to help you discover where and how to find arguments to meet your commitment.

THE ARGUMENT FROM DEFINITION

At one time or another, most of us have begun a serious discussion with someone only to be interrupted after a few minutes by the demand, "Define your terms." The request, although sometimes annoying, is a reasonable one for unless the parties to a discussion share definitions of key terms, they are not likely to get very far in their exchange of ideas. For example, suppose someone says to you, "The next legislature should pass better tax laws for this state." Intelligent discussion of this issue is only possible if both of you can agree on what constitutes a good tax law. You might agree on three criteria: a good tax law is enforceable, taxes each citizen according to his ability to pay, and taxes for luxuries more heavily than for necessities. Once you have settled on these standards, you can go on to debate what specific kinds of tax laws will meet them. If, however, one of you defines a good tax law as one that puts the least burden on him, and the other insists a good tax law is one that raises a lot of money, the conversation quickly comes to a dead end. Traditionally, definitions fall into three categories: logical definitions, figurative definitions, and extended definitions.

Categories of Definitions

Defines briefly,
explicitly, objectively

Use: to avoid confusion

Logical definition Logical definition works by describing the thing to be defined briefly, explicitly, and objectively. For example, "A slave is a person who belongs to another"; "A book is a collection of printed pages bound together"; "Education is the training of the mind." Introducing a logical definition that sets precise limits to a word is often helpful in avoiding confusion in expository writing. For instance, in writing about the problems of narcotics, you would need to know the exact definition of "narcotic." You look in the dictionary and find it defined as a drug that, taken moderately, dulls the senses, relieves pain, and induces profound sleep but that in excessive doses causes stupor, coma, or convulsions. Given these specifics, you would not be justified in calling tobacco a narcotic, but you might well classify alcohol as one. Similarly, you should know precisely what terms such as "capital crime" and "corporal punishment" mean when you use them in a paper.

Usually you will be able to find a clear logical definition by going to the dictionary, but it is well to remember that logical definitions must meet two standards. First, they must be reversible, and second, they must not be circular. A reversible definition of "narcotic" is: "a drug that dulls the senses, produces sleep, and with prolonged use becomes addictive."[2] It would not, however, be reversible if it defined "narcotic" as "anything that induces sleep." That description could fit an anesthetic, warm milk, or even a dull teacher. The circular definition that describes a narcotic as something that induces narcosis has little value because it simply repeats the key word in another form. Not quite so obvious but equally circular is a definition that defines feminine traits as characteristics typical of women.

Figurative definition Figurative definitions are those that define by using a figure of speech, principally metaphor. A figurative definition may be striking and colorful, but because its purpose is usually to persuade rather than to clarify, it should not be used when you are honestly trying to explain or identify. Some famous figurative definitions appear below.

Religion is the opiate of the people. (Karl Marx)

A cauliflower is only a cabbage with a college education. (Mark Twain)

War is hell. (General Sherman)

Man is but a reed, the weakest in nature, but he is a thinking reed. (Pascal)

Patriotism is the last refuge of a scoundrel. (Samuel Johnson)

Notice that the real purpose of all these definitions is to express a point of view, an opinion. Used as a nonlogical rhetorical device, the figurative definition may be effective, but it is an inadequate reply to someone who asks you to define your terms.

Extended definition An extended definition is, in a sense, an expanded logical definition; it gives more information and details about a particular term or phrase. It can range in length from a paragraph to an entire essay or even a whole book. A literary handbook,

Standards:
1. reversible
2. not circular

Defines by metaphor

Use: to persuade

Defines by expanding a logical definition

[2] *The American Heritage Dictionary of the English Language,* s.v. "narcotic."

for example, could define "satire" in one paragraph, but a scholar
might need several pages to give what he considered a really complete
definition of the same term. Several people have written entire books
in order to define the good society or the good life: for example,
Plato's *Republic,* More's *Utopia,* Thoreau's *Walden,* and Bellamy's
Looking Backward.

How to Define

Writers define by using a variety of techniques, singly or in combination. The commonest ones are these: attributing characteristics,
analyzing or enumerating parts, comparing and contrasting, giving
examples, and stating functions. These categories overlap, or even
merge occasionally, but it does not matter if the categories cannot
always be identified distinctly. Knowing how a process works is more
important than giving it exactly the right name.

Attributing characteristics   Defining by attributing characteristics
requires that you concentrate on characteristics distinctive to the thing
being defined. For example, if you were listing the characteristics of
democracy, it would not be sufficient to say that in a democracy the
rulers have the support of the majority of the people and are respon-
sive to their will, because other kinds of government, monarchies or
dictatorships, can also have those characteristics. The necessary and
distinguishing characteristic of a democracy is that the rulers are chosen by the people in free and regular elections. Similarly, if you were
giving the defining characteristics of alcoholics, you would have to
do more than say that they are people who drink too much. Alcoholics
have other distinctive characteristics, such as drinking secretly and
drinking compulsively. Notice that in the following passage Susan Sontag defines woman (or the role that she thinks our culture has assigned
women) by listing what she identifies as uniquely feminine characteristics.

> To be a woman is to be an actress. Being feminine is a kind of
> theater, with its appropriate costumes, decor, lighting, and stylized
> gestures. From early childhood on, girls are trained to care in a
> pathologically exaggerated way about their appearance and are
> profoundly mutilated (to the extent of being unfitted for first-class
> adulthood) by the extent of the stress put on presenting them-
> selves as physically attractive objects. Women look in the mirror
> more frequently than men do. It is, virtually, their duty to look

at themselves—to look often. Indeed, a woman who is not narcissistic is considered unfeminine. And a woman who spends literally *most* of her time caring for, and making purchases to flatter, her physical appearance is not regarded in this society as what she is: a kind of moral idiot.[3]

Analyzing parts   Defining by analysis or enumeration of parts is a similar device in that it lists features that are peculiar to and typical of the thing being defined. For example, the definition of "jargon" on page 75 gives a list of the various writing defects that typically appear in jargon. A definition of "beef stroganoff" would list the ingredients: strips of beef, onions, mushrooms, beef bouillon, and sour cream. A person who is defining the comparatively new term "inner city" needs to specify the particular conditions that make an area qualify for that term. Some of them are traffic congestion, dilapidated housing units, a comparatively high rate of unemployment, a relatively high proportion of residents with low income or on welfare, substandard schools, few recreation areas, and inadequate public services such as garbage collection and maintenance of streets. In the following passage, the physicist and "think tank" director, Herman Kahn, defines a member of the "Silent Majority" by listing what he believes to be the attitudes of a typical member.

> If you wanted to describe the traditional American, the lower middle class, the "forgotten man," you would find that he was intensely preoccupied with things like these:
>
> Religion, tradition, authority. An environment that can be too hot or too cold. The tragic side of life, such as seeing a dead person or coming in contact with disease and suffering.
>
> Defense of national frontiers. Virtues like duty, patriotism, courage. The "Puritan ethic": work-orientation, advancement, deferred gratification, sublimation of sexual desires. Also he is preoccupied with a high degree of loyalty to the country, the city, a secret society perhaps.[4]

Comparing and contrasting   One of the most popular defining techniques is that of comparison and contrast. For example, you can

(margin note: List all the typical parts)

(margin note: Compare one thing with another)

---

[3] Susan Sontag, "The Double Standard of Aging," *Saturday Review of the Society,* October 1972, p. 34. Copyright © by Saturday Review, Inc. First appeared in *Saturday Review of the Society,* October, 1972. Used with permission.
[4] Herman Kahn quoted by Robert J. Donavan, "Class Hostility of Americans," *Austin (Texas) American & Statesman,* October 29, 1972.

define good writing by comparing it with bad writing. Good writing is clear, vigorous, precise, and original; bad writing is confusing, dull, vague, and hackneyed. The comparison-contrast technique is particularly useful in writing extended definitions of concepts or beliefs, for example, Riesman's "inner-direction" and "other-direction" mentioned on page 111; the literary movements of "realism" and "romanticism"; the notions of what is "masculine" and what is "feminine." In this passage from the article "The Double Standard of Aging," quoted above, Susan Sontag goes on to define cultural attitudes toward women by comparing them to attitudes toward men.

Use: to give extended definition of concepts or beliefs

> In a man's face lines are taken to be signs of "character." They indicate emotional strength, maturity—qualities far more esteemed in men than in women. . . . Even scars are often not felt to be unattractive; they too can add "character" to a man's face. But lines of aging, any scar, even a small birthmark on a woman's face, are always regarded as unfortunate blemishes. In effect, people take character in men to be different from what constitutes character in women. A woman's character is thought to be innate, static—not the product of her experience, her years, her actions. A woman's face is prized so far as it remains unchanged by (or conceals the traces of) her emotions, her physical risk-taking. Ideally, it is supposed to be a mask—immutable, unmarked. . . . Because women are identified with their faces much more than men are, and the ideal woman's face is one that is "perfect," it seems a calamity when a woman has a disfiguring accident. A broken nose or a scar or a burn mark, no more than regrettable for a man, is a terrible psychological wound to a woman; objectively, it diminishes her value. [P. 35]

Give a concrete example

Giving examples Probably the simplest and most concrete way to define is by giving examples. At the most elementary level, this technique amounts to pointing to an object that a word stands for; for instance, the easiest way for an architect to define a mansard roof would be to show you one. In writing, however, we usually use examples to supplement and expand other kinds of definitions. If you were defining "antiutopian writing," you would probably first specify that in this kind of literature the author depicts a planned and controlled society that he wants the reader to reject. To support and expand the definition, you could then give Huxley's *Brave New World* and Orwell's *1984* as examples of this kind of writing. Such examples are often invaluable in clarifying a definition. The term "natural sciences," for

Use: to support other kinds of definition

example, can be defined as studies that deal with physical matter and phenomena. This definition seems vague, but your reader will understand the meaning immediately if you list physics, chemistry, biology, and geology as natural sciences. Defining with examples is one of the chief ways in which you can put into practice a cardinal rule of explanation: whenever possible, refer to the concrete and familiar to explain the abstract and unfamiliar.

Stating the function   Finally, we sometimes define by giving the function of a person or object; that is, we answer that key question, "What is it for?" Sometimes specifying function may be the most important part of a definition. For example, a psychiatrist is a doctor who is trained to treat mental disorders; the purpose of sociology is to study patterns and processes in society; a thesaurus is a book that lists synonyms. At other times, listing the function of something may be of secondary importance, or it may be inapplicable or even impossible. You might, for instance, define a commune as an experiment in a new style of living and extend your definition by listing features typical of communes, analyzing the economic and domestic arrangements, and giving examples. Saying precisely what the purpose of a commune is would be more difficult. For some residents it might be saving money; for others it might be expressing protest, seeking friends, or just trying something new. And when it comes to defining certain abstractions such as loyalty, liberalism, wealth, or existentialism, the question of function simply does not arise.

In practice, most of us define by combining some or all of these methods, often without even thinking about what we are doing. But when you must define and are puzzled about how you should go about it, reviewing the commonly used techniques can help. Suppose, for example, that you are one of that great number of freshmen classified as "undetermined major"; you are "undetermined" because you cannot decide what kind of job would suit you best. So you sit down to work out a definition of a good job for you. The process might go like this.

Characteristics: Would involve a variety of activities; would not require that I live in a large city; would make a contribution to society; would be reasonably lucrative ($12,000 to $15,000 a year) and offer chances for advancement; would not require eight hours a day in an office; would involve taking responsibility and making decisions.

Answer "What is it?"

Use: may or may not be relevant

Analysis: A job that allows me to make use of my talents in mathematics and physical sciences; one in which I could make use of my natural mechanical abilities; one that does not require study of a foreign language or literature, subjects in which I do poorly.

Comparison and Contrast: A good job would be interesting, demanding, satisfying, and profitable; a bad job would be dull, frustrating, unrewarding and unprofitable.

Examples: Some jobs that might fit my specifications are: civil engineer, veterinarian, airline pilot, rancher, or ecology consultant. Some occupations that certainly would not fit my standards are: law, advertising, accounting, or writing.

Function: Furnish a comfortable living, give me a sense of accomplishment and self-respect, and provide a satisfying outlet for my energies and talents.

Defining creates an assertion

In working out these techniques of definition, you have done more than simply seek a solution to a problem; you have also created an assertion by spelling out what, in your opinion, a job should be. You have set up an "ought" statement, the kind of statement that is the foundation of rhetoric. In this particular case, your audience is only yourself or perhaps your family, but the techniques of definition you have employed are the same kind that you might use in a variety of rhetorical situations.

Using the Argument from Definition

1. Set a standard and evaluate

2. Set an ideal and persuade

3. Describe what ought to be by what is

The argument from definition, one of the modes you might use to support an assertion, usually does one (or more) of three things: first, it may create a yardstick or standard of measurement and then evaluate something according to that yardstick; second, it may describe an ideal and seek to persuade the audience to adopt that ideal; third, it may give the bad features of a person, institution, or theory and state or imply that the thing being defined ought *not* to be as it is. For example, a student employing the first form might outline the criteria for a good athletic program and then, by applying it to the program at his college, argue that officials need to make major changes. You could use the same method to argue that *Crime and Punishment* is a great novel, Anthropology 302 is a worthless course, or that our welfare system is a failure. The process is simple: formulate a yardstick, apply it, make a judgment.

Martin Luther King provides an example of the second form in this excerpt from his famous "Letter from Birmingham Jail":

One may well ask: "How can you advocate breaking some laws and obeying others?" The answer lies in the fact that there are two types of laws: just and unjust. I would be the first to advocate obeying just laws. One has not only a legal but a moral responsibility to obey just laws. Conversely, one has a moral responsibility to disobey unjust laws. I would agree with St. Augustine that "an unjust law is no law at all."

Now, what is the difference between the two? How does one determine whether a law is just or unjust? A just law is a man-made code that squares with the moral law or the law of God. An unjust law is a code that is out of harmony with the moral law. To put it in the terms of St. Thomas Aquinas: An unjust law is a human law that is not rooted in eternal and natural law. Any law that uplifts human personality is just. Any law that degrades human personality is unjust. All segregation statutes are unjust because segregation distorts the soul and damages the personality. It gives the segregator a false sense of superiority and the segregated a false sense of inferiority. Segregation, to use the terminology of the Jewish philosopher Martin Buber, substitutes an "I-it" relationship for an "I-thou" relationship and ends up relegating persons to the status of things. Hence segregation is not only politically, economically and sociologically unsound, it is morally wrong and sinful. Paul Tillich has said that sin is separation. Is not segregation an existential expression of man's tragic separation, his awful estrangement, his terrible sinfulness? Thus it is that I can urge men to obey the 1954 decision of the Supreme Court, for it is morally right; and I can urge them to disobey segregation ordinances, for they are morally wrong.[5]

The next example, taken from an article urging radical changes in reform schools, illustrates the third form of the argument from definition, negative definition. By showing what reform schools are, the author argues for their abolition.

(1) They are expensive. Officials in a number of states have pointed out that it costs as much to keep one juvenile in an institution for one year as it would cost to send him to the most prestigious and costly prep school. . . .

[5] Martin Luther King, Jr., "Letter from Birmingham Jail," in *Why We Can't Wait* (New York: Harper & Row, Publishers, 1963), pp. 84, 85.

(2) They are populated by children of the poor, generally blacks and Puerto Ricans in the East and blacks and Chicanos in the West . . . 89 per cent of the inmates came from homes where parents were on, or eligible for, public assistance. . . .

(3) They cannot be institutions of learning. The so-called industrial or training schools teach skills, not subjects, and the skills are generally those that are obsolete or designed to anchor the juveniles securely to the bottom of the social and financial scale.

(4) Their professional personnel are generally of low caliber. . . .

(5) Study after study has shown that the recidivism rate of young people is directly proportionate to the amount of time they spend in institutions. . . . A youth who spends several years in an institution is almost certain to spend most of his life behind bars.

(6) Finally, and perhaps most important, reform schools are prime devourers of the lard doled from the political pork barrel. Jobs in the school from top to bottom are political appointments, and local politicians are fighting tenaciously to retain this power to make appointments.[6]

Ethics, the basis for argument from definition

The argument from definition, then, is usually an ethical argument, calculated to appeal to the audience's sense of what is right and moral, what is desirable, what ought to be. As the eminent rhetorician, Richard Weaver, puts it in his book *The Ethics of Rhetoric*, "it seems safe to assert that those who believe in the validity of the argument from genus [definition] are idealists, roughly, if not very philosophically, defined." Although you may not think of yourself as an idealist, when you begin to construct an argument on a matter that interests you, you are likely to find that you have strong opinions about the right course of action; you are, therefore, an idealist on at least that topic. You might, for example, think that a good education should include a study of Western civilization, and consequently courses in it should be required of anyone who receives a college degree. Or, you might argue that your college should not force all students to live in college-approved housing, basing your argument on your belief that everyone should have the right to choose where he wants to live. In both of these cases, you are arguing from your definition of what is good. If by extending and supporting your definition, you can persuade your audience to accept it, you have a good chance of achieving your rhetorical purpose.

[6] Brian Vachon, "Hey Man, What Did You Learn In Reform School?" *Saturday Review of Education,* October 1972, p. 72.

THE ARGUMENT FROM CAUSE AND EFFECT

Definition

The attempt to persuade an audience that one event caused another or that certain effects will follow from certain actions must be one of the oldest forms of argument. One can imagine rulers in ancient times trying to understand the causes of floods or earthquakes or plagues in order that they might explain such disasters to their subjects. Lacking the knowledge to make scientific explanations, they could only make erroneous ones: often they cited the anger of the gods as the cause and recommended that the people make some sacrifice or do penance to keep the effect from occurring again. So strongly does the human mind want to find causes for things it does not understand that everyone believed the explanations. Such naiveté strikes us as childish, but our responses to cause and effect arguments are often equally unsophisticated.

Guidelines: 1. Establish reasonable probability

You can, however, improve your own arguments and better evaluate those of others by observing these elementary guidelines and cautions. First, when making a cause and effect argument, be willing to settle for establishing reasonable probability; don't overstate your case and force yourself into an indefensible position. You cannot really prove that the Supreme Court's abolishment of the death penalty will cause an increase in major crimes or that rising medical costs are going to bring about socialized medicine in this country. At best, you can only hypothesize and say that under the circumstances such results seem highly probable. And after you have made such a hypothesis, you have an obligation to support it by explaining how you arrived at your conclusion and by giving examples that reinforce your reasoning. The selection from Goldwater's *The Conscience of a Conservative* on page 130 is a good example of a cause and effect argument that is weak because it is both overstated and unsupported. The author says without qualification that taking welfare turns a person from "a dignified, industrious, self-reliant *spiritual* being into a dependent animal creature." He does not say "it may" or "it could" or "it probably will," nor does the excerpt explain why he makes such a statement or give any examples to support his assertion. A thinking person simply will not accept such overgeneralizations.

2. Avoid oversimplifying by not assuming a single cause

Second, avoid simplistic thinking about cause and effect. One kind of oversimplification is assuming that an event is the result of a single cause; for example, some social critics have asserted that the student riots of the sixties were the direct result of permissive child-raising practices in the forties. Others claim that increased juvenile crime is the result of children's watching violence on television. Both theories are attractively neat and simple, but they reveal their proponents' ignorance of the complexities of human behavior. If you want to make these kinds of hypotheses—and it is certainly possible that there is an element of truth in each of them—have the good judgment to limit yourself to saying "one of the causes of."

Avoid oversimplifying by not confusing coincidence with cause

Another kind of simplistic causal reasoning confuses coincidence or simple sequence with cause and effect. This can be as primitive as saying that you had a wreck because a black cat ran in front of your car, or it can be as sophisticated as Bertrand Russell's supporting his assertion that conventional living destroys creativity by pointing out that the quality of Wordsworth's poetry declined after he left his mistress and married. We will come back to this kind of erroneous thinking in the chapter on fallacies (Chapter 8). For now, just remember to be wary of this oversimplification both in your arguments and those of others. For example, it is apt to turn up distressingly often in political campaigns. An advertisement from the 1972 presidential contest listed various things that had taken place during Richard Nixon's first term. The writer of the ad pointed out that the grocery bill of the average family was $450 higher in 1972 than it had been in 1968 and that two million more people were unemployed than had been when Mr. Nixon took office. He also noted that four million people had been added to the welfare rolls during Mr. Nixon's administration, that the national debt had increased ninety billion, and that the number of heroin addicts was up by one quarter of a million. The ad suggests that these events took place *solely* because of Richard Nixon's presidency. They coincided with his administration, but their causes were multiple and complex. Whatever your political sentiments, you should be critical of such fallacious reasoning.

3. Avoid using a scapegoat

Finally, be suspicious of cause and effect reasoning that brings in scapegoats or conjures up conspiracies to explain misfortune, and avoid it in your writing. Complex social problems have complex causes, and trying to solve them or to rationalize them away by blaming one group is naive or deceitful. A classic example of this tactic is Hitler's propaganda campaign against the Jews. By blaming them for the economic and social problems that followed World War I, he was able to divert the attention of the German people from their dissatisfactions and concentrate their hostility on a scapegoat. The same thing occurs in our country when people try to explain riots and demonstrations by blaming them on "foreign elements" and "outside agitators." Such simplistic rationalization prevents us from looking for the real causes of social unrest and postpones solutions. The critical thinker avoids this kind of thinking himself and rejects it in the writings of others.

THE ARGUMENT FROM CIRCUMSTANCE

Definition

Signal phrases

The argument from circumstance is a special kind of cause and effect argument in which the speaker or writer seeks to persuade his audience to approve or at least accept a certain course of action on the grounds that no other course is practical or possible. Certain phrases recur so frequently in the argument from circumstance that they signal it. Typical ones are: "It is inevitable"; "We have no choice but to"; "Under the circumstances, our only option is"; "We are forced to"; and "Whether we like it or not, we must." Sometimes the argument contains the appeal "our backs are to the wall" or "we are trapped by forces beyond our control." At other times it takes the fatalistic approach of "we might as well accept the inevitable." In any case, the task of the rhetorician is to convince his audience that the circumstances he is setting up as a cause are so pressing, so serious, that certain effects must follow. He usually does this by giving a detailed analysis and description of the circumstances.

The rhetoric of the Declaration of Independence fits the pattern of the argument from circumstance well. To explain why they advocated revolution, the writers used these words:

> But when a long train of abuses and usurpations pursuing invariably the same object, evinces a design to reduce them [the people] under absolute despotism, it is their right, it is their *duty*, to throw off such government, and to provide new guards for their future security. Such has been the patient sufferance of these colonies; and such is now the *necessity* which *constrains* them to alter their former systems of government. The history of the present king of Great Britain is a history of repeated injuries and usurpations, all having in direct order the establishment of an *absolute tyranny* over these states. To prove this, let facts be submitted to a candid world. [Italics added.]

Fourteen paragraphs follow detailing the oppressive acts of George III and concluding with these dramatic charges:

> He has plundered our seas, ravished our coasts, burnt our towns, and destroyed the lives of our people.

He is at this time transporting large armies of foreign mer- cenaries to complete the works of death, desolation and tyranny already begun with circumstances of cruelty and perfidy scarcely paralleled in the most barbarous ages and totally unworthy the head of a civilized nation.

Apparently, the colonists agreed that the circumstances described were indeed intolerable and accepted revolution as the only solution.

In our own time, Martin Luther King's "Letter from Birmingham Jail" furnishes another example of the argument from circumstance.

You deplore the demonstrations taking place in Birmingham. But your statement, I am sorry to say, fails to express a similar concern for the conditions that brought about the demonstrations. I am sure that none of you would want to rest content with the superfi- cial kind of social analysis that deals merely with effects and does not grapple with underlying causes. It is unfortunate that demon- strations are taking place in Birmingham, but it is even more un- fortunate that the city's white power structure left the Negro community *with no alternative.*

. . . .

As the weeks and months unfolded we realized that we were the victims of a broken promise. The signs remained. As in so many experiences of the past we were confronted with blasted hopes, and the dark shadow of a deep disappointment settled upon us. *So we had no alternative* except that of preparing for direct action, whereby we would present our very bodies as a means of laying our case before the conscience of the local and national community. [P. 79, 80, italics added.]

Other arguments from circumstance: Environment

Arguments that explain human behavior solely in terms of envi- ronment constitute another kind of circumstantial argument. To claim that a person became a criminal because he grew up in a slum is really saying that "under the circumstances, his crime was inevitable." Novelists often use this kind of argument by creating a set of circum- stances to account for their characters' behavior. In *The Grapes of Wrath*, for example, Steinbeck carefully sets up natural and economic events that drove the Joads to become migrants. By portraying them as a poverty-stricken tenant farm family in Oklahoma during a prolonged era of drought, he makes the reader feel that their trek to California is inevitable.

We encounter less dramatic forms of the argument from circumstance in our everyday lives. For instance, when someone uses that old cliché "If you can't lick 'em, join 'em," he is using the argument from circumstance. The person who reasons that if he does not take advantage of an opportunity, someone else will, or who justifies an action by saying that everyone else does it, is also arguing from circumstance. Anyone who argues that people can't help being the way they are is using the same reasoning.

The argument from circumstance can be extremely persuasive and difficult to refute. If the rhetorician can convince his audience that the circumstances are indeed compelling, so overwhelming that they lead to only one logical conclusion, he can win his point. For example, if you were trying to persuade the officials of your college that they should not double tuition and could demonstrate that such a raise would force 40 percent of the students to leave school, they would certainly have to reconsider their proposal. The crucial task in presenting a circumstantial argument is giving enough evidence to make a strong case for your side; merely hypothesizing about what *might* happen under certain circumstances will probably not convince a skeptical reader.

The weakness of the argument from circumstance is that often it is distorted into a justification for immoral or self-serving acts. The person who is going to do something unethical, something that he is ashamed of, usually wants to divert blame from himself. Thus, he may try to avoid taking the responsibility for his acts by pleading that he is the victim of forces over which he has no control. For example, a scholarship athlete may justify his poor grades by pointing out that the four hours a day he has to devote to football practice make it impossible for him to study as much as he should; a politician may excuse broken campaign promises by saying that he had to make them in order to get elected; the owner of a business may claim that if he spends money to install pollution control devices, he will be forced out of business by his competitors. The argument from circumstance can easily degenerate into the argument from expediency. In evaluating both your own circumstantial arguments and those of others, you need to make careful distinctions between the inevitable and the merely probable, between consequences that are disastrous and those that are only inconvenient or unpleasant.

"Can't lick 'em, join 'em."

Advantage, hard to refute: 1. if circumstances are compelling

2. if enough evidence is given

Disadvantage: may be used to avoid responsibility

Distinguish the inevitable from the probable

The Argument from Analogy

Definition

The person who argues from analogy attempts to persuade by suggesting that things that are alike in some respects are probably alike in other respects. The logical process on which this kind of argument is based goes like this: if A and B share the qualities of X and Y, which we can observe, then they are likely to share the quality of Z, which we cannot observe. For example, in recent years some people have tried to demonstrate that women are oppressed by drawing an analogy between their position and that of blacks. They point out that both groups as a whole work at low-paying, menial jobs, have not for the most part been admitted to professions or to positions of power, are considered to have a certain "place" in society, and are often treated as inferiors or incompetents. Thus, they argue that, although women are not numerically a social minority, in other important ways they suffer as much discrimination as minority ethnic groups. Obviously, there are also important ways in which women do not have the same kinds of problems as blacks or Mexican-Americans, but the analogy is partially valid. The directives against race or sex discrimination issued by federal and state administrators testify to its force.

Advantage: it is dramatic

Disadvantage: it cannot *prove* a point

The argument from analogy is often striking and dramatic and, for those reasons, it is frequently persuasive, but at best it only enlightens and clarifies. Used as a reinforcement for other kinds of arguments, however, analogy is an excellent rhetorical device. You cannot actually prove a point solely by analogy because you will rarely find two things alike in every important respect. Also, if two things have minor characteristics in common but virtually no major ones, your argument by analogy will break down. Take, for example, the frequently quoted "domino theory" that some political theorists used to justify United States' intervention in the Vietnam war. They reasoned that the United States must prevent even this single, small Southeast Asian country from surrendering to the Communists because if the first Southeast Asian country fell, all the others would topple in a chain reaction like lined-up dominoes. The analogy is appealingly simple, but it is also weak. Southeast Asian countries and lined-up dominoes have two minor characteristics in common: they are small and they are close together. In other significant ways, they have nothing in common: dominoes are identical, inanimate pieces of wood controlled entirely by external forces; countries are different economically, politically, culturally, and militarily, and their peoples are capable of independent action.

The following is an example of a more cogent and thought-provoking argument from analogy.

> Public education is the nation's largest consumer industry. . . .
> In cases where quality of education is demonstrably poor, there
> is reason to believe that consumers may legitimately take action
> in the courts. Students, parents, taxpayers, and, for that matter,
> Ralph Nader may well claim that the principles of law that govern
> business, industry, and some professions extend to education.
>
> Do they? Here are some parallels that suggest possible lines
> of attack:
>
> When a doctor or lawyer performs negligently, ignoring proper
> practice, he bears legal responsibility. When school boards,
> administrators, or teachers behave negligently in their instruc-
> tional duties, do they bear major responsibility? Do they bear *any*
> responsibility?
>
> When consumer products fail to work, the manufacturer or pro-
> ducer bears some legal responsibility for the failure. When
> teachers fail to teach, do the schools of educations that produced
> those teachers bear responsibility for their failure? Similarly, when
> students fail to learn, are those responsible for their learn-
> ing—schools, teachers, and publishers and purchasers of educa-
> tional materials—legally responsible for student failure?
>
> When a consumer purchases a car, there is an "implied war-
> ranty" from the manufacturer and his agent to the purchaser that
> the car will perform certain minimal functions; for example, it will
> start, propel itself, turn, stop, give a warning signal. Is there an
> implied warranty to the consumer of educational services from
> the state and its local agents that, as a result of schooling,
> graduates will perform certain minimal functions?[7]

The authors of this article prudently frame their analogies as questions, inviting the reader to consider if the reasoning is indeed valid. Such an approach actually strengthens their argument because instead of insulting their audience by claiming more than they can prove, they simply say: Here is a new way to look at the responsibility of educators that has some profound implications. What do you think? You would do well to exercise this kind of restraint when you employ analogy as an argument. If you use good judgment in making your comparisons and do not push them too far, they will be an asset; if you use comparisons carelessly, they turn into fallacies.

Do not push an analogy too far

[7] Gary Saretsky and James Mecklenburger, "See You in Court?" *Saturday Review of Education,* November 1972, p. 50.

The A Fortiori Argument

This Latin term (which is pronounced "ah–for–shee–ór–ee") literally means "all the stronger." It is used to describe a mode of argument that is based on probability. The argument works like this: you hypothesize about two possibilities, the second of which can happen more easily than the first; then, if you can show that the first possibility became a reality, you conclude that the second one should also materialize. In practice, this process is not nearly as complicated as this abstract description makes it sound; you have probably encountered it frequently and occasionally used it yourself. In its complete form the *a fortiori* argument looks like this:

> If we can have the technology to put a man on the moon, we should be able to figure out how to feed the hungry people in the United States.

> We have the technology to put a man on the moon. Therefore, we ought to utilize our technology to feed the hungry people in the United States.

Presumably, landing men on the moon is a much more complicated and difficult task than simply feeding people; the implication, then, is that it is ridiculous for us to be able to do the first and not be able, or at least willing, to do the second. Reduced to the form in which we usually find it, this argument reads, "If we can put a man on the moon, we ought to be able to feed people in this country."

Some *a fortiori* arguments are effective because they appeal to our sense of what seems logical. The argument that if an eighteen-year-old boy is old enough to fight for his country, he is old enough to be allowed to buy a beer is this kind of argument. An *a fortiori* argument that is sometimes advanced in favor of socialized medicine is this: if the state builds public schools and pays teachers in order that everyone may have the right to an education, why should it not build public hospitals and pay doctors in order that everyone might have the right to good health? It is a line of argument that is not easy to refute.

Another form of the *a fortiori* argument appeals to our conviction that people are consistent and predictable. Arguments based on that assumption might run like this: if a man will cheat a member of his family, he will certainly cheat a stranger; if a student will turn in a plagiarized paper, it is likely that he will cheat on an examination; if an army cadet panics in war games, he will go to pieces under enemy

Definition

Appeals to sense of logic

Appeals to our convictions about human behavior

fire; the person who does well in difficult subjects like calculus ought to do well in comparatively easy ones such as Spanish. This kind of argument, which involves speculation about human behavior, is not as solidly grounded as those based on reason, but it can be forceful nevertheless. The 1972 presidential election proved just how forceful. Early in the campaign the Democratic nominee, George McGovern, made two mistakes that were turned into *a fortiori* arguments against him. First, he advocated abolishing welfare payments and giving everyone in the country $1,000 instead; he later admitted that this was impractical and that he had not realized how much it would cost. Second, he said he would stand by his vice-presidential candidate, Thomas Eagleton, after Eagleton admitted that he had been treated for mental illness; but, under pressure, he reversed his decision. McGovern's critics almost immediately put forth the argument that if a presidential candidate could not make careful, rational decisions before the election when the pressures on him were relatively light, he would not be able to make sound decisions as a president when he was under heavy pressure.

THE ARGUMENT FROM EVIDENCE

From the moment that you began the study of rhetoric, you have been counseled: "Be concrete"; "Give examples"; "Support your assertions with evidence." Such advice was really little more than a reminder to do in writing what you do almost instinctively in speech. It seems to come naturally to all of us to draw on external sources when we argue because we realize that our opinions carry more weight when we give outside evidence to support them. We turn to what we have

Purpose: to corroborate and reinforce

seen, read, or heard in order to corroborate and reinforce our own ideas. All information of this kind comes under the general category of evidence. That term, however, encompasses a variety of data that need to be described and analyzed. At the risk of oversimplifying—a risk we always run when we begin pigeon-holing and labeling—we will designate five kinds of evidence: reports, statistics, personal testimony, factual references, and the appeal to authority. At times, of course, these categories will merge and overlap.

Reports

In our mass media culture, we have an unprecedented number of reports; television, radio, books, newspapers, and magazines keep us informed about a multitude of events and topics. The person who keeps up with current events through these channels has an impressive stock of resources with which to reinforce his rhetoric. If you want to argue that this country should subsidize public hospitals, you can quote from an article in *Harper's*[8] magazine that reveals what happens to the quality and cost of health care when businessmen begin building hospitals for profit. You can bolster arguments on defense spending, migrant labor, or political propaganda by quoting television documentaries on those topics. Both the news columns and feature articles in newspapers can furnish you with supporting evidence for papers on topics such as conditions in the local jails, the cheating problem in colleges, or the need for more medical schools in your state. When you are writing on almost any controversial topic, you can find reports that will give you usable information.

Reports are valuable when you are relying on evidence as one of your chief modes of argument, but they do present a problem because obviously all reports are not of equal value. How, then, do you evaluate them? There is no easy answer, but a good rule of thumb is to ask two questions about every report: (1) Is the source reliable?; (2) What is the bias of the person or group doing the reporting? In general, we can assume that major newspapers, national television and radio networks, and magazines of established reputation tell the truth. They may use loaded language and they may leave out certain important details, but what they print or broadcast is reasonably accurate. They cannot afford to have it otherwise. Less well-known newspapers and magazines that specialize in sensationalism or cater to an uncritical and poorly informed audience are less apt to be reliable.

Answering the question about bias involves determining whose interest the report might serve. Often the answer is that it serves no special interest; and you should not be so suspicious or cynical that you assume most reports are distorted in favor of a particular group or party. But only a naive person would fail to realize that a report on the condition of the beef industry put out by the Cattleman's Association is going to differ in tone and emphasis from one put out by the Consumers' Protection League, just as a report on the quality of health care in this country that is made by the American Medical Association is going to differ from one made by the World Health Organization. It is not that the people who make reports deliberately lie; it is rather that someone who has an investment, emotional or financial, in a particular area—education, business, defense, med-

Evaluating reports:
1. Is the source reliable?

2. What is the bias of the reporter?

[8] Roger Rapoport, "A Candle for St. Greed's," *Harper's,* December 1972, pp. 70–75.

icine—can scarcely avoid stressing some points and playing down others. The persons who receive and use those reports should at least be alert for possible bias.

Statistics

Problem of bias

The use of statistics can pose the same problem of bias. After all, whose statistics are they? A good rule here is to trust statistics and data that come from research organizations such as the Brookings Institution, from government bureaus and agencies, from national survey organizations such as the Gallup poll, from a nationally known encyclopedia or publications such as the *World Almanac*, and from research groups funded by universities or nonprofit foundations. But you should be at least slightly skeptical about polls financed by candidates or a lobby and about reports sponsored by individual companies, and very skeptical about any statistical data from unspecified sources. Phrases such as "reports show," "an independent research organization has found," and "statistics prove" do not constitute good evidence.

Personal Testimony

Personal testimony, his own and that of others, provides the student writer with an easy and effective way to support many kinds of arguments. If you are working with a topic about which you have firsthand knowledge, you can use no better source of evidence than your concrete experiences. What you have learned about race problems from incidents in your high school or what you have found out about graft in the construction business by helping to build an apartment house in which shoddy materials were used is impressive testimony, as good as an incident reported in *The New York Times* or *Playboy* magazine. When you recall the variety of experiences you have had in your life or know about in other people's lives, you will find that you have a surprising amount of testimony on which to draw. You should be careful, of course, not to overgeneralize from one or two incidents because the personal experiences of one individual are not enough to *prove* a general theory, but used as reinforcement and illustration, they add interest and concreteness to your papers.

Use your own concrete experiences

Use personal experiences to reinforce or illustrate, not to prove

Using the personal testimony of others can also be effective, but here you may encounter problems about reliability. When you cite the experiences of another person as evidence to support your point, be sure that you have direct knowledge about that experience or know

Use the experiences of others

the person well enough to vouch for his credibility. Anecdotes that you hear in casual conversation, particularly those for which no source is given, may be enlightening, but they do not provide substantial evidence with which to support a serious assertion. A critical audience will dismiss that kind of testimony as no more than "hearsay evidence," not admissible in any court and therefore not to be taken seriously. A statement like the following sentence from Paul Goodman's *Growing Up Absurd* is an example of such hearsay evidence: "The pastor of a large church in an ordinary Midwestern town told me that, in his observation, not one marriage in twenty was worth-while." The reader is unlikely to accept a claim that the institution of marriage is disintegrating simply on the basis of this kind of extreme and completely unverifiable statement.

Avoid using "hearsay evidence"

Factual References

The careful writer looks for solid evidence to back his assertions. For instance, in a column charging that national values are declining, Smith Hempstone uses these factual references to support his allegation:

> An Air Force general admitted to having waged an unauthorized aerial war against North Vietnam before Hanoi launched its current offensive. A prominent author was fined and sent to jail for trying to defraud his publishers. The grades, transcripts and degrees of 600 University of Wisconsin students, accused of submitting as their own work term papers bought from commercial firms, were held up. The chief security officer of both the Republican national committee and the Committee to Re-elect the President was arrested for breaking into the Democratic national committee offices with the apparent intent of committing political espionage.[9]

Anyone who had been reading the papers in the weeks before this column appeared would remember the events to which Hempstone refers and be inclined to agree with his indictment of the national character. When the Women's Liberation spokesman Gloria Steinem seeks to convince her audience that the traditional ideas about the "natural abilities" of women are unfounded, she also turns to factual references.

[9] Smith Hempstone, "Low Estate of Values," *Austin (Texas) American & Statesman,* July, 1972.

Freud to the contrary, anatomy is not destiny, at least not more than nine months at a time. In Israel, women are drafted, and some have gone to war. In England, more men type and run switchboards. In India and Israel, a woman rules. In Sweden, both parents take care of the children.[10]

Effectiveness of facts depends on familiarity to audience

The supporting evidence used by both these authors is effective because it employs references that are familiar to a reasonably well-informed person. If you search your memory when you are writing a paper, you will probably find that you have a stock of similar material readily available. You can draw on historical as well as contemporary material, or you can use what you are learning in other courses. If you are writing a paper in which you try to show that harsh repression of unpopular opinions is not only cruel but also shortsighted, you might cite the examples of the Romans' persecution of the Christians, the Church's persecution of Galileo, and the British government's treatment of Mahatma Gandhi. In a paper arguing for tighter controls on television advertising, you could support your claim that commercials are often misleading by bringing in two facts you learned in your nutrition course: rats fed for three weeks solely on so-called "enriched" bread died of starvation, and cereals that are advertised as "nutritious and full of energy" really furnish the body nothing but calories. Once you develop the habit of looking for rhetorical material in all areas of your experience, you will be surprised at how much information you have stored in your head.

The Appeal to Authority

The final kind of evidence that you can draw on in order to support your rhetoric or exposition is the appeal to authority. In an argument

© 1972 by United Features Syndicate, Inc.

[10] Gloria Steinem, "What It Will Be Like If Women Win," *Time,* August 31, 1970, p. 22.

to support your assertion that there should be unity among the various factions on campus, you might quote Lincoln's warning: "A house divided against itself cannot stand." If you are trying to prove that riots and demonstrations are not phenomena of the twentieth century only, you could quote from the report of the presidential commission on the causes and prevention of violence. You could support a proposal to abolish the grading system by pointing out that low or failing grades have bad psychological effects on children, citing as your authority the famous behavioral psychologist B. F. Skinner, who claims that people learn best when they receive positive, not negative, reinforcement. If you argue against smoking, you would be making an appeal to authority by quoting the inscription on all cigarette packages, "Warning: The Surgeon General has determined that cigarette smoking is dangerous to your health." You are also using authority when you cite a dictionary definition; for example, "Prejudice is an adverse judgment or opinion formed beforehand or without knowledge or examination of the facts; a preconceived preference or idea; bias."[11] References to the Constitution, the Bible, or any other revered document to emphasize or strengthen a point constitute another kind of appeal to authority. You can see that the stock of authoritative sources available to you is vast and varied. Usually the difficulty is not finding an authority to quote, but deciding which one best suits your purposes.

Because most of us are awed by experts, especially those with advanced degrees, titles, and several impressive awards, the argument from authority can be a powerful one. It does, however, pose certain problems. First, does the authority cited have credentials that will command the respect of your audience? You are more likely to win assent to your claims if you give the title, position, and qualifications of the authority you quote. For example, if you want to cite evidence on the problems of college faculties, you might say, "Dr. Reece McGee, professor of sociology at Purdue University and the author of *The Academic Marketplace* and *Academic Janus*, says that"; in an argument against cutting defense spending, you could quote an opinion from Admiral Elmo Zumwalt, Chief of Naval Operations. In both cases, you show that your authorities have the position, the qualifications, and the experience to make their testimony worth listening to. To rely on unverifiable and vague references such as "a well-known economist" or "the president of one of America's major universities" is an evasion of responsibility. And just as you should not rely on such devices yourself, you should not be impressed by them in the rhetoric of others. Remember also that you should not give much weight to the evidence of an authority when he is operating outside

Cite the authority's
credentials

Don't use an authority
speaking out of his
field

[11] *The American Heritage Dictionary of the English Language,* s.v. "prejudice."

of his field. If a Nobel Prize-winning geneticist criticizes the space program, he should be listened to as a private citizen, not as an authority; when Frank Sinatra endorses a political candidate or Joe Namath recommends certain boots, their opinions should be regarded as those of private citizens because their expertise in show business or in professional football does not carry over to politics or footwear.

The other problem with using the argument from authority is that one can, without too much trouble, often find two qualified, reliable authorities who take opposite views on the same topic. Certainly you have heard Biblical quotations brought in as support for both sides of an argument: "An eye for an eye, a tooth for a tooth" opposed to "Father, forgive them; they know not what they do." On the question of disarmament, you will find Senator William Proxmire on one side and Senator John Tower on the other, both experienced, knowledgeable men, but with radically differing opinions. Two well-known, highly trained, and well-thought-of psychologists, Carl Rogers and B. F. Skinner, disagree violently on the best ways to influence human behavior. And so it goes. In situations like these, you can conclude only that intelligent authorities of good will often view matters differently and that there may be no single right answer available. For your rhetorical purposes, it is perfectly legitimate to try to find a qualified authority who supports your point of view. If you give his credentials and quote him both accurately and in context, you are arguing fairly.

Problem of opposing authorities

COMBINING ARGUMENTS

In practice, of course, any rhetorician combines several modes of argument (including some we have not yet discussed) and a variety of persuasive techniques in order to make his arguments convincing. You will be doing the same. It should be easier now that you realize how many places there are where you can look for ways to develop and support your assertions. As an illustration of how many means are available to the arguer, let us analyze the kinds of arguments that one man put together in a short, persuasive essay.

Does the Devil Make Us Do It?

From evidence: personal testimony

New York——I was passing a sex shop on 42nd Street recently when the police were conducting a raid. The cops went in and the patrons came out. One customer, trying to duck the television cameras, exited quickly and then pretended he was merely a passer-by. He sidled up to me, to blend into the crowd, and watched.

"What's happening?" I asked him.

"A raid."

"What for?"

"Because," the man said, indignant now, "they got all that filth in there."

The incident says a lot about the confusing American view of pornography. That view has always been a hypocritical one. As a nation we have never made up our mind, when handed a dirty picture on the corner, to smile, to call the cops, or both.

I vote we just smile. What's all the big sweat, anyway?

We are a people titillated by sex. Increasingly so. Where once the smut business in this country was largely manufactured in France or at least made in Japan, it is now fully an American industry. It is big, big business. New York City has two dozen weekly sex newspapers selling from 50 cents to $1 an issue. Forty-second Street hawkers sell everything from phony stimulants to pathetic photos of "genuine schoolteachers from Ohio."

Silicone-breasted go-go dancers perform in the shadow of Washington's capitol, not rarely for nightclub-touring government officials. X-rated movies have become so common many drive-ins have begun offering them, along with customer anonymity. . . .

Indeed, pornography has gone socko. Why? Because the nation wants it (although the nation won't admit it). People now spend as much as $2 billion annually, by some industry estimates, to further the phenomenon.

Undeniably, much of what has happened has been unfortunate. Manhattan's 42nd Street, which used to be a tourist attraction, is now, with its bosom-boosting, a mean tourist trap. The sex clubs along Washington's 14th Street are, late at night, overly aggressive, with their loud music, their nude window photographs and their pimps at the door begging customers. Many people are genuinely offended that newspapers now advertise X-rated movies with their drippy titles ("The Midnight Plowboy"). This kind of aggressiveness is, perhaps, open to legislative restriction—if only because it foists pornography on that part of the population which is definitely not interested.

But beyond this protection of the innocent (including children), there seems to be no logical or even moral reason to call the cops on smut. You look or you don't look. You buy or you don't. If nobody forces you, what really is the crime? . . .

Two years ago, the President's Commission on Pornography and Obscenity released the results of a thorough, three-year,

The following appear as margin notes alongside the text:

From definition: attributing characteristics; giving examples

From definition: attributing characteristics

From definition: stating function
From evidence: factual reference

From evidence: factual reference

From cause and effect
From evidence: factual reference

From definition: stating function

From definition: giving examples

From definition: giving examples
From cause and effect

From cause and effect

From evidence: appeal to authority

From evidence:
testimony

From evidence: appeal
to authority; testimony

From evidence: appeal
to authority; testimony

From definition: attrib-
uting characteristics.
From evidence: appeal
to authority
From comparison:
a fortiori

From definition: com-
paring and contrasting

From evidence:
testimony

From evidence: personal
testimony

From circumstance

extremely objective study of smut in America. It was a blanket admission that the nation, the John Birchers, the J. Edgar Hoovers, had been worrying for naught for generations. The commission says that exposure to sexual material does not cause crime, emotional problems or lead to character deterioration. It said that it is "extremely unwise" for governments to attempt the legislation of morality beyond behavior. It said that all laws prohibiting or limiting sale or showings of sexual material should be repealed. And it said, moreover, that most Americans believe in sexual propaganda.

The commission's report, predictably, was buried under a blanket of condemnation. But its findings are, two years later, no less relevant and revealing. The First Amendment of the Constitution (free speech, free press) applies to all or it does not really apply to any. If we allow this newspaper to print, we have to also, constitutionally, even though we personally object, allow the beady-eyed peddlers to go to press too.

So smile. Smile! Is sex really so decadent?

O.K. So you don't like pornography. Stout fellow. But others do, a good many others, and hypocritical though some of them are, they are remarkably human. The fellow outside the 42nd Street shop, for example. When he started cheering the police raid, I told him to can it, that I had seen him slink out of the door, that even then he had a dirty book in his pocket.

"Oh," he said, turning colors, ending up in green, "well, ah, that is," he took out the book and grinned, "the devil made me do it."[12]

EXERCISES

1. Identify the mode or modes of argument appearing in the following examples:
a. Running a university is like running a business, and, therefore, it is a good idea to have businessmen for regents. The purpose of a university, after all, is to turn out a reliable product.
b. If a man can find time to jog and play handball every day to keep his body in shape, you would think he could find time now and then to read a book to keep his mind in shape.
c. I see nothing wrong with selling dirty books at the college book store. If it doesn't do it, the store next door will.

[12] Tom Tiede, "Does the Devil Make Us Do It?" *The Taylor (Texas) Daily Press,* November 24, 1972. Reprinted by permission of Newspaper Enterprise Association.

d. "A State which dwarfs its men in order that they may be more docile instruments in its hands even for beneficial purposes—will find that with small men no great thing can really be accomplished; and that the perfection of machinery to which it has sacrificed everything, will in the end avail it nothing. . . ." (John Stuart Mill)

e. The head of the psychology department at our university says that this country is on the brink of a sexual and social revolution.

f. "In all things that are purely social we [the black and white races] can be as separate as the fingers, yet one as the hand in all things essential to mutual progress." (Booker T. Washington)

g. A true liberal is one who believes in progress and is willing to listen to new ideas. Senator Hubert Humphrey's voting record has convinced me that he fits the description.

h. Henry cannot really be blamed for stealing that car. His home life, the pressures of poverty, and our culture's stress on the automobile as a status symbol made it impossible for him to resist.

i The Department of Labor recently put out a bulletin showing that there would be a 26 percent increase in the demand for nurses and other health workers in the next decade. Obviously these professions provide the ideal choice for an ambitious young person.

j. Professional football is now the king of sports in this country. When I try to visit my friends on Sunday afternoon or Monday night from August through December, I find them sprawled in their living rooms with their eyes glued to the television. Half of the sports section each week is taken up with analyses of games past and games to come. Like well-paid gladiators who cannot last in the arena more than a few seasons, the battered but arrogant pros endure their weekly agony so that the citizenry may be entertained. Our new national heroes are Joe Namath, Sonny Jurgenson, and Roger Staubach, and the effect on our young people is bound to be degrading.

2. Using at least three of the standard methods of defining, write an extended definition of one of the following:

a. A slum
b. An unscrupulous politician
c. A successful athlete
d. A bad environment for a child
e. Pornography
f. A foolish parent
g. A racist
h. A conservative

3. Analyze the various methods of defining that the author is using in the following selection.

> "Ghetto" was the name for the Jewish quarter in sixteenth-century Venice. Later, it came to mean any section of a city to which Jews were confined. America has contributed to the concept of the ghetto restriction of persons to a special area and the limiting of their freedom of choice on the basis of skin color. The dark ghetto's invisible walls have been erected by the white society, by those who have power, both to confine those who have *no* power and to confine their powerlessness. The dark ghettos are social, political, educational, and—above all—economic colonies. Their inhabitants are subject peoples, victims of the greed, cruelty, insensitivity, guilt, and fear of their masters. . . .
>
> The ghetto is ferment, paradox, conflict, and dilemma. Yet within its pervasive pathology exists a surprising human resilience. The ghetto is hope, it is despair, it is churches and bars. It is aspiration for change, and it is apathy. It is vibrancy, it is stagnation. It is courage, and it is defeatism. It is cooperation and concern, and it is suspicion, competitiveness, and rejection. It is the surge toward assimilation, and it is alienation and withdrawal within the protective walls of the ghetto.[13]

4. How good are the following analogies?

a. One common argument for supposing that crowding as such is bad for people starts from experiments that have been carried out with laboratory animals, principally rats. The best-known experiments, performed by Dr. John B. Calhoun, showed that rats kept in unusually crowded conditions developed all kinds of psychological disturbances—mother rats took to infanticide, males became unnaturally aggressive, and the mortality rate rose. So is it not reasonable to suppose that people living in metropolitan areas will be more disturbed than those who live in rural areas? With growing population densities, will not violence within and between countries become much more prevalent? These are common suspicions.[14]

b. The House version of the bill gave the President the right arbitrarily to cut back [Congressional] spending in any area at all—including, theoretically, social security, or veterans' pensions, or interest on the national debt. . . . There is plenty of resistance in Congress,

[13] Kenneth Clark, *Dark Ghetto: Dilemmas of Social Power* (New York: Torchbooks, 1967), pp. 11–12.
[14] John Maddow, "The Doomsday Syndrome," *Saturday Review of the Society,* October 21, 1972, p. 32.

in part for the same reason that an extravagant wife resists when her husband proposes to take over sole control of a joint checking account. Senate Majority Leader Mike Mansfield has even said that if the House bill became law, "you might as well abolish Congress," which is the kind of exaggeration to which extravagant wives are prone.[15]

c. For if women are willing to acknowledge the remotest emotional obligation to husband and children, especially to children during their fragile first five or six years of life, then they can't summon the time, physical energy, and psychic equipment to do two jobs simultaneously. You can't split a woman's life down the middle and expect each half, like a severed worm, to go happily crawling off, to survive and function in perfect health.[16]

d. What could become of such a child of the seventeenth and eighteenth centuries, when he should wake up to find himself required to play the game of the twentieth? Had he been consulted, would he have cared to play the game at all, holding such cards as he held, and suspecting that the game was to be one of which neither he nor anyone else back to the beginning of time knew the rules or the risks or the stakes? . . . Probably no child born in the year held better cards than he. Whether life was an honest game of chance or whether the cards were marked and forced, he could not refuse to play his excellent hand. . . .

As it happened, he never got to the point of playing the game at all; he lost himself in the study of it, watching the errors of the players.[17]

5. Carefully examine the analogies that are drawn in the passage from the article "See You In Court?" on page 161. What likenesses are the authors suggesting between the processes and products of an educational system and those of a corporation? What likenesses are there between the professional obligations of a doctor, lawyer, or engineer and those of a teacher? What major similarities do you see? What major differences do you see? What strengths and what weaknesses do you find in the analogies? If, as the authors imply by their title, the charge of the schools' turning out substandard products were taken into court, what do you think the decision would be?

[15] Stewart Alsop, "What Nixon Hears the Voters Saying," *Newsweek,* October 23, 1972, p. 120.

[16] Ann Bernays, "What Are You Supposed To Do if You Like Children?" *The Atlantic,* March 1970, pp. 107–109.

[17] Henry Adams, *The Education of Henry Adams* (New York: The Modern Library, 1931), p. 4.

6. Which of the following cause and effect arguments and arguments from circumstance do you find convincing? Why?

a. The high standard of living in the United States has brought about our energy crisis.

b. We must grant the Department of Justice the privilege of tapping phones and installing listening devices in homes or offices because if criminals make use of this modern technology, law enforcement agencies cannot afford to do without it.

c. Doing away with the grading system in college would put a stop to students' cheating.

d. Television advertising is responsible for the "revolution of rising expectations" in this country.

e. The power of the farm bloc in Congress has declined in the last twenty-five years because the number of people living on and making a living from farms has dropped from 15 percent to 7 percent.

7. Analyze the kinds of arguments the writer of the following passage is using.

Americans seem especially susceptible to the social callousness brought about by random experiments with technology. Rootless by nature, we prize mobility and "progress"; we choose to display our techniques (the earth gouged, the weather altered, the enemy blown to pieces by "smart" bombs) in the manner of a mindless virtuoso. Still blinded by fabulous visions of self-advancement, we seek personal riches and pleasures in the same selfish spirit that arms us with ninety million guns and kills 55,000 people a year in automobile accidents.

The truth about technology is not simply that we are small cogs in big machines, but that each small cog has a remarkable power to affect the machine for good or evil. Our systems run amok because individuals misuse that power. In terms of personal responsibility, there is a common bond between the assassin and the polluter, the skyjacker and the drunken driver, the self-appointed air raider (General John Lavelle) and the Pentagon bureaucrat who blindly orders to Saigon a tanker loaded with enough herbicides to poison the Pacific Ocean if the ship should sink. Each manipulates lethal power in the most thoughtless manner, all the while protesting his own helpless innocence.

The illusion of powerlessness may yet prove to be the most dangerous by-product of an advanced technology. If we believe that we cannot govern our own lives, then we fall into the error of thinking that everything is permissible because nothing makes

any difference. Which makes children of us all and further contributes to the proliferation of the huge systems that we so
enthusiastically condemn.[18]

Theme 1

Purpose: To make you aware of ways in which definition may
be used for rhetorical purposes.

Procedure: Using the argument from definition, write a theme
that seeks to persuade your audience to share your attitude about
the subject you are defining. Remember, the paper must show your
bias. First, review pages 148 to 152, on the methods of developing
definition, for example, comparing and contrasting, giving examples,
and enumerating parts. Then, pick one or two techniques with which
to work. Choose a topic from the list below. Limit your topic to a manageable size; pick out a few main points you want to emphasize; be
specific and concrete, and avoid broad generalities that do little more
than repeat routine prejudices.

Topics
a. A liberated woman
b. A student radical
c. A male chauvinist
d. A member of the Establishment
e. An individual's character by describing his room or apartment
    Decide before you begin what your attitude is and choose details
to support it. In addition to your argument from definition, you may
use connotation, figurative language, selected illustrations or whatever
you need to persuade. Your thesis sentence should show the main
points you intend to include in your definition.

Theme 2

Purpose: To make you aware of the modes of argument you may
use to develop a thesis by having you write a paper in which you
use two or more of the standard argumentative devices. The possibilities are the arguments from *definition*, *cause and effect*, *circumstance*, *comparison*, and *evidence*.

Procedure: Choose one of the topics listed below and write an
argumentative paper. Before you start, think out the stand you want

[18] Editorial, "An Antidote for Despair," *Harper's,* September 1972, p. 47. Copyright © 1972,
by Minneapolis Star and Tribune Co., Inc. Reprinted from the September, 1972, issue
of Harper's Magazine by special permission.

to take; then, do some exploratory thinking about what kinds of arguments you can use to develop your paper. For example, if you were writing a paper supporting the assertion that the world should achieve Zero Population Growth, you might use these arguments as the main points in your paper:

Definition: attributing characteristics   An overcrowded world will not be a decent one to live in.

Cause and effect   Continued population growth will cause poverty, hunger, and war.

Comparison: analogy   Experiments with rats have shown that overcrowding increases hostility.

Circumstance   The present rate of population growth is so catastrophic that we have no choice except to legislate restrictions.

Comparison: a fortiori   If we believe in controls on education and health, we should believe in controls on population even more.

Evidence: testimony   Statistics or examples to support your points.

Evidence: authority   Quotations from experts such as Paul Ehrlich.

Remember that you would not have to use all of these kinds of arguments. (Of course, all points would have to be expanded.)

When you have finished your paper, go back and label your arguments in the left-hand margin opposite each paragraph. This is an important part of the assignment.

Please begin with a thesis sentence that summarizes the main points you are going to make. It need not be a part of your actual theme.

Topics

a. This university [should, should not] make a concerted drive to bring larger numbers of minority students to this campus.

b. Our city [should, should not] pass and strictly enforce an ordinance prohibiting nude dancers from performing in local nightclubs.

c. All papers that a student writes for freshman English [should, should not] be returned with comments but no grade; and, the final grade in the course [should, should not] be "Satisfactory" or "Unsatisfactory."

d. Every high school [should, should not] require all students to take a course in home and family relations that would include sex education, the study of nutrition, money and credit management, and child psychology.

7

Three
Modes
of
Reasoning

INDUCTION

Definition

In the previous chapter we talked about the argument from evidence, about the ways in which data, reports, testimony, and facts can be used to support opinions and beliefs. The person who argues inductively is using a variation of the argument from evidence; he gathers data, reports, testimony, and facts and, by examining his evidence, arrives at an opinion or conclusion. Another way of describing inductive reasoning is to say that it is a method of reasoning in which one moves from observations about specific cases to a generalization about all of those cases; that is, one notes the characteristics of some parts of the whole and generalizes that what is true of the parts is true of the whole.

All of us employ this kind of reasoning constantly, but do we use it well or poorly, responsibly or carelessly? Unfortunately, far too often we use the inductive method carelessly and irresponsibly: we generalize from too little evidence or from evidence that is biased or irrelevant. By doing so, we brand ourselves as sloppy thinkers. Suppose, for example, you are trying to convince a member of your college's board of trustees that most students simply cannot afford a proposed 25 percent increase in tuition and laboratory fees and that it will actually hurt the college by decreasing the enrollment. In reply, a trustee might say to you, "Oh come on; I drive by those fraternity houses every day and see the T-birds and Toronados parked out in the drive. And you should go up to the Regency Room on Saturday night and see those kids spending $20 for dinner. You can't tell me that students on this campus are poor. I know better." You would be outraged by such a sweeping statement based on so little information and by the failure to take the trouble to find out if there was other, conflicting evidence that should be taken into account. Yet it would be just as bad for you to generalize that all teaching assistants are incompetent because you have one who is, to assume that all football players are stupid because you know some who are on scholastic probation, or to claim that all politicians are crooks because two members of the state legislature have been indicted for fraud. Any thoughtful person ought to realize that this kind of argument is a misuse of evidence. Such reasoning (so-called) is distressingly common, however, as the logician Lionel Ruby points out:

Faulty generalizations common

> Hasty generalization is perhaps the most important of popular vices in thinking. It is interesting to speculate on some of the reasons for this kind of bad thinking. One important factor is prejudice. If we are already prejudiced against unions, or busi-

nessmen, or lawyers, or doctors, or Jews, or Negroes, then one or two instances of bad conduct by members of these groups will give us the unshakable conviction that "They're all like that." It is very difficult for a prejudiced person to say, "Some are, and some aren't." A prejudice is a judgment formed *before* examining the evidence.

A psychological reason for asserting "wild" generalizations is exhibitionism. The exhibitionist desires to attract attention to himself. No one pays much attention to such undramatic statements as "Some women are fickle," or that some are liars, or "Some politicians are no better than they ought to be." But when one says that "all women are liars" this immediately draws attention. Goethe once said that it is easy to appear brilliant if one respects nothing, not even the truth.[1]

Necessity of generalizing

Nevertheless, as Ruby goes on to say, in spite of our knowing that generalizations are dangerous, we must generalize. If we did not, we could not learn from our experiences or make any inferences from information that we gather. What we must do, then, is to find guidelines and rules for the legitimate use of the inductive method, guidelines to follow in constructing our own arguments and to use as a check in evaluating the inductive arguments of others.

Criteria for Valid Induction

As usual, we cannot expect perfection in any argument, but we can set up and apply reasonable criteria. The criteria for the proper use of evidence in an inductive argument are, briefly, as follows:

1. The evidence should be of sufficient quantity.
2. The evidence should be randomly selected.
3. The evidence should be accurate and should be objectively presented.
4. The evidence should be relevant to the conclusion drawn.

Sufficient evidence When you construct an inductive argument in this manner, the first question you should ask yourself is "How big should the sample be?" The answer, of course, depends on the size of the whole about which you are going to generalize. Although there are no hard and fast rules about proportion, common sense tells you that the larger the population (to use sociological terms) to be included, the larger your sample should be. Thus, if you are going

Size of sample depends on size of population

[1] Lionel Ruby, *The Art of Making Sense* (New York: J. B. Lippincott Co., 1954) p. 259.

to generalize about a student body of 10,000, you should probably gather data about at least 500 individuals in that body; to use fewer would be to run the risk of missing important evidence. Note, however,

Small groups require
large sample

that in generalizing about a comparatively small group, you have to use a proportionately larger sample. It stands to reason that if you have an assortment of cards bearing ten different designs, you will not get a representative cross section of those designs by turning up only 5 cards out of 100; if you were to turn up 500 cards out of a total of 10,000, however, your chances of getting a fair sample are much better. Similarly, if you were polling a class of 100, you could not come to any supportable conclusions by interviewing only 5 people from that class.

In practice, few writers specify exactly how many individual items their sample includes or mention the size of the total population about which they are generalizing. Rather, they give several examples, and the reader must decide whether the examples are sufficient. The reader

Reader must judge
validity of sample

must also estimate the size of the total group, but in most cases that is not too difficult to do. The writer usually makes evident whether he is generalizing about a whole population or a comparatively small subgroup, such as factory workers, professors, or housewives. Since there are, after all, time and space limitations when presenting an argument, a reader should not be too critical or always ready to reject an argument because the sample may not be as large as, ideally, it ought to be. He must be satisfied with what seems like a reasonable number of examples.

Random samples   Ensuring randomness or representative sampling in inductive evidence may often be more important than the actual amount of data collected. The term "random sample" here has

Definition: random
sample

either or both of two meanings: first, data chosen strictly by chance, and, second, data that represents a true cross section or representative picture of the whole. The second kind of sample is exemplified by the Voter Profile Analysis method the major television networks use in order to predict final results very early in the evening on election night. You may have been surprised (and a little irritated by the apparent wisdom of computers) to hear Walter Cronkite say, "On the basis of 2 percent of the vote now in in our sample precincts, we predict that Senator Percy and President Nixon will win by a landslide in Illinois." And usually he turns out to be right, not because he or the computers possessed any supernatural wisdom, but because the sample precincts have been carefully chosen to be as representative as possible of the state as a whole. If Illinois has 39 percent Protestants,

13 percent Jews, 38 percent Catholics, and 10 percent other, so do the precincts; if the state has 12 percent of the population earning above $30,000, 27 percent earning between $20,000 and $29,000, 40 percent earning between $10,000 and $19,000, 22 percent earning between $5,000 and $9,000, and the remainder below $5,000, so do the precincts. Other relevant data, such as level of education, occupation, percentage of eligible voters going to the polls, and political party registration, also enter into the calculations. The tremendously complex process is made possible by sophisticated computers that can retain and analyze huge amounts of diverse information. The result is a nearly perfect piece of inductive reasoning.

Representative sampling   In ordinary rhetoric you have neither the need nor the means to do such detailed and meticulous sampling, but you can learn much from the Voter Profile method. If you are generalizing about a group, you must have evidence from a representative cross section of that group; if you do not, your sample will be warped or skewed. For instance, if you want to find out what the dominant political opinions are on your campus, you will need to get evidence from students in a variety of departments: engineering, business, fine arts, languages, English, pharmacy, and physics might make a representative sample. You will also need to include students from different income levels and to make sure that both independents and fraternity and sorority members are represented. The accurate distribution of your sample will be as important, or more important, as the number of students you poll, for people in certain occupations and income levels have a predisposition to think alike. If you take your sample from only one group—the group easiest to reach—you will not get a true cross section.

Chance sampling   If you do not have enough information about the subdivisions of your total population to construct a "sample precinct," you can use another technique that will ensure a random sample: selecting your evidence solely by chance. One way to do this would be to pick every tenth name out of the student directory; another would be to interview every tenth student who goes into the university book store at textbook-buying time or every twenty-fifth student who comes through the line to pay his registration fees. If your sample is large enough it will be a reasonably accurate cross section. Professional pollsters like Gallup or Roper use both the representative and chance methods to ensure an unbiased, truly random sample of public opinion. They are also careful to frame their questions in neutral terms because loaded questions produce biased evidence. Asking people "Are you opposed to forced busing to achieve integrated schools?'' will evoke quite different answers from ''Are you in favor of busing as a tool to achieve racial balance in schools?''

Dangers of skewed samples

A few examples will illustrate the dangers of generalizing from a skewed sample. The classic instance is the 1936 presidential poll conducted by the now defunct magazine *Literary Digest*. On the basis of responses from people chosen by chance from the telephone books of several cities, the editors predicted thet Landon would defeat Roosevelt. They couldn't have been more wrong. What they failed to consider was that in 1936, when the Depression was still severe, only the relatively prosperous segment of the total electorate had telephones. In 1970, Charles Reich, a professor of law at Yale University, predicted a peaceful revolution in this country as the younger ecology- and peace-minded generation moved into positions of power (*The Greening of America,* 1970). What Reich seemed not to realize was that he was judging the temper of the younger generation by the highly select and privileged group of young people whom he knew at Yale. Some critics of Dr. David Reuben, author of the famous *Everything You Always Wanted To Know About Sex But Were Afraid To Ask,* claim that the generalizations he makes about prostitutes and homosexuals are based on a few individuals he knows or has heard about and, hence, that his conclusions are invalid.[2] A similar criticism might be leveled at those who conclude that Vitamin C has curative powers from the three or four short case histories given in Adelle Davis' *Let's Eat Right to Keep Fit*. The inference may be correct, but the small and biased sample cited does not meet the criteria for good inductive evidence.

Biased evidence

We all should keep in mind how easy it is to fall into the habit of basing conclusions on biased evidence. Most people prefer to spend their time with others who think like they do: businessmen talk to other businessmen, professors talk to professors, doctors to doctors, students to other students, and radicals to other radicals. Occasionally, we may have a serious conversation with someone whose views differ from ours, but usually we seek out individuals whose opinions reinforce our own. It's more comfortable that way. The danger is, however, that we will take the small part of the world that we know best as representative of the larger whole. So doctors may find it difficult to believe that any substantial number of people are in favor of socialized medicine, and radicals think that only the rich and powerful are

[2] See Betty Rollin, ''Everything Dr. Reuben Doesn't Know About Sex,'' *Playboy,* November 1972, p. 123.

satisfied with our economic system. Because we tend to believe what we want to believe, it is all too easy to interpret agreement from others like ourselves as broad-based support. Politicians, pollsters, and research scientists are among the few classes of people who make a conscious, consistent effort to take a truly random sample before they draw conclusions; the rest of us could learn from their methods.

Accurate evidence   Judging the accuracy of inductive evidence may pose problems. In this age of specialization and experts, many of us are not qualified to decide which data are genuine and which spurious. Most of the time we have to rely on the integrity of the speaker or writer; we must assume that most people tell the truth and that they do not falsify reports that could easily be checked. If, for example, a government official says, in arguing for a continuation of our Intercontinental Ballistic Missile program that the Soviet Union has 1,712 intercontinental missiles, he may be exaggerating, but probably he is not. The senator who opposes the program also has access to such information and would be quick to refute him.

Sometimes we can use our common sense to check evidence. For example, an article in the December, 1972, issue of *Ms.*, a Women's Liberation magazine, argued that in spite of equal opportunity legislation, substantial salary discrimination against women still existed. Knowing that the editors of the magazine are biased (they would admit it freely), we might question the accuracy of the data on which the article is based. To forestall such doubts the author included with the article a chart that lists twenty-seven different jobs and gives the comparative qualifications, experience, and salaries of men and women in those jobs. For sixteen of the jobs, the chart named the specific employer so that any reader might verify the figures. The author's use of this kind of verifiable data reinforced her assertions.

A reader may also judge the accuracy of evidence by considering whether the evidence is given objectively or presented in slanted language. Compare the following passages, each of which supplies information leading to the conclusion that America is a nation plagued by crime and violence.

> Especially disturbing to many Americans—black and white—is an upsurge of crime and violence in the schools. . . . During one sixteen-day period this fall, at least fourteen New York City teachers were robbed or assaulted inside their schools.
>
> Pressure from parents and teachers led the New York school board to allocate $6 million for a small army of guards: 600 cur-

Integrity of speaker or writer

Common sense

Language

rently stationed in high schools and junior highs, another 1,200 who will be posted to the city's elementary schools. In Los Angeles, similarly, a series of thefts, knifings and gang-style shootings prompted Mayor Sam Yorty to tap Federal model-cities funds to hire parents for patrol duty in fourteen schools (L.A. already spends about $3,000 per school for special guards). Houston school officials are also adding guards and thinking about student ID cards to help keep out loiterers.[3]

[In southeastern Ohio] Many cases of incest are known; inbreeding is rife. Imbeciles, feeble-minded, and delinquents are numerous, politics is corrupt, and the selling of votes is common, petty crimes abound, the schools have been badly managed and poorly attended. Cases of rape, assault, and robbery are of almost weekly occurrence within five minutes' walk of the corporation limits of one of the county seats, while in another county political control is held by a self-confessed criminal. Alcoholic intemperance is excessive. Gross immorality and its evil results are by no means confined to the hill districts, but are extreme also in the towns.[4]

The first report, although not entirely impartial, is a reasonably objective account; the second is contaminated by such terms as "corrupt," "excessive," "gross immorality," and "evil results," words that carry strong value judgments. Moreover, Mencken's sources are suspect because he identifies them only as "two inquirers who made an exhaustive survey."

The student writer also has an obligation to identify his sources when he quotes material or attributes an opinion. If you use statistics, you should be sure they are reliable and should let the reader know where you found them. If you make a positive statement about a matter on which there are conflicting views, show in some way that you have sufficient information to back up your statement; you could, for example, quote a professor from whom you took a course, or you could cite a documentary film that you saw. And you should, of course, as pointed out in Chapter 5, state your evidence in neutral language.

Relevant evidence, relevant conclusions Finally, we must ask whether the conclusion drawn from the evidence is relevant and whether the facts given actually do point to the conclusion that we or a writer or speaker have drawn. While it is true, for example, that

---

[3] *Newsweek,* December 18, 1972, p. 33.
[4] H. L. Mencken, "The Anglo-Saxon," in *The Vintage Mencken* (New York: Vintage Books, 1955), pp. 127–137. Originally published in the Baltimore *Evening Sun,* July, 1923.

Americans spend more of their personal income for medical care than the people of any other nation, we are not justified in concluding that consequently we get the best health care. Doctors' fees, drug prices, and hospital charges are significantly higher in the United States than in other countries, but there is no provable correlation between cost and quality. Similarly, concluding that today's farmers are lazy because most of them no longer keep a milk cow or raise chickens would not be warranted, for it ignores the fact that they are simply devoting their energies to other, more profitable work. In his article on the American use of convenience foods, "Science Has Spoiled My Supper," Philip Wylie commits the error of drawing an irrelevant conclusion from the evidence given.

> Without thinking, we are making an important confession about ourselves as a nation. We are abandoning quality—even, to some extent, the quality of people. The "best" is becoming too good for us. We are suckling ourselves on machine-made mediocrity. It is bad for our souls, our minds, and our digestions. It is the way our wiser and calmer forebears fed, not people, but hogs; as much as possible and as fast as possible, with no standard of quality.
>
> The Germans say *"Mann ist was er isst*—Man is what he eats."* If this be true, the people of the U.S.A. are well on their way to becoming a faceless mob of mediocrities, or robots. And if we apply to other attributes the criteria we apply these days to appetite, that is what would happen! We would not want bright children any more; we'd merely want them to look bright—and get through school fast. We wouldn't be interested in beautiful women—just a good paint job. And we'd be opposed to the most precious quality of man: his individuality, his differentness from the mob.[5]

While Wylie may make a good case that the frozen and packaged foods described in the essay are inferior, he establishes no necessary or even probable link between Americans' eating processed food and their loss of individuality and good taste—qualities which, by the way, he does not prove that they had before they started eating convenience foods.

Drawing an irrelevant conclusion about convenience foods does no great harm, except perhaps to one's reputation as a fair-minded thinker, but misusing the inductive method can have more serious

[5] Wylie, "Science Has Spoiled My Supper," *The Atlantic Monthly,* April 1954, pp. 45–47.

consequences. Probably you know of instances in which unthinking people have made rash and sometimes harmful judgments on the basis of wholly inadequate evidence. Beliefs many people share about welfare furnish one example. An individual may know or hear of one or two families on welfare who have color television sets. When he drives through the poorer areas of a city, he may also see expensive cars parked along the curb and several apparently able-bodied men standing around talking and laughing with each other. On the basis of these observations, none of which he has investigated—he doesn't know, for instance, if the family won the television in a supermarket promotion contest, who actually owns the cars, or whether the men he saw are on the night shift or are construction workers not currently employed—he may conclude that all people on welfare are freeloaders who are defrauding the state. Moreover, he may not hesitate to use his so-called evidence to justify strong opposition to all welfare programs.

Equally faulty inductive reasoning led many nineteenth-century defenders of slavery in this country to assert confidently that a slave was really happier and better off living as a slave than he would be as a free man competing in the mainstream of society. Because most slaves did not dare express their discontent, such defenders were hardly getting either an accurate or random sample of the slave population as a whole. Furthermore, the relatively few slaves an average Southerner knew well scarcely constituted an adequate sample from which to generalize. Yet many of the people who took a proslavery stand genuinely thought that they were making valid arguments based on solid evidence.

These kinds of conclusions illustrate one of the major pitfalls of inductive reasoning: selecting and interpreting evidence in such a way that it will confirm a bias already held. Individuals who do this may honestly believe that they have solid grounds for their opinions; what they do not realize is that they are reasoning from *a priori* premises, premises formed before the evidence was examined. Consequently, if they are called upon to defend those opinions, they select evidence that reinforces their premises and reject or ignore that which does not. This process cannot be called valid induction.

Confirming a bias

There is, of course, nothing inherently wrong with forming a hypothesis before examining the evidence. Much scientific research begins in this just way because if the investigator does not have some idea of what he is looking for, it is difficult to know where to start gathering data. Nevertheless, if he uses the inductive method conscien-

Forming a hypothesis

tiously, he holds his hypothesis only tentatively and is willing to alter or modify it when he finds conflicting evidence. The person who is committed to a theory before he begins his research must be particularly scrupulous both in selecting and evaluating his evidence if he is not to succumb to the temptation to find what he wants to find.

Using Inductive Arguments

Judging the arguments of others   By now, this analysis of the ways in which inductive arguments can go wrong may have you ready to challenge any that you encounter and even a little dubious about the wisdom of trying to use the method yourself. A challenging attitude is healthy if you don't carry it to extremes. If a writer or speaker gives you a reasonable number of examples that seem to be accurate and randomly selected, and his conclusion is a statement of probability rather than a sweeping generalization, give him the benefit of the doubt. After all, we can scarcely expect a rhetorician to present *all* the relevant data on an issue; if he were to attempt to do so, the audience would become so bored it would never hear his argument to the finish. Furthermore, we must accept generalizations and hypotheses from qualified, reliable people if we are to learn anything. Your best approach to the inductive arguments of others is, then, to be receptive but not gullible, open-minded but not naive. Be alert to possible bias, omission, or distortion but don't assume that everyone seeks to deceive.

Constructing your own arguments   You should not assume either that the task of constructing a respectable inductive argument is too complex and difficult for you to master. It is not. You have access to perfectly good evidence on a variety of topics, and you now have some guidelines for shaping it into an effective argument. For example, you might get the impression from walking across your campus that students talk better ecology than they practice. If you wanted to write a letter to the college newspaper pointing this out, you might pick three problems to investigate: litter on campus, graffiti on walls and desks, and lawns damaged by students taking short cuts. To start, you could check two areas on each side of the campus for discarded candy wrappers, beer cans, soft-drink bottles, leaflets, and advertisements. After writing down your findings, you could go on to inspect two or more recently constructed buildings. If you find the desks inscribed with initials, fraternity crests, and doodles, and the restroom walls decorated with names and slogans, you have more evidence

---

Margin notes:

Evaluate number, accuracy, and selection of examples

Give benefit of the doubt

Trust qualifications and reliability

Be alert to bias, omissions, distortion

Collect evidence

Use the guidelines

to add to your list. Finally, you could quickly check the lawns between main buildings and assess the damage. The entire tour should not take more than two hours, and it would provide you with enough evidence to put together a reasonable inductive argument, perhaps not as strong a one as you had originally intended, but an honest and supported one all the same. The same kind of investigative techniques could furnish the data for papers on study conditions in the dormitories, living facilities for married students, or even broader topics, such as public transportation in your city.

Making the "inductive leap" As long as we are working from a sample rather than examining every single unit of the whole about which we are generalizing, the inductive method cannot yield perfect results. For instance, we cannot prove beyond any doubt that attending college in the North or East is always more expensive than attending college in the South unless we have data on every single school. The possibility of error is always present when we are projecting from a sample—even the Voter Profile Analysis is wrong sometimes. Nevertheless, we can, by careful sampling, establish high probability: a survey of representative institutions in the North, South, and East would show that going to college in New York or Minnesota is very likely to cost more than going to a school in Alabama or Louisiana. Moving from an examination of some of the available evidence to a generalization about the whole population from which that evidence is drawn is known as the "inductive leap." If our sample is sufficient, random, accurate, and relevant, we can be confident that the leap is warranted. If the sample does not meet these criteria, we are not reasoning, but jumping to conclusions.

Draw relevant conclusions (margin note)

DEDUCTION

The study of classical deductive logic is a complex process that, if done properly and thoroughly, takes several weeks and involves learning many rules and definitions. But it is not really necessary that you learn all the intricacies of the deductive method in order to understand how it works and how to use it in arguments. In practice, you have been both encountering and using deductive logic, or syllogistic reasoning, for a long time, so in this section you will be simply examining and evaluating a procedure you are already familiar with.

Two main deductive forms (margin note)

The two principal forms of deduction are the categorical syllogism and the hypothetical syllogism. Each does what its name suggests.

The categorical syllogism sets up classes or categories, and, by show-ing that something is or is not in a certain class, it affirms or denies that an item has the characteristics of that class. The hypothetical syl-logism sets up a hypothesis, an "if—then" statement, and, by showing that the hypothesis is or is not true, it leads to a conclusion. As usual, the abstract definition makes the process sound more difficult than it is; a concrete example will clarify it.

The Categorical Syllogism

Affirmative syllogism   A typical affirmative categorical syllogism (that is, one in which both the major and minor premises are affir-mative) would look like this:

middle term   major term
Major premise   All U.S. astronauts have college degrees.

minor term   middle term
Minor premise   Eugene Cernan is a U.S. astronaut.

minor term   major term
Conclusion   Therefore, Cernan has a college degree.

What we have done here is set up three classes: A—People with a college degree; B—U.S. astronauts; and C—Eugene Cernan. All of class B is included in class A; therefore, the individuals in B share the characteristic of those in A. Class C is included in Class B, thus it too must share the characteristic of A, that is, a college degree. Diagrammed, the syllogism looks like this:

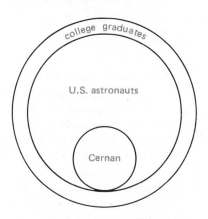

Minor term

Middle term

Major term

Validity

All affirmative syllogisms that are valid, that is, show positive proof, *must* look like the above figure when they are diagrammed. The *minor term*, that is, the subject of the conclusion, must be enclosed within the circle representing the *middle term*, the term that appears in both premises but not in the conclusion. The circle for the middle term must be completely within the circle representing the *major term*, that is, the term that is the predicate of the conclusion. If an affirmative syllogism is valid, you will be able to draw a straight line that runs through the centers of all the circles representing the various terms.

Negative syllogisms   Negative categorical syllogisms make negative assertions about classes. A typical one would look like this:

major term   middle term

Major premise   No Eskimos have blond hair.

minor term   middle term

Minor premise   Jones has blond hair.

minor term   major term

Conclusion   Therefore, Jones is not an Eskimo.

Diagrammed, the syllogism looks like this:

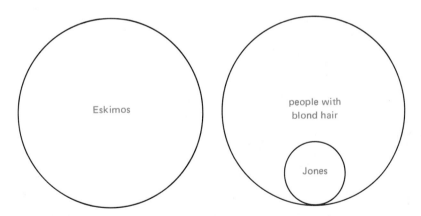

Notice that here there are two circles and that they must not touch, since by definition Eskimos are completely excluded from the class of people with blond hair. The circle representing Jones, or the minor term, comes wholly within the circle representing people with blond hair, or the middle term. Therefore, Jones cannot have the characteristics of a class from which he is necessarily excluded.

Affirmative/negative syllogisms   Another kind of categorical syl-

logism has an affirmative major premise, but a negative minor one.
A typical syllogism of this type might look like this:

major term   middle term

Major premise   All Texans are wealthy.

minor term   middle term

Minor premise   George is not wealthy.

minor term   major term

Therefore, George is not a Texan.

Diagrammed, it would look like this:

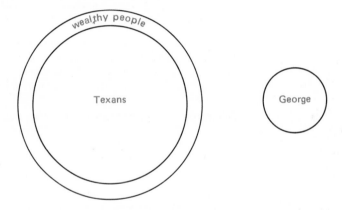

Validity

Again, the diagram proves the syllogism is valid because the circle
representing the minor term, George, must come completely outside
of the circle representing wealthy people. Since Texans cannot, by
the definition in the major premise, be outside of that circle, George
cannot be a Texan.

    Testing validity—the concept of distribution   Although there can
be more than one reason for the invalidity of a categorical syllogism,
the chief reason, and the only one to be discussed in any depth here,
is that it contains an undistributed middle term. Grasping this concept
of distribution seems to be the major stumbling block for students
just beginning the study of syllogisms, so I will try to explain it as
clearly as possible. As it is used in logic, the term "distributed" means
including or excluding every member of a class or group. When a
quality—intelligence, for example—is distributed throughout a class,
then each and every member of that class, by definition, possesses
that quality—every member is intelligent. The phrase "all intelligent

Definition of
"distributed"

people" indicates a distributed term; the phrases "some intelligent people" or "most intelligent people" indicate an undistributed term because the entire class of intelligent people is not covered. Distribution can also be negative; that is, it can exclude every member of a class. For example, the phrase "no Germans" indicates a distributed term; so does "no atheists" or "no reasonable person." Distributed terms may be expressed in varied ways: "every Englishman" or "any Englishman" really means "all Englishmen"; "not a single German" or "no one who is a German" are variations of "no Germans." On the other hand, terms that are preceded by modifiers indicating a part of the whole are undistributed terms. The words "some," "few," "many," "several," "the majority," and others like them signal undistributed terms.

Negative distribution *(margin)*

Undistributed terms *(margin)*

Some rules A few rules about distributed and undistributed terms in syllogisms and an illustration of the problems that may arise in connection with them follow.

1. The middle term (that is, the term that appears in both major and minor premises, but not in the conclusion) must be distributed at least once in a valid syllogism.
2. No term that has not been distributed in the premises may be distributed in the conclusion.
3. The *predicate terms* of all *affirmative premises* are *undistributed*.
4. The *predicate terms* of all *negative premises* are *distributed*. (Remember that a predicate term is one that completes the verb "to be" or another linking verb.)

Examples

distributed   undistributed
All Austrians are lovers of whipped cream.

undistributed   distributed
Most women are not ardent women's libbers.

distributed   distributed
No dogs are five-legged creatures.

undistributed   undistributed
Some brilliant people are poor.

undistributed   undistributed
Few illiterates are qualified to vote.

distributed   distributed
No one under thirty is a person who can be trusted.

Try your hand at labeling the following:

No satellites are planets.

Most long hairs are radicals.

All brilligs are slithy toves.

Most people are not concerned about international affairs.

No man is a prophet in his own land.

All A is Z.

The reason for all this fuss about distributed and undistributed terms is that when you are drawing conclusions about things or people on the basis of the class to which they belong, you must know precisely what that class includes; what it *must* include and what it only *may* include. If your conclusion, because of an undistributed term, means no more than *may*, then you have not positively proved your case. Notice how the following examples demonstrate such lack of proof.

Major premise   All members of the Politburo are Communists.

Minor premise   Sergei is a Communist.

Conclusion   Therefore, Sergei is a member of the Politburo.

Diagrammed, the syllogism looks like this:

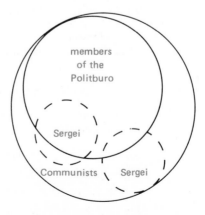

Sergei, the minor term, can go anywhere in the large circle that designates Communists; it does not *have* to go within the Politburo circle and, consequently, Sergei does not *have* to be a member. It is true that he may be, but it is not proved that he is. Because the middle term in both premises is undistributed, the syllogism is invalid. Moreover, the diagram proves it. Whenever the circle for the minor term can be put in more than one place in a diagram, or whenever it overlaps a larger circle rather than coming completely within or without it, the syllogism is invalid. Here is another example:

Major premise   Most U.S. senators are wealthy men.

Minor premise   Collins is a U.S. Senator.

Conclusion   Therefore, Collins is a wealthy man.

The middle term, U.S. Senator, is not distributed in either premise. You know then, that the syllogism is invalid. You can prove it with a diagram.

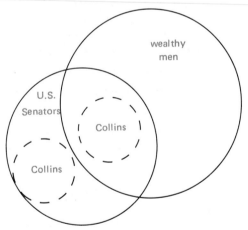

The following invalid syllogism works a little differently:

Major premise   All Southerners are gentlemen.

Minor premise   McKinney is not a Southerner.

Conclusion   Therefore, McKinney is not a gentleman.

The problem here is that a term is distributed in the conclusion that is not distributed in the premises, but even if you do not see precisely what is wrong, diagramming the syllogism will reveal that it is invalid.

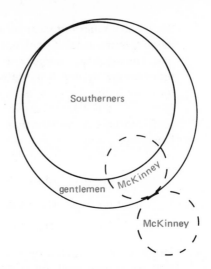

After you draw the first two circles and look for the correct place to put the circle representing McKinney, you realize that it could go either outside of Southerners or gentlemen. It might go outside of gentlemen, but it does not have to; thus, you know the reasoning is invalid because there is more than one place to put the circle. Here is another example:

Major premise   Not all politicians are dishonest.

Minor premise   Clark is a politician.

Conclusion   Clark is not dishonest.

The middle term, politician, is not distributed in either premise, so the syllogism is invalid. You know this as soon as you make the following diagram.

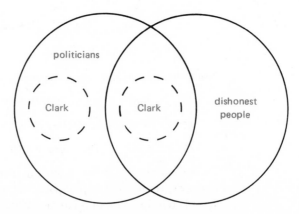

Diagramming is your quickest way to detect the fallacy of the undistributed middle term, which can also be labeled "the fallacy of the shared characteristic." It is closely related to the "guilt by association" fallacy. Notice how this works.

Radicals like Angela Davis study the works of Herbert Marcuse.

Professor Schwartz studies the works of Herbert Marcuse.

Therefore, Professor Schwartz is a radical.

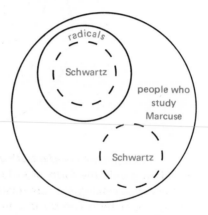

Most liberals are fuzzy thinkers.

Gerald is a liberal.

Therefore, Gerald is a fuzzy thinker.

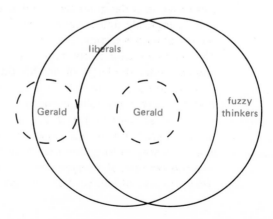

Ignorant people are racists.

Jackson is a racist.

Therefore, Jackson is an ignorant person.

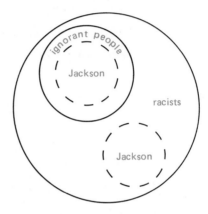

Testing validity—the truth of premises So far we have been considering only the *form* of syllogisms. We have been asking whether the various statements are related in such a way that a diagram proves the minor term can go in only one place. If they are, the syllogism is valid; if they are not, and the minor term can be put in more than one place, the syllogism is invalid. Obviously, this is a mechanical process, a matter of observing the rules. It shows us what we can and cannot actually *prove* beyond any doubt. If, for example, parents know that all individuals studying for the priesthood are males, they can prove to a daughter who says she wants to be a priest that her goal is logically unattainable. The circle representing candidates for the priesthood is completely enclosed by the circle representing males. The daughter cannot enter the circle of males, so there is no way she can enter the circle of priesthood candidates. In this same way, parents could demonstrate to a son who aspired to be an astronaut that he must get a college education. This kind of proving is useful and often enlightening. But a syllogism can be *valid*, that is in the correct form, and be quite useless and even deceptive because its premises are not true. You may have suspected this earlier when you saw the example of the syllogism beginning, "All Texans are wealthy." They are not, of course, but the *form* of the syllogism is correct. So

Validity of form

Truth of premises

is the form of the following syllogisms even though the major premise of both is absurd.

All cows have purple wings.

Bessie is a cow.

Therefore, Bessie has purple wings.

No red-headed woman is trustworthy.

Millie is a red-headed woman.

Therefore, Millie is not trustworthy.

Two tests for syllogisms

An acceptable syllogism, then, must pass two tests: first, its form must be valid; second, its premises must be true. When a deductive argument satisfies these two requirements, then you, as a rational person, are bound to accept the conclusion. To quote Lionel Ruby again, "It is not the mark of the rational mind to say, 'Your argument is valid, and your premises are true, but I refuse to grant the truth of your conclusion.' "

Criteria: knowledge and common sense

Truth of major premise important

Testing for validity is fairly simple, but, unfortunately, we cannot diagram for truth. To test for that we must examine the premises and decide whether, in the light of our knowledge and common sense, they seem to be reasonable statements. Assessing the truth of the major premise is especially important because usually it is the one that contains the chief generalization or definition on which the conclusion is based. For example, if a person argues that Byron White must be a brilliant man because he was a Rhodes scholar, his major premise is that all Rhodes scholars are brilliant men. The strength of his conclusion depends on the truth of the major premise. Someone who asserts that Tom Harris is a bigot because he comes from Mississippi is using as his major premise the generalization that all people from Mississippi are bigots. In the same way, the person who argues that Julie Harris must be a poor wife because she favors Women's Liberation is backing his argument with the major premise that no advocate of Women's Liberation can make a good wife. The minor premise that puts an individual person or unit into a specific class can usually be quickly checked—after all, you probably know whether Byron White was a Rhodes scholar or if Tom Harris is from Mississippi—but the major

Difficulty of verifying major premise

premise is not so easy to verify, particularly because it is often an *a priori* premise. Moreover, when we use or encounter syllogistic reasoning in everyday discourse, frequently the major premise is not directly stated because the categorical syllogism appears in the form of an *enthymeme*.

Enthymemes

Definition

Enthymemes are syllogisms that omit one of the three statements. In actual conversation the syllogism used earlier to demonstrate that Mr. Jones is not an Eskimo might sound like this: "Jones an Eskimo? Oh, he couldn't be. He's a blond." The speaker thinks that the major premise, "No Eskimos have blond hair," is so obvious that it is not worth mentioning. Some other syllogisms condensed into enthymemes might look like this.

> We can count on McGinnis to support the tax reform bill because he is a liberal.

> The Smiths must have plenty of money. They sent their daughter to Radcliffe this year.

> *Playboy* is sent through the U.S. mails, so obviously it's not hard core pornography.

All of us revert constantly to this abbreviated form of the deductive method both to save time and because it would be impractical and tedious always to spell out fully the assumptions and generalizations that underlie our reasoning. There is nothing inherently wrong or fallacious in arguing in enthymemes, but too often when they are expanded into their full form the major premise proves to be unsound. For instance, the premise, "All people who send their children to Radcliffe have plenty of money," is false because some students get scholarships, some parents begin saving money for their children's education as soon as the children are born, and some college students receive grants or loans that pay much of their expense. Similarly, if someone assumes that a person is a Marxist because there are several books on Marxism on that person's shelves, he is arguing from a false premise. Simply owning books on any philosophy—socialism, Marxism, Catholicism, or atheism—does not prove adherence to that belief. It shows only interest, perhaps even a hostile interest.

In practice, what we usually do when we reason in enthymemes is to establish probability. If the subject of politics comes up when you are talking to a medical doctor, you might reason that he would be a conservative on most issues. The unstated premise backing your conclusion would be that most doctors are political conservatives. As a formal syllogism, your reasoning is invalid because your middle term, medical doctors, is not distributed; nevertheless, your conclusion would have some merit if your reading, personal experience, and observation support that conclusion. So your expectation that Dr. Green will prove to be a conservative is a reasonable one, although certainly not infallible. We might argue in the same way that the young person who does not finish high school is sacrificing his chance to earn a good salary, and that the person who drinks, smokes, and eats too much will damage his health. Enthymemes like these are cause and effect arguments of high probability even though the major premises cannot be called absolute truths.

Using Categorical Syllogisms

Understanding categorical syllogisms and enthymemes can help you with your writing in two ways. First, it will enable you to trace the pattern of your own thinking and test both its truth and validity. Suppose, for example, that you are petitioning the dean of your school to be exempted from the freshman mathematics requirement on the grounds that algebra will be of no use to you in your chosen profession of nursing. The major premise of your argument would be that no student should be required to take a course that will not be directly useful to him. Once you see that your reasoning rests on that assertion, you will probably realize that you have put yourself in an indefensible position. Or suppose that you are trying to convince a judge that you should not be penalized for smoking marijuana because in your opinion the law that prohibits it is stupid and unreasonable. You are basing your argument on the assertion that no one should be punished for disobeying a law that he finds unreasonable; you will find that premise difficult to support.

You can also make good use of syllogistic reasoning in constructing arguments. For instance, if you are asked to write a persuasive paper for or against a proposal to legalize and license the sale of heroin or to have the federal government pay the campaign expenses of major political candidates, you will probably not have too much trouble deciding how you stand on either issue. You may have considerable difficulty, however, in clarifying your reasons for thinking as you do. Often it will help if, as a part of the prewriting process, you try to construct your argument in syllogistic form, beginning with the conclusion and working backwards. Here is how this method might work with the proposal recommending federal funding for political candidates.

Syllogisms aid in tracing your thinking and testing its validity

Syllogisms aid in constructing arguments

You would start out by writing down your opinion: "I am for federal funding of political candidates because I think the present system is unfair." As soon as you write down the statement you will probably realize that you have to find backing for your assertion. So your next step is to jot down your reasons for claiming that the present system is unfair. You come up with these:

It favors candidates who have the support of wealthy people.

Wealthy people who give a lot of money to a candidate will want favors in return. This could lead to corruption.

It prohibits poor people from running for office. This is undemocratic.

Once you have thought out your reasons, you are ready to combine them into a major premise. It could look like this: "Any system of campaign funding that favors one class over another, encourages corruption, and is undemocratic should be changed." Your minor premise would be this: "The present system of campaign funding does these things." The conclusion is obvious. Your theme would explain your reasoning more fully and give concrete examples to support your points. If you felt it necessary, you could construct a second syllogism to serve as the basis for your conclusion.

Political campaigns should be funded by a method that gives equal opportunity to both major candidates.

Federal funding would be such a method.

Therefore, political campaigns of major candidates should be federally funded.

Working an argument out in this way is more than an exercise in organization; it is also an exercise in applied reason. If after you finish the study of the categorical syllogism you forget the precise meaning of "undistributed middle," "validity," and "enthymeme," but you remember always to look for the basic premises upon which you base your conclusions, you will have taken a major step toward improving both your writing and your thinking.

The Hypothetical Syllogism

Definition

The hypothetical syllogism also consists of a major premise, a minor premise, and a conclusion, but, as the name suggests, the major premise is a hypothesis, a conditional statement which asserts that if a certain condition or event occurs, it follows that another condition or event will also occur. The minor premise asserts that the first condition or event did or did not occur; the conclusion states that the second condition did or did not follow. The first condition in the major premise is called the antecedent, and the second condition is called the consequent. For example:

antecedent   consequent

If a book wins the Pulitzer prize, it is a good book.

antecedent   consequent

If students do not complain, it shows that our school is running efficiently.

antecedent   consequent

If children are neglected, they will have emotional problems.

Testing validity: form There are two and only two kinds of minor premises that will produce a valid conclusion for a hypothetical syllogism. First, the minor premise may affirm the antecedent; that is, it may say "yes" to part A of the major premise. Second, the minor premise may deny the consequent; that is, it may say "no" to part B of the major premise. Another way of saying this is that if you can show that the prior condition exists, then it must follow that the second one will also exist; or, if you can contradict the statement made in the consequent, then the first part of the major premise is not acceptable either. In practice, the method works like this:

> If a book wins the Pulitzer prize, it must be a good book.
>
> This book won the Pulitzer prize.
>
> Therefore, it must be a good book.

Here the minor premise affirms the antecedent, that is, says "yes" to part A, so the syllogism is valid.

> If children are neglected, they will have emotional problems.
>
> These children have no emotional problems.
>
> Therefore, these children have not been neglected.

Here the minor premise denies the consequent, that is, says "no" to part B, so the syllogism is valid. To repeat, a hypothetical syllogism is valid *only* if the minor premise affirms the antecedent of the major premise or denies the consequent of the major premise.

(margin notes)

Antecedent and consequent

Minor premise *must* affirm the antecedent or deny the consequent

Denying antecedent
makes conclusion
invalid

If either process is reversed, the syllogism becomes invalid. If the minor premise denies the antecedent, that is, says "no" to part A, the conclusion is incorrect; it is also incorrect if the minor premise affirms the consequent, that is, says "yes" to part B. A common-sense analysis will show why setting up a hypothetical syllogism in which the minor premise does either of these things will invalidate the conclusion, for instance:

If a book wins the Pulitzer prize, it is a good book.

This book did not win the Pulitzer prize.

Therefore, it is not a good book.

The minor premise denies the antecedent and the conclusion therefore is invalid. The reason is that the formula "if A, then B" is not necessarily reversible into "if not A, then not B." In many cases, B can exist independently of A, that is, A's *not* happening will not prevent B from existing. In this case, obviously a book can be good and not win a prize. In this next syllogism you have the same kind of invalid form.

If Carl cuts all his classes, he will flunk out of school.

Carl does not cut all his classes.

Therefore, he will not flunk out of school.

A will produce B, but many students who attended class regularly have still flunked out of school. Excessive cutting is not the only reason for failure.

Affirming consequent
makes conclusion
invalid

Affirming the consequent produces the same kind of fallacy, that is, B's being true does not prove that it was caused by A, because the valid formula "if not B, then not A" cannot be reversed into "if B, then A." For example, the following syllogism is invalid because the minor premise affirms the consequent.

If a car runs out of gas, it will stop.

The car has stopped.

Therefore, it has run out of gas.

The syllogism is invalid not only because it breaks a rule but because it violates the rational precept that while a certain cause may produce a predictable effect, the presence of that effect does not necessarily indicate that cause. There are many reasons why a car may stop.

No gas ─────────────────────⟶ Car stops

No gas ⟍
Hitting an obstacle ⟍
Wheel falling off ───────⟶ Car stops
Ignition turned off ⟋

Similarly, if we were to affirm part B of the second and third hypothetical premises on page 203, we would get invalid syllogisms. An efficiently run school is no guarantee that the students will not complain, and children's emotional problems do not indicate they have been neglected; there can be other causes for such problems.

Reasoning about the truth of premises   Formal validity by itself, however, does not make a hypothetical syllogism persuasive; we must also be convinced of the truth of the premises. If a person bases his reasoning on a flimsy or deceptive hypothetical proposition, we will reject it no matter how logically he argues. Simplistic assertions such as "if he is over thirty, he is a reactionary" and "if a person is loyal to his country, he does not criticize it" cannot form the basis for legitimate arguments because they are false. If, however, you accept the major premise as reasonable and the minor premise as true, a properly developed hypothetical syllogism can be an extremely effective rhetorical device.

False premises negate the argument

Using hypothetical syllogisms   Hypothetical syllogisms are particularly useful in arguing about intangible concepts. Arguments for the existence of God often take this form.

Intangible concepts

> If there is order in the world, there must be a God who established it.
>
> There is order in the world.
>
> Therefore, there must be a God.

C. S. Lewis uses a hypothetical syllogism to "prove" that there is a natural law of right and wrong.

> If people quarrel, they must have a common standard of right and wrong.
>
> People do quarrel.
>
> Therefore, they must have a common standard of right and wrong.

The black, nineteenth-century writer Frederick Douglass used the syllogism with great skill in an essay called "The Color Line," in which he undertook to prove that prejudice against blacks was not, as some people claimed, a natural instinct in white people. He built his argument almost exclusively around hypothetical syllogisms; the chief ones are quoted below.

First. If what we call prejudice against color be natural, i.e., a part of human nature itself, it follows that it must manifest itself whenever and wherever the two races are brought into contact.

Second. If it can be shown that there is anywhere on the globe any considerable country where the contact of the African and the Caucasian is not distinguished by this explosion of race-wrath, there is reason to doubt that the prejudice is an ineradicable part of human nature.

Third. If this so-called natural, instinctive prejudice can be satisfactorily accounted for by facts and consideration wholly apart from the color features of the respective races, . . . we may venture to deny the claim set up for it in the name of human nature.

Fourth. If any considerable number of white people have overcome this prejudice in themselves, . . . the fact shows that this prejudice is not at any rate a vital part of human nature, and may be eliminated from the race without harm.

Fifth. If this prejudice shall, after all, prove to be, . . . simply a prejudice against condition, and not against race or color, and that it disappears when this condition is absent, then the argument from the nature of the Caucasian race falls to the ground.[6]

In the body of the essay, Douglass systematically validated each of these hypothetical syllogisms with evidence, testimony, and factual reference. First, he showed by appealing to experience that prejudice does not manifest itself wherever the races mix; therefore, it could not be natural. Then, by historical reference, he proved that people are prejudiced not against color, but against poverty, servitude, and ignorance. And he went on to show that innumerable white people had conquered it in themselves. His argument is impressive because every syllogism is in valid form and the truth of his premises is virtually indisputable.

Cause and effect arguments

You can put the hypothetical syllogism to good use in your own papers, particularly when you are setting up cause and effect arguments. You might choose to assert, "If the grading system promotes dishonesty and destructive competition, then it should be abolished," or, "If efficient public transit systems would help to solve our air pollu-

[6] Frederick Douglass, "The Color Line," *The North American Review,* June, 1881.

tion problems, then we should use public funds to build such a system." In either paper your two chief tasks would be first, to support the reasoning behind your major premise; second, to give evidence to show that your minor premise is true. The technique is a comparatively simple way to develop a convincing theme.

A NEW KIND OF ARGUMENT: THE ROGERIAN APPROACH

The modes of argument that we have been examining in Chapters 6 and 7 are the traditional ones that men have been using and studying for centuries. Their constant recurrence in political speeches, editorials and newspaper columns, and debates on social problems testifies that they are rhetorically sound. People do respond to reasoned, well-supported, and skillfully phrased attempts to persuade. Yet we are all aware that occasionally we find ourselves involved in an argument in which we feel helpless to convince the other person of our point of view. Ironically, such arguments often concern the issues about which we care most strongly—racial or sexual matters, moral questions, personal loyalties. In these kinds of situations too often communication breaks down because both parties are so emotionally involved, so deeply committed to certain values, that they can scarcely listen to each other, much less have a rational exchange of views. So we say, "There's no use arguing" or "You just can't reason with him" and give up. Aristotle himself would probably react the same way and admit that there are times when logic seems to fail.

Dr. Carl R. Rogers, the noted psychotherapist and authority on human relations, thinks that we do not have to admit defeat, that individuals can communicate about sensitive issues on a rational plane and move beyond controversy to understanding and change. And that, after all, is what rhetoric is all about. In his article "Communication: Its Blocking and Its Facilitation," Rogers points out that the chief impediment to personal communication is the tendency we all have to react to value statements with other value statements. If someone remarks to you, "I thought *Deliverance* was really a fine movie," your first impulse is probably not to ask him why he liked it, but to give your own opinion: either "So did I" or "Oh, I couldn't stand it." Almost inevitably, once two people have committed themselves to opposite stands on an issue, even one as trivial as the merits of a movie, the possibility of their listening to a dissenting point of view with an open mind is sharply reduced. Each is on the defensive, more concerned

The effect of value statements

about justifying his own opinion than in understanding why the other person believes as he does.

If we unthinkingly throw up this kind of barrier to communication on relatively unimportant matters, how much more likely we are to do so on issues that touch our basic values. As Rogers points out:

> Although the tendency to make evaluations is common in almost all interchange of language, it is very much heightened in those situations where feelings and emotions are deeply involved. So the stronger our feelings, the more likely it is that there will be no mutual element in the communication. There will be just two ideas, two feelings, two judgments, missing each other in psychological space. . . . This tendency to react to any emotionally meaningful statement by forming an evaluation of it from our own point of view, is, I repeat, the major barrier to interpersonal communication.[7]

The failure of rhetoric

It is at this point of communication breakdown that ordinary rhetorical tactics quit working. You can reason brilliantly or cajole in your most ingratiating tones, but the person whom you are addressing will not listen as long as you are presenting only your own side of the case. He *must* defend himself because you are threatening his values and thus his self-image. What can be done about such an impasse? Very little, if you are as unwilling as your audience is to yield or compromise. If, however, you are genuinely interested in solving the communication problem and coming to some kind of agreement, Rogers suggests that there is much you can do. You can begin by looking at the issue from the other person's point of view, that is, by trying to empathize with him.

> Real communication occurs, and this evaluative tendency is avoided, when we listen with understanding. What does that mean? It means *to see the expressed idea and attitude from the other person's point of view, to sense how it feels to him, to achieve his frame of reference in regard to the thing he is talking about.*

Rogers suggests an experiment.

> The next time you get into an argument with your wife, or your friend, or with a small group of friends, just stop the discussion for a moment and for an experiment, institute this rule. "Each

[7] Carl R. Rogers, "Communication: Its Blocking and Facilitation," (Paper delivered at Northwestern University's Centennial Conference on Communications, October 11, 1951).

person can speak up for himself only *after* he has first restated the ideas and feelings of the previous speaker accurately, and to that speaker's satisfaction." You see what this would mean. It would simply mean that before presenting your own point of view it would be necessary for you to really achieve the other speaker's frame of reference—to understand his thoughts and feelings so well that you could summarize them for him. . . . Once you have been able to see the other's point of view, your own comments will have to be drastically revised. You will also find the emotion going out of the discussion, the differences being reduced, and those differences which remain being of a rational and understandable sort.[8]

Obviously, this would be a time-consuming and difficult approach to argument, and to undertake it you would have to care deeply about coming to an understanding with a person or group. When feelings are running high, however, the traditional kinds of argument are more apt to infuriate than convince an audience. Under such circumstances, a new approach at least is worth a try. Let us imagine how it might go in a situation that has undoubtedly come up in the homes of some women college students in recent years.

I didn't realize that you and mother would be so set against my wanting to be a doctor. I guess being around girls who are planning on going into medicine made me feel as if there wasn't anything unusual about it, and I hadn't stopped to consider how you might feel about it. I see now that you think it's a pretty shocking idea—I'm trying to understand why—I guess one of your objections is that if I go to medical school, I really can't plan on getting married until I'm 28 or 29 and that seems bad to you. Maybe you also think that medical school is so hard that I wouldn't have any social life or any fun and I'd miss a lot, even after I get to be a doctor. You might also be thinking that cutting up cadavers and seeing people who have terrible diseases will be more than I can handle emotionally. And I certainly realize how expensive a medical education is going to be, and you've already spent an awful lot of money on my education. I think, though, that if I can get into medical school I can get a loan. Why don't we talk about some of these other problems?

This hypothetical young woman is making a real effort to understand her parents' point of view and to state it fairly. Notice that she uses almost no connotative language, refrains from suggesting that

[8] Rogers, "Communication."

they are old-fashioned or have superficial values, and, above all, resists the temptation to defend herself rather than concentrate on their objections. Few audiences could remain indifferent to such a show of consideration. When the daughter goes on to state her own position, still being as objective as possible, her parents are almost certainly going to be more willing to listen than they would have been if she had immediately begun to justify her view. They no longer have to defend or explain their position because they know she understands it. The outcome of the discussion is not likely to be a total victory for either side. The important thing is that the parties have established communication; now rational discussion is possible.

This Rogerian approach to argument has real potential for reducing hostility and producing some agreement between people who have previously been talking *at*, not *to* each other. Although you may not completely win your argument, with traditional tactics you would almost surely lose it. But the Rogerian approach is not an easy one. As you probably realize by now, to handle it successfully a person must be mature and open-minded, genuinely interested in seeing the other fellow's point of view. To do so takes courage. As Rogers points out,

> If you really understand another person in this way, if you are willing to enter his private world and see the way life appears to him, without any attempt to make evaluative judgments, you run the risk of being changed yourself. You might see it his way, you might find yourself influenced in your attitudes or your personality.[9]

Rogers' strategy for improving communication about sensitive issues was developed principally in small face-to-face encounter groups. There is no reason, however, that it cannot be adapted to written rhetoric. In fact, those of us who do not have the patience and forebearance of a trained psychologist might handle such an argument better in writing than we would in a direct conversation, where tempers are apt to flare and defensive barriers spring up. A plan for using Rogerian argument in a paper, letter, or prepared speech might look something like this.

Rogerian approach may be used in rhetoric

1. A brief, objectively phrased statement of the issue to be discussed.
2. A complete and impartially worded summary of your audience's opinions on the issue, demonstrating that you have made an honest

[9] Rogers, "Communication."

effort to understand how they feel and why they feel that way. It would also be useful to mention the values that you think underlie those opinions: honesty, decency, concern for safety, sensitivity to public opinion, or whatever seems important.

3. An objective statement of your own opinions on the issue, along with your reasons for feeling as you do. You should carefully avoid loaded language or any suggestion that you are more moral or sensible than your audience. Here again it would be useful to give the values on which you base your opinions.

4. An analysis of what your positions have in common; probably you will find that you share some goals and values.

5. A proposal for resolving the issue in a way that injures neither party.

No one would claim that this approach is foolproof or even that it will work most of the time. When both you and your audience have deep emotional differences on an issue, it is difficult to sustain the objectivity and real empathy that are necessary if you are to reach an understanding. It will not work at all if one party uses the strategy as a trick to win agreement from his opponent, then twists that agreement into his victory. But the Rogerian method can be effective when you are more concerned with increasing understanding than you are with winning. And it is the only new thing in rhetoric that has come along in a very long time.

Objectivity and empathy needed

Understanding, not winning, is the goal

EXERCISES ON INDUCTIVE REASONING

1. The following paragraphs illustrate some patterns of inductive reasoning. From the evidence given or suggested in each one, what judgment would you make about the conclusion that is drawn?

   a. Both this summer and last, I taught a section of freshman English with an enrollment of twenty students. In each of those sections I had a student who was an active member of the Socialist party. This leads me to believe that 5 percent of the students in summer school are Socialists.

   b. At a recent meeting the leaders of our local Parent-Teacher Association expressed concern because the afternoon meetings held on the first Monday of every month do not attract enough parents, particularly fathers. Someone suggested holding the meetings at night, but the president rejected that idea because those present decided 2-to-1 that night meetings would be inconvenient.

   c. The Cuban refugees who came to this country after Castro's rise to power have done quite well. A survey by the U.S. Bureau of Immigration shows that 48 percent of the refugees have entered the professions they were in in Cuba, 35 percent have gone into other businesses, 10 percent are in college or technical training, and only 7 percent are receiving aid from a government source or relatives.

d. Our student newspaper has recently conducted an experiment that demonstrates rather conclusively that the landlords in the university area are not abiding by the no-discrimination clause required in all leases. The reporters called 100 apartment houses chosen at random from the yellow pages of the telephone directory asking if they had vacancies and if they rented to students. The supervisors of 67 of those called said they did. Yet when a black couple applied to rent those apartments, in 54 instances they were told that there were no vacancies and none was expected.

e. A survey of members of the U.S. Chamber of Commerce, men who represent the outstanding achievers in our country's free enterprise system, supports this committee's belief that new corporate taxes would seriously impede industrial expansion and new investment in the next fiscal year.

f. A recent grand jury investigation of conditions in the county jail indicates a drastic need for reforms. They found three and four prisoners confined in two-man cells, inadequate lighting and ventilation, no recreational facilities for prisoners, two suicides and nineteen instances of assaults by inmates on other inmates in the past month, and sanitary conditions that one juror described as "simply unbelievable in an institution that is under government supervision."

g. I knew when I came down here that Theta Beta Eta was a great fraternity, and I am now more convinced than ever. One of their members was student body president last year and last night I was at a party with two of their pledges. They're just the nicest guys you ever could meet.

h. The tremendous popularity of the book and movie *Love Story* shows that public taste in this country is finally turning away from the existentialist, antihero type of fiction and that there will be an upsurge of romantic, sentimental movies and books.

2. What kind of evidence would you need to support the following generalizations? Which ones would you phrase in more moderate terms?

a. The college students of the seventies are no longer interested in protest and social reform.

b. English 101 is a flunk-out course on this campus.

c. The student who graduates from a German high school is much better educated than the average high school graduate in the U.S.

d. People who have taken a defensive driving course are much safer drivers than those who have not.

e. Professional football has replaced baseball as the national American pastime.

f. We are living in the most corrupt era this country has ever seen.

g. Television advertising is a major cause of the economic discontent of low-income groups in America.

h. The automobile has caused radical changes in the American way of life in the last forty years.

i. The decline in the number of students earning exemption from English 101 may be at least partially due to the fact that we now have a whole generation of students who have been reared on television.

j. Raising and showing Arabian horses is a rich man's hobby.

3. Below are three generalizations, followed by evidence that might be used to support them. For each generalization decide which pieces of evidence constitute good support and which are of dubious value. Give your reasons.

a. Football is a character-building sport.

   1. The successful football player must practice self-discipline.

   2. Football is the most popular of all high school sports.

   3. A good football player learns that teamwork is the key to winning.

   4. Learning plays develops the memory and drills improve the player's physical coordination.

   5. A high percentage of football players have been chosen as Rhodes scholars.

b. In the fifty years following the Civil War in this country, a series of scandals occurred that caused many people to feel that the American dream had succumbed to greed and corruption.

   1. In 1905 six U.S. Senators were under indictment for fraud.

   2. Mark Twain wrote "The Man That Corrupted Hadleyburg."

   3. Under the Grant administration cabinet officers sold positions in the Bureau of Indian Affairs.

   4. Upton Sinclair's book *The Jungle* revealed that in the meat packing industry the owners exploited and sold meat from animals that were diseased and condemned as unfit for human consumption.

        5. Andrew Carnegie used his fortune to establish free public libraries across the country.

c. During the next decade the make-up of the college population in this country is going to change significantly.

        1. Because of the increasing number of community colleges that make it possible for students to go to school at night, more and more adults will be entering college.

        2. The open admissions policies that are being adopted by many publicly financed colleges will make a college education available to those who were not previously qualified.

        3. More and more adults are going to return to school as automation makes many present jobs obsolete.

        4. The oversupply of teachers with advanced degrees is going to make it possible for community colleges to improve their faculties.

        5. Fewer young men will be going to college now that the draft is no longer in effect.

4. Evaluate the following paragraph as a piece of inductive reasoning.

> The present cultural circumstances of the Negro have their roots in the very beginning of his unsought association with America. From the start the groups of Africans transported to America were treated in such a way as to discourage either the continuation of old cultural habits or the establishment of new ones strong enough to replace the old. Though practically all slaves were from West Africa, they came from different areas and tribal groups, spoke different languages, and observed different customs and mores. Those who spoke a common language, possessed a common religion or body of mythology, and honored a common system of institutions were separated in order better to assure compliance in the new environment. Those cultural elements responsible for the internal cohesion of any ethnic group were consciously eliminated by slave traders and slave masters.[10]

SUGGESTED WRITING ASSIGNMENT

Purpose: To practice constructing an inductive argument.

Procedure: Gather evidence for a paper on one of the following topics. Include with your theme, but on a separate sheet, a description

[10] Donald Gibson, "The Negro: An Essay on Definition," *The Yale Review,* March 1968, p. 337.

of your sample, indicating its size and how you chose it. You may state your conclusion first and then give your evidence, or you may give the evidence first and then draw your conclusion.

Topics

a. Recreational facilities on this campus (do, do not) meet the needs of the student body.
b. The newspaper advertisements for movies are a good indicator of the tastes of the movie-going public.
c. A significant proportion of the students I know feel that they (would, would not) learn more in their courses if they were graded solely on a pass/fail system.

EXERCISES ON
DEDUCTIVE
REASONING

1. There are at least three major syllogisms in the following passage; they may not be in absolutely perfect logical form, that is, the middle term may not be distributed, but the form is there. Begin by looking for the conclusions Orwell is trying to prove, then work back through the argument.

> As a matter of fact, very little of the concept of the tramp-monster will survive inquiry. Take the generally accepted idea that tramps are dangerous creatures. Quite apart from experience, one can say *a priori* that very few tramps are dangerous, because if they were they would be treated accordingly. A ward will often admit a hundred tramps in one night, and these are handled by a staff of at most three porters. A hundred ruffians could not be controlled by three unarmed men. Indeed, when one sees how tramps let themselves be bullied by the work-house officials, it is obvious that they are the most docile, broken-spirited creatures imaginable. Or take the idea that all tramps are drunkards—an idea ridiculous on the face of it. No doubt many tramps would drink if they got the chance, but in the nature of things they cannot get the chance. At this moment a pale watery stuff called beer is seven-pence a pint in England. To be drunk on it would cost at least half a crown, and a man who can command half a crown at all often is not a tramp. The idea that tramps are impudent social parasites . . . is not absolutely unfounded, but it is true in only a few percent of the cases. Deliberate, cynical parasitism is not in the English character. The English are a conscience-ridden race with a strong sense of the sinfulness of poverty. One cannot

imagine the average Englishman deliberately turning parasite. And this national character does not necessarily change because a man is thrown out of work. Indeed, if one remembers that a tramp is only an Englishman out of work, forced by law to live as a vagabond, then the tramp-monster vanishes.[11]

2. Test the following categorical and hypothetical syllogisms for both validity and truth. Use diagrams when applicable.

a. All crimes punishable by death are felonies.
   Smoking marijuana is a felony.
   Therefore, smoking marijuana is punishable by death.

b. No man who has been divorced can win this election.
   Stevenson has been divorced.
   Therefore, Stevenson cannot win this election.

c. If two people are in love, they never say "I'm sorry."
   John and Mary sometimes say "I'm sorry."
   Therefore, John and Mary are not in love.

d. All brilligs are slithy toves.
   No slithy toves are borogroves.
   Therefore, no brilligs are borogroves.

e. If people did not believe in God, they would not want a life after death.
   People do want a life after death.
   Therefore, people do believe in God.

f. All girls who belong to sororities are rich.
   Jeanne belongs to a sorority.
   Therefore, Jeanne is rich.

g. No gentleman would cheat at cards.
   Jeff cheats at cards.
   Therefore, Jeff is not a gentleman.

h. All people who are members of Alcoholics Anonymous are ex-alcoholics.
   Stanley is not a member of Alcoholics Anonymous.
   Therefore, Stanley is not an ex-alcoholic.

i. If someone is a working cowboy, he will have a weather-beaten face.
   Joe has a weather-beaten face.
   Therefore, Joe must be a working cowboy.

[11] George Orwell, *Down and Out in Paris and London* (London: Secker & Warburg, 1960), pp. 201–2. Reprinted by permission of Secker & Warburg and Sonia Brownwell Orwell.

    j. No lawyer is a person who has been convicted of a felony.
        Jane is a lawyer.
        Therefore, Jane has never been convicted of a felony.

    k. Most geniuses are fundamentally lazy people.
        George is a genius.
        Therefore, George is a lazy person.

    l. If you love me, you would be jealous when other men paid attention to me.
        You are not jealous when other men pay attention to me.
        Therefore, you do not love me.

3. Expand the following enthymemes into full syllogisms.

a. It can't be very good because it is made of synthetics.

b. I know he's making lots of money because he is a veterinarian.

c. Since Joe doesn't pay school taxes, he won't care if we have good schools.

d. I know he's a Texan because he's wearing cowboy boots.

e. Of course she believes in birth control! She's an intelligent woman.

f. Jones must have his Ph.D. After all, he's a full professor.

g. With his criminal record he'll never get a decent job.

h. Louis will not be readmitted to high school as long as his hair is down to his shoulders.

i. Well, you know that Tom didn't embezzle that money. He's a warden in his church.

j. You can count on Jim's behaving well. He's a graduate of the Naval Academy.

k. Clarence really isn't an alcoholic; he doesn't drink anything but beer.

l. Nixon was virtually sure of re-election simply because he was the incumbent.

4. Compose a categorical syllogism that shows how you would back one of the following conclusions.

a. Single people (should, should not) be allowed to adopt a child.

b. An X or R rating should be assigned to any movie that features violence or torture.

c. Our college (should, should not) do away with admission on the basis of SAT scores.

d. Classics by such authors as Shakespeare, Dickens, and George Eliot (should, should not) be required reading in high school English courses.

Theme 1

Purpose: To show how an ordinary argument can be built on the basis of a categorical syllogism.

Procedure: Construct an argument supporting one of the following propositions. Using the proposition as the conclusion of your syllogism, work backwards to set up the whole syllogism. Your argument should be a supported expansion of the premises of your syllogism.

Example: You want to argue that the abolition of the curfew at dormitories is a good thing.

Major premise   All policies that encourage independence and maturity in college students are wise policies.

Minor premise   The abolition of the curfew will encourage independence and maturity in college students.

Conclusion   Therefore, the abolition of the curfew is a wise policy.

Your theme would support first the major premise, then the minor one, then end with the conclusion.

Remember that your first step in thinking out your argument is to decide on your conclusion; then work back to setting up your major and minor premises. If you have trouble setting up your syllogism, ask for help before you begin your paper.

Choose one of these topics, taking only *one* side of the issue.

Topics
a. The increasing number of X-rated movies being made and widely distributed today [does, does not] constitutes a threat to the morality of young people. (Assume that no one under eighteen is admitted.)
b. An employer [does, does not] have the right to require that his employees cut their hair and wear conventional clothes.
c. Contraceptive devices [should, should not] be available to anyone who wants them regardless of age, marital status, or ability to pay.
d. Choose one of the propositions given in Exercise 4 above.

Theme 2

Purpose: To show how the hypothetical syllogism may be used to work out an argument.

Procedure: Choose one of the paragraphs below and read it carefully. Decide how you think the person involved should solve his problem and why you believe that solution is the best. Then put your reasoning into a hypothetical syllogism which summarizes your points. Develop that hypothetical syllogism into a theme.

Example: In case A, the major premise of your syllogism might look like this:

> If a man is an elected law official, he has an obligation to enforce the law impartially regardless of who may be affected.

Or this:

> If a man has to choose between loyalty to his family and duty to his profession, he should put personal obligations before business obligations.

Or this:

> If a man thinks that a particular course of action is going to corrupt young people, his obligation is to stop that action at all costs.

Of course, you may not agree with any of these interpretations. Work out your own for one of the cases, then develop your theme by expanding and supporting the premises of your syllogism. *Be sure you set up the minor premise so that your reasoning is valid.*

a. Mr. Chase, the local district attorney, is earning himself a statewide reputation by vigorously tracking down and obtaining convictions of pushers of hard drugs. He is, understandably, proud of his work and feels that he is contributing to cleaning up his town and protecting the young people in it. Just before a planned raid Mr. Chase gets an anonymous phone call that warns him that his son is one of the key figures in the ring of pushers that will be picked up. The phone call may be a trick to get him to call off the raid; on the other hand, when he thinks about some of the strange behavior of his son in past weeks, he realizes that the caller may be telling the truth. The raid is due to start in ten minutes and he could give his men no good reason for calling it off, but if he goes ahead with it, his son may be arrested and sent to prison for ten years. What should Mr. Chase do?

b. Young Jim Dodson is a cadet at the U.S. Air Force Academy, an institution that demands of its students a very strict code of honor. Not only must the cadets pledge not to lie, cheat, or steal but they must also pledge to reveal any code violation by another cadet. Dodson knew this when he entered the Academy and approved of the regulation because he feels that a dishonest man is not fit to be an officer or to lead other men. The night before a final examination he finds that his roommate has made a complete set of crib notes to take into the exam with him and has done it so cleverly that there is little chance that he will be caught. Dodson knows that it is his duty to turn in his roommate; he also knows that if he does the boy will be expelled from the Academy and probably will not get an education since his family is very poor. But if the boy is caught and Dodson is asked if he knew about the cheating, he will lose whether he lies or tells the truth. What should he do?

Theme 3

Purpose: To help you understand the concept of the Rogerian approach to argument by putting it into practice.

Procedure: Write an argument in which you put yourself into *one* of the situations described below and try to persuade your audience to accept your point of view. Consider carefully how and why your audience is going to be threatened by the proposal you are making and think how you can best alleviate their fears and persuade them to see your point of view. Before you start, reread the text. Organize your paper according to the five phases of argument summarized on pages 210 and 211.

Your thesis sentence should precede your theme and should show the main idea you are presenting and the principal points you will use to support it.

Topics
a. You are married to a pleasant, prosperous, but stubborn man who feels strongly that wives should be home-makers and should not work unless it is absolutely necessary. You are a college graduate qualified to hold down a good job and want to go to work. Your children are in school.
b. You are a college sophomore who cannot decide on a career and you want to drop out of school for a year to rethink your goals and values. You must convince your parents who are very much opposed to the idea.
c. You are a college sophomore girl who wants to move out of the college dormitory and take an apartment with two other girls. Many

of your friends have done this, but you know your parents are going to object on the grounds that a dormitory is a safer place to live. You are going to try to persuade them to give their consent to your moving.

d. You are a man of thirty-five who makes about $10,000 a year as a salesman, but after ten years of the work you have come to detest your job and want to go back to college in order to become an engineer. As a veteran, you will receive about $230 a month while you are in school, but that will not be enough to live on. You want to convince your wife that in the long run you will both be happier if you make this change, but she is skeptical. She has a job that pays $350 a month. You have no children.

8

Fallacies and
Propaganda:
How Not
to Argue and
What Not
to Believe

Fallacies are sometimes called "counterfeit arguments." The figurative description is apt because, like bogus money, fallacious arguments resemble the real thing (logic) but have flaws that cancel their value as sound rhetoric. Fallacies are usually classified as "formal" if those flaws are in form or structure, and as "material" if the flaws are in content or matter.

FORMAL FALLACIES

Fallacies of deductive reasoning

Fallacies of inductive reasoning

Circular arguments

We have already covered the main formal fallacy of the categorical syllogism: the fallacy of the shared characteristic or the undistributed middle; and of the hypothetical syllogism: denying the antecedent and affirming the consequent. The errors of generalizing from an insufficient sample or from a sample that is biased or poorly chosen might be called the formal fallacies of inductive reasoning.

Another kind of formal fallacy is the circular argument. This kind of reasoning appears to move from a premise to a conclusion, but in reality it does no more than move in a circle, the circular reasoning being disguised by a slight change in wording or terminology. Such a pseudoargument might go like this: "The proposed gun control legislation in this country is a left-wing plot because only radical liberals would scheme to take guns away from citizens." "The Arabs cannot be trusted because everything they do proves they are treacherous" is just as circular. The main assertion is not supported but simply repeated. Students sometimes slip into this kind of fallacy when doing rhetorical analysis. They may, for instance, conclude a theme with a statement like this: "The writer is not persuasive because he does not convince the reader to accept his idea." Unfortunately, their teachers sometimes do no better. Several years ago the authors of an article in an educational psychology journal claimed to have proved that feminine and masculine traits exist among very young children. They cited as evidence for their theory an experiment conducted by putting an equal number of male and female three-year-olds in a room with an assortment of toys. Their observations convinced them that boys had a definite preference for "masculine" toys, and girls showed a marked preference for "feminine" toys. Then they defined "masculine" toys as those preferred by boys and "feminine" toys as those preferred by girls! A government official who replies to a journalist's inquiry about why certain documents have been marked "Classified" by saying that they contain confidential information is using the same kind of evasive reasoning.

MATERIAL FALLACIES

Faulty Analogy

Two major material fallacies, faulty analogy and *post hoc, ergo propter hoc* or false cause, have already been touched on in the first chapter on modes of argument, but they are important enough to warrant a brief review. The prudent writer seldom uses analogy as his main rhetorical device because, although a good analogy can clarify and reinforce an argument, it cannot actually furnish proof. And most

Analogies break down if pushed too far

analogies break down if they are pushed too far. For instance, proponents of our multibillion dollar space program have sometimes drawn an analogy between that program and the opening of our American frontier to justify the expenditure and human resources that we have invested in space exploration. The comparison is a faulty one, however, because there are far more differences than similarities between the two enterprises. Each may introduce man to unknown territory, but people cannot rocket to the moon on their own, and they cannot settle and cultivate the area after they get there. The moon, so far as we know now, has no economic assets to develop, and it offers no solution to our problems of crowding and overpopulation. The comparison of trips to the moon to Columbus's voyages has the same weaknesses. Analogies of this kind have more emotional than rational force. Because Americans are likely to respond favorably to words such as "exploration," "pioneer," and "frontier," too often they do not carefully examine the validity of the arguments in which they are used. As a precaution against being misled by such easy comparisons, when you use or encounter an analogy you should ask yourself, "Are there enough important similarities between the two things being compared really to support the conclusions that are being drawn?"

Post Hoc, Ergo Propter Hoc

"False cause"

The material fallacy of *post hoc, ergo propter hoc* or "false cause" is another form of simplistic reasoning. Human laziness or the desire to see dependable patterns in a complex world tempts us to solve problems by setting up neat cause and effect relationships. It is much easier to say "Permissive child rearing causes juvenile delinquency," "The Vietnam war caused our economic problems," or "Pornography causes sex crimes" than it is to try to trace and understand the complicated chain of circumstances that underlie most problems or events.

In the 1950s, shortly after the United States government had conducted a series of hydrogen bomb tests in the Pacific, the country was hit by an unusually severe winter. Despite the meteorologists' protestations that the weather was the predictable result of a change in the Gulf Stream, some people insisted that the bomb tests had caused it. *The New Yorker* magazine satirized this kind of thinking in a cartoon showing two Neanderthal men peering out of a cave at a torrential rain. The caption was, "We never used to have this kind of weather before they started using bows and arrows."

Giving evidence validates post hoc argument

Chapter 6 pointed out the fondness of political campaigners for the *post hoc* fallacy. They use the strategy of "after this, therefore because of this" in several ways. Invariably, they attempt to discredit their opponents by suggesting that any misfortunes that took place during an administration were the direct result of that administration's bungling. Such reasoning is not necessarily fallacious if the attacker can give supporting evidence for his charges. It is fallacious, however, if it shows only a sequential connection. Candidates also project the *post hoc* fallacy into the future by suggesting that their election alone will cause good things to happen. This same technique is used extensively by advertisers, who rely on it heavily to convince their customers that delightful effects will follow their purchase of a certain product. "Drive our car and the girls will swarm all over you," "Bleach your hair and rekindle your husband's lagging affection," "Take our correspondence course and earn $20,000 a year," "Use Endocreme and look young again." What deceptively simple cause and effect arguments! And how sad when they turn out to be fallacies.

Begging the Question

Another material fallacy that crops up as often as weeds in a garden is "begging the question." The term describes the process of assuming in the premises of an argument what you ought to be establishing by proof; another name for it might be "loading the assertion." It resembles circular reasoning in that the writer does not construct a legitimate argument; he merely asserts that something is because it is. For example, the statement "Henry Miller's filthy books should not be allowed in our library," which neither proves that the books are filthy nor shows why they should be taken out of the library, is a loaded assertion masquerading as an argument. So are the following sentences: "Useless courses such as Greek and Hebrew are a waste of time"; "This fine public servant deserves our support"; and "This cor-

"Loading the assertion"

rupt official should be thrown out of office." A reader would probably agree that useless courses are a waste of time, fine public servants deserve support, and corrupt officials should be gotten rid of; such statements are almost redundant. But in each case the writer has not proved his allegation, nor has the writer of the following paragaph:

> Our government has become the captive of vain, callous, ambitious, special interests who stoop to spying, bribery, espionage and blatant police state tactics to continue themselves in power and to obtain special privileges at the expense of all. This corruption, with its resultant suppression of moral values and civil freedoms, has achieved a level surpassed only in completely total dictatorships. [From a letter to the editor of the *Austin (Texas) American & Statesman,* October 19, 1972.]

The fallacy of begging the question creeps into writing in subtler ways as well. A common form is the question-begging epithet, that is, a favorable or unfavorable label attached to the subject of the assertion, for example, "John's *disgraceful* conduct ought to be censured" or "This *treasonable* act must not go unpunished." Such statements substitute connotation for argument. Other expressions that appear frequently in question-begging arguments are "It is common knowledge," "Everybody knows," "Everyone would agree," "It is obvious," and "The fact is." When these are followed by no more than statements of opinion, the chances are that the writer is trying to evade the burden of proof. "Everyone knows that socialized medicine has been a failure in England" and "It is common knowledge that the Syndicate controls the numbers racket" prove nothing unless they are followed by supporting evidence.

The question-begging epithet

"Everybody knows"

Argument Ad Hominem

"To the man"

Ad hominem means "to the man." The phrase identifies the kind of argument that focuses on an individual's character or personal life rather than on the issues involved. If a man is running for office, the debate should center on his qualifications, his experience, and the kind of program he is advocating, not on his religious beliefs, his military record, or his marital status. The campaigner who overemphasizes his war record and his church affiliation and keeps appearing on television with his family, but who says little about taxes or legislation, may reasonably be accused of evading the real issues. He is trying to appeal to his audience's emotions rather than their reason. Unfortunately, such tactics often work. Until recent years, a divorced person stood little chance of being elected to public office, and John F. Kennedy was the first successful Catholic presidential candidate. But the thinking person tries to look beyond personalities and personal biases when he is making a judgment about an individual's qualification or achievements. To condemn an author's works because he is reputed to be a heavy drinker, or to say that a man ought not to be elected senator because he once fathered an illegitimate child, is the mark of a narrow mind.

People who pride themselves on being thoughtful and rational individuals will pay little attention to mud-slinging, gossip, or unsupported charges about candidates or other public figures. They will try to focus on the relevant issues as they see them. There are times, however, when an *ad hominem* attack is not necessarily beside the point. If a person who is running for a major office actually is an alcoholic, he may not be able to handle the responsibilities of that office. If you want very much for the next legislature to liberalize controls on contraceptives, you are not necessarily showing religious bias if you vote against a candidate because he is a Catholic. There are times when referring to a person's character, beliefs, or past actions may not be irrelevant; the fair-minded person tries to make a careful distinction between personal attacks and information that bears on the issue. The following hypothetical political advertisement illustrates the problem.

Relevant ad hominem arguments

VOTE FOR HONESTY AND DECENCY

John Q. Candidate stands four-square on his record of thirty scandal-free years as county treasurer. You *know* he's honest. On the other hand, his opponent is a man who declared bankruptcy in 1968, has been married three times, and last year was brought into court twice on charges of reckless driving.

Is it an *ad hominem* fallacy or a justified baring of relevant information?

Argument Ad Populum

This fallacy, similar to the *ad hominem*, takes the form of impassioned emotional appeals "to the people," that is, to the deep biases people have for institutions such as God, motherhood, country, family, and may have against Fascism, Communism, atheism, or other such abstract concepts. This fallacy too seeks to arouse emotions rather

"To the people" Appeals to deep biases

than confront issues. The passage from Hitler's writings on page 85 is a classic example of the *ad populum* fallacy. In Albert Camus' *The Stranger*, the state prosecutor pleads to the jury to send the protagonist, Meursault, to the guillotine not so much because he killed a man in a moment of irrationality, but because he did not cry at his mother's funeral and was unmoved when the prosecutor showed him a crucifix. And the jury convicted. As we shall see, propaganda relies heavily on the *ad populum* technique.

Basis for propaganda

Tu Quoque

"You're another"
Deflects or evades the issue

A free translation of this Latin term is "You're another." This fallacy takes the form of evading the issue or deflecting a hostile charge or question by making a similar charge against the opponent. For example, a man who had been charged with cheating on his expense account might counter the accusation with, "Who are you to criticize me for padding my expense account when I know you cheat on your income tax?" Lionel Ruby quotes a typical *tu quoque* argument on the issue of the draft. A younger man might say to an older one, "You're in favor of the draft because you're too old to go." The older one might reply, "Maybe so, but you're against it because you're afraid you'll have to go."[1] The so-called argument is entirely beside the point; neither has mentioned the merits or defects of the draft law.

Exchanges on a low personal level are not difficult to spot for the counterfeits they are, but *tu quoque* arguments sometimes become rather sophisticated—in fact, one finds them in surprising company. Take, for example, this paragraph from a Jean-Paul Sartre essay on existentialism.

> As is generally known, the basic charge against us [Existentialists] is that we put the emphasis on the dark side of human life. Someone recently told me of a lady who, when she let slip a vulgar word in a moment of irritation, excused herself by saying, "I guess I'm becoming an existentialist." Consequently, existentialism is regarded as something ugly; that is why we are said to be naturalists; and if we are, it is rather surprising that in this day and age we cause so much more alarm and scandal than does naturalism, properly so called. The kind of person who can take in his stride such a novel as Zola's *The Earth* is disgusted as soon as he starts reading an existentialist novel; the kind of person

[1] Lionel Ruby, *The Art of Making Sense* (New York: J. B. Lippincott Company, 1954), p. 89.

who is resigned to the wisdom of the ages—which is pretty sad—finds us even sadder. Yet, what can be more disillusioning than saying "true charity begins at home" or "a scoundrel will always return evil for good"?[2]

Sartre has not at all refuted the charge that existentialism is a gloomy philosophy that focuses "on the dark side of human life." He has only deflected the criticism by saying, in effect, "You call us gloomy! You're just as gloomy with your cynical slogans and admiration for naturalistic novels."

Black/White Argument

"Either/or"

Insufficient options

Oversimplification

This fallacy may also be called the "fallacy of insufficient options" or the "either/or" fallacy. The writer or speaker who uses it is trying to force his audience into choosing between two conflicting alternatives by suggesting that there are no other options. In fact, there may be several options or even the option of making no choice. This kind of oversimplification is attractive to people who have what the psychologists call "two-valued orientations," that is, they see the world in terms of black and white, right and wrong, good and bad. As you can imagine, they don't have many philosophical problems. A typical example of their outlook on life is illustrated by the bumper sticker "America—Love It or Leave It." This kind of attitude is as prevalent on the left as it is on the right. "Either you believe in socialism or you're a dirty fascist pig" is as bad as "If you're not an advocate of free enterprise, you're a Communist sympathizer."

The rational thinker neither relies on this tactic nor allows himself to be intimidated by it. For example, if he is concerned about industrial air pollution in this country, he does not argue that we have to choose between factories and clean air. He knows there are other options: filtering devices and other controls that will give us clean air if we are willing to pay for it, relocating factories to reduce the concentration of pollutants, and so on. He does not subscribe to the simplistic view that the solution to our technological problems is a return to nature. Moreover, he sees the flaws in arguments such as the following:

Johnny goes by the official title of "student." Yet Johnny is the face every professor would prefer to see anywhere but in his classroom where it blocks with its dreary smile, or its stoical yawn,

[2] Jean-Paul Sartre, "The Humanism of Existentialism," *The Philosophy of Existentialism* (New York: Philosophical Library, 1965), p. 32.

the educational process on which we are proud to spend annually billions of dollars. By his sheer inert numbers he is making the common pursuit of professors and students—real students—impossible.[3]

Kenner goes on to define the "real student" as one who insists on knowing.

> . . . what it does not know it will encounter with pleasure. And it *must* learn, as a cat must eat. . . . its tireless curiosity is unmistakable. In time, if all goes well, it will accept training, and the life-long responsibilities of keeping itself trained.
>
> But Johnny has no such appetite, no such momentum. When Johnny applies his brand-new ball-point to his first blue book, each sentence comes out smudged with his unmistakable pawprint.

Throughout the essay Kenner recognizes only two kinds of students: Johnnies and real students. The real student is always described in favorable terms—"tireless curiosity," "a mind that insists on knowing," "encounters knowledge with pleasure"—while Johnny is defined by his "dreary smile," "stoical yawn," and "the smudge of his unmistakable pawprint." The argument is totally black and white; Kenner does not acknowledge the possibility that there may be students who do not fit into one of his categories. As a result his argument, although cleverly written, falls to the ground.

Loaded rhetorical questions

The loaded rhetorical question that allows for only one acceptable answer is a form of the black/white argument.

> Are we going to take steps to maintain law and order in our community, or are we going to allow the thugs and dope addicts to take over this town and ruin our homes and families?
>
> Shall we vote against this bill for increased welfare payments, or shall we abandon our fight to stop creeping socialism in our society?

The Complex Question

"Double question"

The complex question is fallacious because it sets up a question in such a way that a direct answer can only support the questioner's

[3] Hugh Kenner, "Don't Send Johnny to College," *Saturday Evening Post,* November 14, 1964, pp. 12–16.

assumption. The classic example is "Have you stopped beating your wife?" To answer either "yes" or "no" is incriminating. The deceptive part about this fallacy is that the questioner is apparently asking only one question, but in reality he is asking two: "Did you ever beat your wife?" and "Do you now beat your wife?" Other variations of this fallacy might take these forms.

Does everyone in your town still get drunk and raise hell on Saturday night?

How long have you been consorting with known criminals and other Syndicate-types?

What made you think you could get away with plagiarizing that paper?

When did you start cheating on your income tax?

Questions like these are designed to trick an audience and therefore do not deserve a direct answer. You can cope with them only by insisting that the questioner break the question down into two distinct parts to be answered separately and independently.

Red Herring

"Diverting attention"

Deliberately sidetracks an argument

This term, which refers to smoked herring, a particularly strong-smelling fish, is a figurative phrase that describes the tactic of bringing in an irrelevant point to divert the audience's attention from the main issue. It refers to the old belief that dragging a red herring across a trail would divert the attention of hunting dogs from the scent they were expected to follow and send them off in another direction. There are many kinds of diversionary tricks used in arguments, but we usually reserve the term "red herring" for the digression a speaker or writer uses to sidetrack an argument. For example, if a labor leader were arguing that unions ought to be exempt from antitrust laws but spent much of his speech describing the hardships union men endured in the early part of this century, he would be employing a red herring fallacy. Labor's fight for the right to bargain collectively is important historically but has nothing to do with the present issue. The fallacy also crops up when a speaker interrupts a debate on a specific issue to bring in matters that are not under discussion. For instance, a college faculty member who tried to sidetrack a discussion about faculty salaries into an attack on the school's publish-or-perish rules would be using a red herring fallacy. The latter problem may be worth discussing, but it is not the issue under consideration.

The Genetic Fallacy

Predicting from origins

People who argue from the genetic fallacy assert that we can predict a person's nature and character if we know his origins. They would hold that the same is true for institutions, works of art, or ideas. We often find this fallacy expressed as an enthymeme.

He wouldn't do that because he's from a good family.

Jane must be a racist since she spent her early life in South Africa.

The Reivers must be a Gothic novel since Faulkner wrote it.

Acupuncture cannot be an acceptable technique for modern doctors since it was developed in ancient China.

Jack is bound to be exceptionally bright because his father is a professor.

That radio won't last very long if it came from Japan.

Some of these conclusions *may* be true but proving them requires evidence, not simply speculation about origins.

Hypostatization

A person who uses this fallacy gives concrete reality to what is actually no more than a concept. Most often, this fallacy takes the form of a sweeping generalization disguised as an argument from authority. For example, someone may write, "History has proved that absentee ownership leads to peasant revolts," or, "Psychology tells us that a person's character is formed by the time he is six." The people who make such statements are assuming that there is a body of individuals or works which represents all historians or all psychologists and can speak for them. The implication is that there are no differences of opinion, no dissenting voices. That, of course, is not a reasonable assumption; experts in those fields of study could readily cite numerous examples that would conflict with such assertions. If you want to use this kind of argument as support for a point—and often you will—have the good judgment to qualify it and be specific. Modify

Generalization in form of argument from authority

Assumption: no differences of opinion

the statements to read, "Many historians have pointed out that absentee ownership frequently leads to peasants' trying to take over the land." Better still, give a specific reference if possible. "The noted psychologist Eric Fromm points out that the attitudes children absorb from their parents usually persist through adulthood." Don't, however, fall into unsupportable generalizations such as "Medicine has proved that an accumulation of cholesterol occurs most often in tense individuals" or "Science has proved that there is no life in outer space." Science and medicine, as actual entities, do not exist. Your audience may remind you of that fact.

Special Pleading

"Whole-truth" argument

Bias invalidates evidence

This term describes a totally one-sided argument that is presented as the whole truth. The points that the arguer makes for or against the issue may be quite true or at least supported with reasonable evidence, but his position is so biased that it cannot be considered valid. Mark Twain used this kind of argument against the church and Christianity in his novel *The Mysterious Stranger*. He focused on the crimes that have been committed in the name of the church, on the misery and injustice that God allows to exist in the world, and on the suffering of good Christians and the triumph of those who flout God's laws. Bertrand Russell took the same approach in his book *Why I Am Not a Christian*. Neither man conceded any good to Christianity. Even those people who are inclined to share the writers' prejudices should realize that their arguments, although supported with examples, are completely unfair. Any argument that concentrates solely on the merits or defects of an institution or system and ignores whatever points may be made on the other side is open to the same charge.

No rhetoric is free of fallacy

This catalog of common fallacies by no means includes all the ways in which an argument can go wrong. Studying it, however, should alert you to the more obvious weaknesses in the arguments of others and help you to avoid such pitfalls in your own rhetoric. If, while you are constructing an argument, you can spot those places at which an opponent might justly say, "Oh, but you're not being logical" or "Ah ha! Your conclusion does not follow from the evidence you have given," you can strengthen your own writing. But we also have to remember that almost no rhetoric is totally free of fallacy—even Plato or John Stuart Mill could not produce an argument that might not be justifiably criticized at some point. We cannot demand

Balanced judgment
necessary

Blatant fallacies
undermine arguments

perfection and unswerving consistency from any speaker or writer; such a demand is in itself a kind of fallacy. What we must do, then, is make a balanced and charitable judgment of other people's arguments. An occasional question-begging epithet, hypostatization, or genetic fallacy does not constitute sufficient grounds for rejecting an entire editorial, essay, or speech. If, however, an argument contains blatant *post hoc* fallacies or personal attacks, and the author twists his evidence, you have every right to say that it is not a sound or just argument. Finally, you should remember that your opponents are not the only ones who indulge in fallacies. You must be honest enough to search out the fallacies in arguments you agree with as well as in those to which you are hostile.

WHY NOT USE FALLACIES?

Ethical considerations   Students often ask, "Well, what's the matter with using fallacies in an argument if they help you to win?" There are two answers to that question, one ethical, one practical. The first involves definition. Using dishonest means—and that is what fallacies amount to if a person is using them consciously—to attain an end brands you as a dishonest person. A fallacy is a swindle, a counterfeit argument, an evasion of your responsibility to support your beliefs with logical and legitimate methods. Viewed from an ethical standpoint, this question is on the same level as "What is the matter with cheating if it gets you a good grade?" or "Why shouldn't I lie if it's to my advantage?" Deception by any other name remains deception.

Practical considerations   Viewed from a practical standpoint, fallacies in your argument may contribute to defeating your purpose. If you use fallacies deliberately and cynically, you are assuming that your audience is not very bright and cannot detect twisted reasoning. Even people with untrained minds are not totally gullible; they can recognize loaded statements and spurious appeals to their emotions and they will realize you are insulting them. The person with the trained mind will immediately dismiss a fallacious argument as not worth bothering with. If you cannot construct a rational defense for your ideas, he will label you as a sloppy thinker. If he thinks you are capable of putting together a reasonable and careful argument but prefer to make an irrational one in the hope of winning, you will lose his respect and support.

PROPAGANDA

Definition

All rhetoric seeks to persuade, but propaganda, as we shall use the term here, seeks to persuade principally by appeals to the emotional, irrational side of our nature. As Lionel Ruby put it:

> A propagandist, in the strict sense, is not interested in the truth for its own sake, or in spreading it. His purpose is different. He wants a certain kind of action from us. He doesn't want people to think for themselves. He seeks to mold their minds so that they will think as he wants them to think, and act as he wants them to act. He prefers that they should *not* think for themselves. If the knowledge of certain facts will cast doubts in the minds of his hearers, he will conceal those facts.[4]

Uses fallacies

Given these goals, we might expect the propagandist to rely heavily on fallacies to achieve his ends. And so he does. Whether he is promoting a product, an ideology, a frame of mind, or a person, he will employ counterfeit arguments designed to short-circuit the reasoning process and go straight to the emotions. Sometimes this technique is employed to achieve useful, even admirable, goals; nevertheless, a propagandist quite often reveals a real contempt for his audience. He operates from the assumption that his audience is irrational, shallow-minded, more swayed by myths than by facts, and incapable of abstract or logical thinking. A propagandist who has contempt for his audience agrees, in effect, with Adolf Hitler that "the people in their overwhelming majority are so feminine by nature and attitude that sober reasoning determines their thoughts and actions far less than emotion and feeling."[5] This propagandist is confident that he, with his superior intellect and his knowledge of human weaknesses, can manipulate and condition the masses into buying, literally or figuratively, what he has to sell.

Commercial Propaganda

In recent years the advertising industry has raised the art of manipulation almost to a science. Agencies spend a substantial portion of their budgets on motivational research, the systematic study of people's needs, and their fears, anxieties, hopes, and desires, as well. They hire sociologists to advise them about patterns of social behavior and the attitudes and life-styles of various economic groups; they hire

[4] Ruby, *The Art of Making Sense,* p. 76.
[5] Adolf Hitler, *Mein Kampf,* trans. Ralph Manheim (Boston: Houghton Mifflin Company, 1933), p. 183.

psychologists to tell them what stimuli will trigger favorable responses toward a product and what symbols they can use to set up good associations with their products in the minds of prospective customers. And their photographers and artists produce visual images with which the customer can identify. Armed with these tools, the advertisers mount their campaign to persuade the great buying public to part with its dollars. In return for those dollars, the buyer gets the manufacturer's product, which to him may represent some of the good things in life: pleasure, love, security, popularity, prestige, a new image of himself. What appeal do you think the following hypothetical ads might have and for what types of audiences?

> The Jupiter is *the* auto! Built by true craftsmen for those few who demand the finest. And those few who can afford the finest. Its sleek styling, its understated elegance, its unmistakable *éclat* says—but ever so subtly—that you've arrived!

> *You Can't Afford to Wait!* You feel young doing those fun things you love—swimming, skiing, riding. But the sun, the wind, the water are the enemies of that fresh complexion. Don't wait for them to dry out those precious oils your skin must have. Be young! Keep that dewy look your man loves so much! Start today to use Ponce de Leon Essence of Youth. Smoothed over your skin twice a day, it will erase those tiny wrinkles that steal away your youth! Only $15 for the half-ounce jar.

> Mother McCrea's bread is as good as that wonderful bread your mother used to make. You could make it too, if you had time. But because we know you don't have those hours and hours it takes to make really delicious bread, we want to help you. Just take a Mother McCrea's ready-to-brown loaf, brush a little butter on the top, pop it in the oven and you'll have that delicious, golden-crusted bread you remember. Your family will love it! And you! Because you've taken time to bake for them. *(According to Vance Packard, author of* The Hidden Persuaders, *advertisers use this kind of copy to overcome the guilt women feel about using prepared foods. Notice the emphasis on "you" and "your.")*

> VIXEN! It's not for the timid. Only a *real* woman would dare to wear it, dare to hint at that exciting, provocative you that simmers just beneath the surface. But if you're not afraid, VIXEN is your perfume. And you'll find a *real* man.

Do you want to serve a wine to those special guests but are afraid to? Afraid you'll reveal your ignorance when you bring out the bottle? Want to cover up the label for fear it might not be the right kind? Don't be. You'll never be gauche if you choose our *vin extraordinaire*. White or red, it's superb. Serve it proudly—it says all the right things about your taste. And may even get you that promotion.

Not all or even most advertisements are deceptive or contrived solely to appeal to the emotions. In fact, a thorough check of a variety of magazines—*Psychology Today, Newsweek, Ladies' Home Journal, Playboy, Cosmopolitan, Esquire, Ebony, Harper's,* and *Good Housekeeping*—reveals that a majority of the advertisers want to appeal to the readers' desire for a quality product at a reasonable price. The copy is often connotative and the accompanying pictures are frequently provocative, but the tone is rational. Such ads cannot be called propaganda in the pejorative sense. But commercial appeals like the hypothetical ones above must, I think, be classified as attempts to move people by manipulating their fears and insecurities, their desire for love, and their need to feel important. They sell illusions, and perhaps there is nothing wrong with that. The rational woman should know, however, that when she pays $15 for a half-ounce jar of face cream to make her look ten years younger, she is buying an illusion—nothing more.

Political Propaganda

Political propagandists also sell illusions, sometimes of a potentially more dangerous kind. One of the chief illusions they promote is that there are simple solutions to complex problems. A candidate may exploit people's fear of violence and crime by repeating over and over again that if he is elected he will restore law and order and make this country safe for law-abiding citizens. He doesn't say how he intends to accomplish this feat or what should be done to reduce the causes of crime; he simply repeats "law and order," "law and order" as if it were a magic incantation. He bases his speeches and his campaign literature on what the Institute for Propaganda Analysis calls "Glittering Generalities."

"Glittering Generalities"

"Glittering Generalities" is a device by which the propagandist identifies his program with virtue by use of "virtue words." Here he appeals to our emotions of love, generosity, and brotherhood.

He uses words like truth, freedom, honor, liberty, social justice, public service, the right to work, loyalty, progress, democracy, the American way, Constitution defender. These words suggest shining ideals. All people of good will believe in these ideals. Hence the propagandist, by identifying his individual group, nation, race, policy, practice, or belief with such ideals, seeks to win us to his cause.[6]

The passages of cant on page 87 are this type of propaganda.

"Name-calling"

The other side of this coin is "Name-calling," the technique of attaching invidious labels to the opposition, labels such as "alien philosophy," "Communist aggressor," "pseudo-intellectual," "atheist," "agitator," "welfare chiseler," "Fascist," "honky," "white devil," "reactionary," and "racist pig." Epithets like these not only beg the question but they attempt to circumvent the issues by placing the blame for problems on a scapegoat, an evil "They" who are conspiring to overthrow the forces of good.

Ad populum fallacy

Demagogues are particularly fond of the *ad populum* fallacy. Not only do they try to align themselves with God, mother, and country but they make frequent references to "plain folks," "the working man," "the little guy," "the solid middle class," and "the ordinary taxpayer." They flatter their hero, "the common man," with references to his "grassroots wisdom" and his "horse sense." They are also skilled in

Black/white argument

the black/white argument—"Either we fight Communism abroad or we'll have to fight it on our own shores"; "We must choose between people's socialism or exploitation by the capitalist bourgeoisie"—and

Red herring

they are masters at dragging a red herring across the trail of an argument. A debate on school financing becomes a tirade about busing or one about defense needs turns into an attack on the Pentagon "brass hats."

Fortunately, in this country no single power group monopolizes the media so that it can pour out a constant, unchecked stream of lies, distortions, half-truths, and hatred for any opponents, and a steady diet of praise for its own leaders and policies. (Not everyone would agree with that statement, however. The Socialist Herbert Marcuse and other dissidents contend that the media are totally under the control of the white power structure.) We also, for the most part, seem to have a tradition of fair play and restraint that keeps all but the extremist groups from indulging in the kind of completely irrational,

[6] The Institute for Propaganda Analysis, "How to Detect Propaganda," *Propaganda Analysis,* November 1937, pp. 5, 6.

and warped propaganda produced by Nazi Germany. But we should not take comfort in the thought that we have nothing to worry about simply because things are not as bad as they could be. As Lionel Ruby put it, "Insofar as propaganda seeks to get us to act by emotional appeals coupled with a concealment of facts—facts that might make us think about the merits of the proposal—it is 'bad' *as a method.*"[7]

Thus, if an individual wants to remain an individual—a person who makes rational choices on the basis of the best information he can gather rather than one who is swayed by appeals to his fears, his anxieties, and his ego—he needs to be constantly alert to the tactics the political propagandists might employ. Unfortunately, in the last decade this has become much more difficult because the commercial and the political propagandists have joined forces, especially through the increasingly pervasive medium of television. Joe McGinniss describes this alliance in his book *The Selling of the President, 1968*.

> Politics, in a sense, has always been a con game. . . .
>
> Advertising, in many ways, is a con game too. Human beings do not need a new automobile every third year; a color television set brings little enrichment of the human experience; a higher or lower hemline no expansion of consciousness, no increase in the capacity to love.
>
> It is not surprising, then, that politicians and advertising men should have discovered one another. And, once they recognized that the citizen did not so much vote for a candidate as make a psychological purchase of him, not surprising that they began to work together.[8]

McGinniss' book is a detailed, documented account of how the professional writers and advertising men who were hired to help with the 1968 presidential campaign "marketed" Richard Nixon to the public through television. Our concern here is not with the merits of the candidate himself—presumably the "salesmen" would have handled Abraham Lincoln or Franklin Roosevelt the same way if they had run those campaigns. Our concern is, rather, with the professional propagandists and their methods. McGinniss quotes one of them as writing,

> "Voters are basically lazy, basically uninterested in making an *effort* to understand what we're talking about. . . . Reason requires

---

[7] Ruby, *The Art of Making Sense*, p. 77.

[8] Joe McGinniss, *The Selling of the President, 1968* (New York: Pocket Books, 1970), pp. 19, 20. Copyright © 1969 by JoeMac, Incorporated. Reprinted by permission of Trident Press, a division of Simon & Schuster, Inc.

a high degree of discipline, of concentration; impression is easier. Reason pushes the viewer back; it assaults him, it demands that he agree or disagree; impression can envelop him, invite him in, without making an intellectual demand. . . . When we argue with him we demand that he make the effort of replying. We seek to engage his intellect, and for most people this is the most difficult work of all. The emotions are more easily roused, closer to the surface, more malleable. . . .

"[Nixon] has to come across as a person larger than life, the stuff of legend. People are stirred by the legend, including the living legend, not by the man himself. It's the aura that surrounds the charismatic figure more than it is the figure itself, that draws the followers. Our task is to build that aura. . . .

"So let's not be afraid of television gimmicks . . . get the voters to like the guy and the battle's two-thirds won." [Pp. 32, 33.]

The promoters built their campaign on this philosophy. They assumed that voters didn't want to think about the issues, that they wanted to feel, to be impressed, to be swept along in a warm swell of emotions.

The advertising men created a new slogan: "This time vote like your whole world depended on it"—ambiguous, vague, but catchy. Their marketing masterpiece, however, was a series of sixty-second television commercials based on still pictures. McGinniss describes them this way:

Treleaven could use Nixon's voice to accompany the stills but his face would not be on the screen. Instead there would be pictures, and hopefully, the pictures would prevent people from paying too much attention to the words.

The words would be the same ones Nixon always used—the words of the acceptance speech. But they would all seem fresh and lively because a series of still pictures would flash on the screen while Nixon spoke. If it were done right, it would permit Treleaven to create a Nixon image that was entirely independent of the words. Nixon would say his same old tiresome things but no one would have to listen. The words would become Muzak. Something pleasant and lulling in the background. The flashing pictures would be carefully selected to create the impression that somehow Nixon represented competence, respect for tradition, serenity, faith that the American people were better than people anywhere else, and that all these problems others shouted about meant nothing in a land blessed with the tallest buildings, strong-est armies, biggest factories, cutest children, and rosiest sunsets in the world. Even better: through association with the pictures, Richard Nixon could *become* these very things. [P. 83.]

Eighteen of these sixty-second commercials were produced, each care-fully edited to remove anything controversial. They became one of the major propaganda devices used in the last weeks of the campaign. McGinniss reports the comment of one of the men who helped make them:

> "You know," . . . "what we're really seeing is a genesis. We're moving into a period where a man is going to be merchandised on television more and more. It upsets you and me, maybe, but we're not typical Americans. The public sits home and watches *Gunsmoke* and when they're fed this pap about Nixon they think they're getting something worthwhile." [P. 117.]

Did the professional propagandists con the American public? No one knows the answer to that question. Richard Nixon did win in 1968, to be sure, but by a very narrow margin. He did not even receive a majority of all the votes cast, so the propagandists' success was certainly not overwhelming. Moreover, he might well have received all his votes entirely on his own merits, or because of a number of events quite beyond his or anyone else's control. It would be foolish to overestimate the power of the Big Sell. But it would be foolish also to be unaware of the new techniques of propaganda that technology has made possible. Your only weapon against them is reason and critical thinking—and being more perceptive and better informed than some manipulators give you credit for being.

EXERCISES   1. Identify and analyze the following fallacies. Although you should be able to identify each by name (sometimes more than one designa-tion could apply), the most important thing is that you be able to tell why the reasoning is faulty.

a. You see, the priests were right. After we threw those virgins into the volcano, it quit erupting.

b. The Bible says, "By their fruits ye shall know them." The fact that there have been riots on college campuses proves that universities are subversive institutions.

c. This campaign to legalize filthy and corrupting movies is the irresponsible work of a few perverted individuals.

d. We ought to elect Bill Duncan to the Senate because he was a Medal of Honor winner in World War II.

e. Are all the people in Alabama still red necks and bigots?

f. It is common knowledge that socialized medicine has not been successful in England.

g. Are we going to vote a pay increase for our teachers or are we going to let our schools deteriorate into substandard custodial institutions?

h. The people of Rome lost their vitality and desire for freedom when their emperors decided that the way to keep them happy was to provide them with bread and circuses. What can we expect of our own country now that the government gives people free food and there is a constant round of entertainment provided by television?

i. Fraternities and sororities are regaining favor with college students everywhere. At both the University of Virginia and Texas Tech the pledge classes were 12 percent larger this year.

j. Of course, Madame, since you loved your husband so dearly you will want to buy this $1,800 casket, our very finest.

k. The policy that Jones is proposing is unsound because it won't work.

l. Philosophy tells us that reason is only the tool of the passions.

m. Jack must be a very tough young man. He just got out of the Marines.

n. Two kinds of young women go to college: those who want an education and those who want a husband. If a girl drops out without graduating, it is a sure sign that she wasn't really interested in an education.

o. Vote for Burns. He'll make a good governor—honestly.

p. My opponent for the state legislature, Mrs. Jenkins, may be a capable woman, but in my opinion, and I think yours, capable women should be using their talents to provide a good home for their husbands and children. If they have extra time after doing that, they should devote their energies to volunteer work in the community.

q. The question before us today is how we can raise the money to provide this state with a new medical school. I am for a medical school; the citizens of this state need it if we are to have adequate care. But I shall refuse to vote for the appropriation as long as the doctors of this state continue to charge such excessive fees for their services.

r. Women should not be allowed to go to stag parties because they are for men only.

2. Analyze the fallacies in the following paragraphs.

a. Now, in the 1970s, every intelligent person would agree that marijuana ought to be legalized. Only a few puritanical types who think that anything that is fun must be bad for people still want to keep our ridiculous laws on the books. They claim that getting stoned on marijuana now and then is harmful, but they think nothing of tossing off a couple of martinis before dinner every night. As for the argument that smoking marijuana leads to experimenting with hard drugs, I know for a fact that that is not true. I know several people who have smoked pot but as far as I know none of them is on heroin. And science has demonstrated that there is no necessary connection between the two.

b. There is no doubt that the present deplorable state of morals among our young people is due to the increasing popularity of sex education in the schools. Showing films on sex to youngsters and then expecting them not to experiment with it is like putting them in a room full of food and expecting them not to eat. And statistics prove that one out of every three high school students who has been enrolled in a sex education course has gone on to have intercourse at some time within the next two years. We should realize that one of the avowed aims of the Communists is to weaken the moral fiber of our young people. We must choose: either we return to the old Christian way of chastity and continence before marriage, or we let our society degenerate into a shameless hedonism of the kind that destroyed ancient Rome.

c. The iniquities of our American capitalist system are now so apparent to every person of compassion that it is hard to see how the majority can continue to support the wicked exploitation it promotes. In the past four years, 5 percent of our people have been unemployed. The media are controlled by a few big chains that are more interested in making money than they are in informing the public. They accuse socialist regimes of censorship while they control the news to suit themselves. That fact is proven by the incident of a television station in Topeka, Kansas, that refused to give a socialist candidate equal time to reply to a speech by a Republican. History proves that all governments that denied the working classes their rights have eventually toppled. It is only a matter of time until the little people of this country will rise against their masters like animals that have been driven into a corner and finally turn and fight.

3. For several days read your daily newspaper carefully, particularly the editorials, syndicated columns, letters to the editor, and news stories in which public officials are quoted. Clip and bring to class any fallacies that you may find. Be prepared to say specifically what you think those fallacies are and to make a judgment about whether they seriously damage the effect of the article.

4. Carefully examine the advertisements in two magazines, preferably two with very different audiences. Clip or photocopy advertisements that you think are based on fallacious reasoning or that represent commercial propaganda.

SUGGESTED
WRITING
ASSIGNMENTS

Theme 1

Purpose: To give you practice in identifying the kind of fallacies that may appear in a column by a popular writer.

Procedure: Begin by summarizing in one short paragraph, and in *your own words*, the main idea of the article below. Go beyond the mere assertion that Hoffer is against socialism; try to show what specific criticisms he makes of the system.

Then identify and illustrate with brief examples three or four kinds of fallacious arguments Hoffer uses to persuade the reader to reject socialism. Organize your discussion by types of fallacies instead of doing a paragraph by paragraph analysis.

Conclude with a short statement about the general effectiveness of the passage. Would it persuade the average, reasonably well-informed newspaper reader? Why?

In your thesis sentence list the various fallacies you are going to discuss, for example:

In this article Eric Hoffer employs the fallacies of ———, ———, and ——— to convince his readers that ———.
Warning: Do not either argue or agree with the author's ideas. You should concentrate on his methods of argument.

No Redemption Via Socialism

There is no evidence that socialism has worked a perceptible improvement in man's nature. No one would maintain that the present-day population of Russia is more honest, decent, tolerant, or humane than were the Russians 50 years ago. A Britain subjected to socialist influence for years seems as prone to racial prejudice as any other country. There is more antisemitism in Russia than in any capitalist country.

It is also highly doubtful whether socialism can release new creative energies in literature, art, music, science and technology. There can hardly be a more striking contrast than that between the cultural aridity of Communist Russia and the rich creative ferment of Russia's pre-revolutionary days.

As to happiness: The Scandinavian countries, with a high degree of socialism, have some of the highest suicide rates. Russia has already exceeded the 40 years Moses needed to bring the Israelites to a promised land, and the good life is still a dream. Socialization has become synonymous with greyness and joylessness.

As molders of new humanity the socialists and the Communists are remarkably uninterested in the fantastic alchemy of man's soul. They expect "history" to do this and that and their task as they see it is to drive the masses up the steep incline of the future.

Are there groups anywhere in the Occident at present dreaming of socialism as a redemption and a new birth? Socialism has become a shabby thing. Everyone now knows that when a country goes socialist it loses its sparkle and zest. The intelligentsia and the politicians usurp the privileges of the rich while the common people are condemned to meagerness and boredom.

. . . .

The real dividing line which is now opening across societies everywhere is that between experimenters and "experimentees." The socialists and the Communists strive with all their might to strap humanity to an operating table, and the truth is now abroad that these social surgeons are maniacal quacks who would operate on us with an ax.[9]

Theme 2

Write a paragraph similar to those in Exercise 2 in which you construct a fallacious argument on some topic of current interest on your campus. Consult the editorials and letters to the editor in your local student newspaper for ideas and, perhaps, for some sample fallacies. Leave a wide margin at the left side of the paper and in it label each of the fallacies that you have used.

[9] Eric Hoffer, "No Redemption Via Socialism," *Austin (Texas) American & Statesman,* July 6, 1968.

9

Writing
about
Literature

At some time in your college career you will almost certainly face the assignment of writing one or more papers about literature. If most of the writing you have done up until that time has focused on argumentation and factual material, you may feel unprepared to meet this new challenge. Analyzing a poem or comparing two characters in a play seems, at first glance, to call for different skills and tactics than arguing for additional services at the student health center or analyzing an editorial that calls for student participation in faculty promotions. Actually, the two kinds of writing are more similar than you might realize. Both call for you to make an assertion and support it; both require that you use language precisely and clearly, and that you understand how other people are using it; both demand that you reinforce your statements with examples and concrete evidence. In practice, then, the approach and techniques that you have been using for writing exposition and argumentation will, with certain limitations, serve you well in writing about literature.

Your study of rhetoric can help you with literary assignments in other ways. Probably nothing is more crucial to an appreciation of literature than a sensitivity to language; therefore, your study of diction—connotation, figurative language, concreteness, tone—will help you to understand how a poet, playwright, or novelist achieves his

Understanding effects
Finding the theme

effects. You can also use rhetorical analysis to find the theme or main idea of a work, and the habit of analyzing the evidence a writer brings in to support his assertions will aid you in tracing the devices an author uses to develop that theme. Authors of fiction, like essayists or orators, have a purpose; at times, especially if they are writing suspense or adventure stories, it may be no more than to entertain. More often, however, the writers that you are likely to study in college have a moral

Discovering purpose

purpose. They want to persuade you that some ways of behaving are good, some ways are bad; they want you to admire certain characters, dislike others. They may want to persuade you of the need for change. Sometimes they simply want you to understand people and their problems. Unlike writers of nonfiction, however, they do not usually announce their purposes. You must infer them from internal evidence in the work. In Mark Twain's *Huckleberry Finn,* for example, the theme of Huck's gradual disillusionment with conventional morality is developed by incident after incident in which so-called "good people" act selfishly and cruelly. The ability to recognize and evaluate this kind of evidence is invaluable in writing about literature.

FINDING YOUR PURPOSE, AUDIENCE, PERSONA, AND ARGUMENT

Purpose and Audience

Preliminary steps

Purpose

Preparing to write a paper about literature involves going through the same preliminary steps that you would take before beginning on any other writing assignment; deciding on your purpose; deciding who is your audience and what its expectations of you are; choosing a persona or voice; deciding on the main points of your argument. Your immediate purpose is to demonstrate to your instructor that you understand the literature you are working on and can articulate your ideas about it. A corollary purpose should be to learn more about the literature by writing about it. Obviously you know that your audience is

Audience

your instructor (and perhaps the class), but analyzing that audience's expectations may require some reflection. You can begin by assuming that unless an instructor specifically says so, he does *not* want your paper to be merely a summary of the literary work you are writing on. You can also assume (again, unless he specifically states otherwise) that he does *not* expect your paper to be solely a subjective emotional response to the work. While your emotional response to literature is important, the instructor cannot very well evaluate your understanding of a literary work on the basis of your feelings about

Audience's expectations

it. Probably what your instructor does expect from you is this: first, that you understand the theme of the work; second, that you have some insight into the way the author achieves his effects; third, that you can make a supported judgment about its quality. These expectations, of course, closely parallel the formula we have been using in rhetorical analysis: what is the author's main idea, what means does he use to communicate that idea, and is he successful?

Persona and Argument

Persona

Techniques of argument

Deciding on your persona should not be difficult; you are in the straightforward role of student, and your tone will probably be objective and informal. The kinds of argument or expository techniques that you decide to use in your paper will depend, at least partially, on the assignment, but you may be surprised at how readily you can adapt the rhetorical modes to developing the topics most frequently assigned for literary papers. For example, if you are asked to analyze the character of Oedipus in *Oedipus Rex* and to relate his character to his fate in the play, the logical way to develop your topic would be by using arguments of definition and cause and effect. If you are asked to evaluate a short story, you can use deductive reasoning: a good short story has traits A, B, and C; this short story has these traits; therefore, this is a good short story. If you are asked to discuss the effect of imagery in a poem—for example, T. S. Eliot's "The Hollow Men"—you can argue inductively. By listing the main images from the first stanza—"stuffed men," "hollow men," "leaning together," "filled with straw," "dried voices," "wind in dry grass," "rats' feet," "broken glass," and "dry cellar"—you can demonstrate that Eliot is trying to create a depressed and sterile atmosphere, and then go on to support your thesis with examples from other stanzas. In a theme on character motivation, you may want to show how the author builds an argument from circumstance. In William Faulkner's *Light in August,* for instance, the author develops a complex and almost air-tight circumstantial argument to explain why Joe Christmas murders a woman.

PREWRITING FOR LITERARY PAPERS

Rough out a plan

Do not write even one sentence of your theme until you have roughed out a plan for your paper. For some reason, literary topics tempt many students just to start writing with little real idea of what they are going to say. The result is usually a collection of random comments that does not even qualify as a good book report. Such a paper has almost no value for either you or your teacher. To avoid this kind of disaster,

Narrow the topic

begin by narrowing your topic to a manageable size. If, for instance, the assignment is to write on the significant character traits of Jay Gatsby in F. Scott Fitzgerald's novel *The Great Gatsby*, you would not describe his actions through the entire book in order to show his character. You need to focus on a few key traits, but in order to choose those traits, you should write down everything you can remember about him.

> Ambitious—wanted to be rich, hard working as boy
> Dishonest—tells lies about war experiences, shady business deals
> Materialistic—likes big cars, big house, parties, fancy clothes
> Naive—believes Daisy perfect, no social sense
> Romantic—impossible dreams, wants to sacrifice self for Daisy

Out of this list you choose materialism and romanticism as the most interesting, particularly because the combination is paradoxical. Now you can go on to plan what is essentially a theme of definition. You can define Gatsby by his possessions—fancy car, gaudy clothes, pretentious mansion—by his actions toward Daisy, and by his dreams, giving examples to illustrate all your points. Your thesis sentence could be: "Jay Gatsby's character is a paradoxical combination of the materialistic and the romantic."

A rough outline would look like this:

I. Gatsby's Possessions
    A. Clothes
        1. White suit, silver tie
        2. Dozens of flashy shirts
    B. Pretentious mansion
        1. Twenty-room house
        2. Library with fake books
        3. Swimming pool
    C. Large, ostentatious car
II. Gatsby's Actions toward Daisy
    A. Arranges secret meetings
    B. Wants to rescue her from her husband
    C. Takes blame for her killing Myrtle
III. Gatsby's Dreams
    A. Boyhood dream of wealth
    B. Plans to marry Daisy; thinks of her as still a virgin

Another assignment might be to discuss conflict in *Othello.* If you try to discuss all the conflicts in *Othello* in one short paper, you're going to have trouble organizing your ideas and finding room to bring in the supporting details you need. Therefore, in order to focus your paper you need to review the conflicts in the play and decide which one you want to deal with: Iago and Othello, Othello and Desdemona, Desdemona and Iago, or the conflict within Othello himself. Since the last is really the crux of the play, you choose that. Your thesis sentence might read: "Despite the abundance of killing, plotting, and fighting in *Othello,* the major conflict in the play is within Othello himself: the conflict between honor and love."

Limiting your topic presents less of a problem when the assignment is to write about a short poem because you have a comparatively small amount of material to work with. Nevertheless, you need to decide on the main points you are going to make, in what order you are going to discuss them, and which examples you are going to use to support your ideas. Suppose, for example, you were asked to analyze the following poem.

A Fire Truck[1]

Right down the shocked street with a siren-blast
That sends all else skittering to the curb,
Redness, brass, ladders and hats hurl past,
   Blurring to sheer verb.

Shift at the corner into uproarious gear
And make it around the turn in a squall of traction,
The headlong bell maintaining sure and clear,
   Thought is degraded action.

Beautiful, heavy, unweary, loud, obvious thing!
I stand here purged of nuance, my mind a blank.
All I was brooding upon has taken wing,
   And I have you to thank.

As you howl beyond hearing I carry you into my mind,
Ladders and brass and all, there to admire
Your phoenix-red simplicity, enshrined
   In that not extinguished fire.

Probably the main points you would want to bring out about this poem
would be its dominant impression, the tension in it, and the poet's
theme. Your working notes might look like this:

Dominant impression	*action*; motion—noise—power
Support	shocked, siren-blast, skittering, hurl past —uproarious gear, squall of traction, head-long bell, howl, brass, red, beautiful, heavy, loud, obvious
Tension	Contrast of fire engine and poet's mind; motion vs. reflection and inaction
Support	action verbs vs. "stand here," "purged of nuance," "mind a blank," "brooding."
Poet's theme	Action is easier than thinking; temptation to avoid reflection and thought and just *do*. Italicized phrase "Thought is degraded action" obviously important but can't be sure statement represents poet's beliefs since he says only that it is the message he gets from the engine's bell.

More consideration of the poem would probably give you additional ideas, but with these points you have a good basis to begin writing. Your thesis sentence might read, "In 'A Fire Truck' Richard Wilbur contrasts the sensations of watching a fire truck in motion with the persona's melancholy frame of mind to show the temptation the persona feels to abandon the intellectual life for a life of action." A specific outline would follow clearly the pattern of your working notes.

Finding Evidence

When you are writing a paper on a literary topic, you are, after all, still writing an expository theme; that is, you are making assertions about that literature, and you must support and develop them in the same way that you would handle assertions in argumentative writing.

Sources of evidence

You can look for supporting evidence in several places: the author's use of connotation and imagery, his attitude toward his characters, the value statements of characters who seem to speak for the author, and his attitudes toward institutions, beliefs, manners, or morals.

Connotation and Imagery

In *Sister Carrie* Theodore Dreiser repeatedly uses the terms "drift," "swept along," "carried on the tide," and "a moth of the lamp" in describing his heroine, a woman who has little control over her life. You could assert, on the basis of this connotative evidence, that the author sees this character as a victim of circumstances. You might make the same assertion about a character who is described by words like "pawn" and "puppet," terms such as "defeated," "helpless," or "beaten," or associated with jail or trap imagery.

Attitude Toward Characters

Characters whom the author obviously either admires or dislikes furnish you with strong supporting evidence for statements about the theme of a book or story. In *The Scarlet Letter*, for example, Hawthorne portrays Chillingsworth as contemptible and Dimmesdale as weak and hypocritical (the names themselves are connotative). You could assert, therefore, that he disapproves of cowardice, rigid codes of morality, the motive of revenge, and a religion that concerns itself more with punishment than with love. His obvious approval of Hester indicates that he believes in the values she represents: courage, fortitude, loyalty. Thus, Hawthorne's attitude toward his characters provides evidence for the assertion that a major theme in the book is the destructive effect of judgmental, narrow morality. In *Babbitt* Sinclair Lewis criticizes small town mores by portraying an outstanding citizen as a ridiculous and pompous person.

Spokesman Characters

You should be cautious about assuming that an important character in a book or story is the spokesman for the author, but if the ideas expressed by that character seem consistently to be a reflection of the philosophy you think the book is expressing, you can probably use his speeches as supporting evidence in a paper. It is obvious, for example, that Hank Morgan's comments on slavery in *A Connecticut Yankee in King Arthur's Court* are an accurate statement of Mark Twain's own views; therefore, we can reason that other attitudes he expresses are also Twain's. John Steinbeck comments on the actions of his characters in *In Dubious Battle* through the philosophical doctor; the events in the book reinforce the impression that the doctor/observer speaks for the author.

Finding Evidence in Poetry

Diction and tone

Evidence in poetry may be more subtle and therefore more difficult to extract because usually it consists of image clusters and the general tone that the poem conveys. Nevertheless, it is there in the form of connotation, metaphor, and the author's attitude toward his material. Look, for example, at the two final stanzas from Matthew Arnold's "Dover Beach."

> The Sea of Faith
> Was once, too, at the full, and round earth's shore
> Lay like the folds of a bright girdle furled.
> But now I only hear
> Its melancholy, long, withdrawing roar,
> Retreating, to the breath
> Of the night wind, down the vast edges drear
> And naked shingles of the world.
>
> Ah, love, let us be true
> To one another! for the world, which seems
> To lie before us like a land of dreams,

> So various, so beautiful, so new,
> Hath really neither joy, nor love, nor light,
> Nor certitude, nor peace, nor help for pain;
> And we are here as on a darkling plain
> Swept with confused alarms of struggle and flight,
> Where ignorant armies clash by night.

The lines reveal Arnold's sense of despair and desolation and also hint at his loss of faith in God and his failure to find anything to replace it. The metaphor of faith as a sea that once surrounded him like a "bright girdle" conveys the spiritual support he felt in the past; the slow tempo and the negative words "melancholy," "retreating," "night wind," "drear and naked shingles" in the following lines reveal his present mood. In the next stanza a key word is "seems": the world may "seem" various and beautiful and new, but the next two lines deny that this is so. The negative phrases "darkling plain," "confused alarms of struggle and flight," and "ignorant armies clash by night" complete and reinforce the total impression of despair.

Thus, the diction in a poem is evidence, evidence as substantial as examples or data that you might use to support another kind of argument. The associations that we attach to words have a kind of reality, and we cannot ignore that reality when interpreting poetry or

Figurative language   any other kind of literature. A poet's figurative language is similar evidence. Shakespeare's metaphors comparing age to autumn, sunset, and a dying fire leave little doubt that the persona has a melancholy view toward aging. When Gerard Manley Hopkins writes in his sonnet "God's Grandeur," "The world is charged with the grandeur of God./It will flame out, like shining from shook foil," we must recognize that he is a religious man who wants his reader to be awed by God's power. The rest of the imagery in the poem supports the interpretation.

It is simply not true, then, to say, as readers sometimes do, that a poem can mean anything you want it to mean. It is true that a poem may have more than one fixed meaning or that it can mean different things to different people. A valid interpretation, however, cannot contradict the evidence. Given the imagery we quoted earlier from the first stanza of Eliot's "The Hollow Men," one can scarcely assert that it is a cheerful poem. All the evidence is against such an interpretation. Nor could one find evidence in "A Fire Truck" to claim that it is somber or dismal although there may be a faint undertone of discontent. What it comes down to is this: in searching for the meaning of a poem—or any other literary work—you go through the same intellectual process that you would use in any other field. You look at the material before you, form a hypothesis, then look for evidence to confirm it. If the evidence supports your hypothesis, it is valid; if it does not, you should reexamine your data until you find a hypothesis that fits the facts. The main difference between interpreting literature and writing an account of other kinds of material is that in literature there may be more than one hypothesis that fits the evidence.

MAKING JUDGMENTS ABOUT LITERATURE

Finally, in writing a theme about literature, you will probably have to give a supported answer to the question: "Is this a good piece of literature; why or why not?" The question is one that many of us would prefer not to face. We would rather say simply we like the book, play, or poem and not have to justify our opinion. Nevertheless, if we study literature seriously, we must make judgments about it and try to analyze the grounds for those judgments. Only in this way can we develop our tastes and learn to make intelligent distinctions about what is worth reading and what is not.

Fortunately, we can use many of the same techniques that we have been using in judging other kinds of rhetoric. We can fashion a yardstick of values and determine in what ways the work measures up and in what ways it does not. Such a yardstick would have much in common with the ones we have been already using, but it would

Criteria
also contain some other features. Criteria for judging literature should include at least these points:

1. *Timelessness.* Is the work of lasting interest? Are the comments the author makes about people, about the pressures, rewards, and problems of life still relevant? Is the theme of the work as pertinent now as it was at the time it was written? *Oedipus Rex*, for example, was written over 2,000 years ago, but we are still awed and moved by its portrayal of the inner conflicts of a proud ambitious man who brings on his own doom.

2. *Universality.* Does the work, regardless of when and where it was written, have meaning for people throughout the Western world? (I specify "Western" because most of us are not sufficiently familiar with the Oriental cultures to judge the impact a piece of literature might have on them.) *Huckleberry Finn*, for example, although it has been called the first truly American novel, deals with a universal theme, the loss of innocence.

3. *Truthfulness.*   Is the work credible? Does the author make us believe what he is telling us? Such a standard cannot, of course, be applied literally. We do not believe in the literal truth of *Gulliver's Travels* or *Candide,* but we understand that the authors are using fantasy and exaggeration to communicate basic truths about mankind. Moreover, a good novel, story, or drama should give us the feeling that what happened to the characters was inevitable; that, given their temperaments and the situation in which they were placed, the outcome could not have been otherwise. Everything we know about Willie Loman in *Death of a Salesman,* for instance, makes his suicide inevitable. A different ending would have been disappointing and untrue.

4. *Effective Language.*   This is a matter for which it is difficult to set precise standards. The study of such authors as James Joyce, William Faulkner, Mark Twain, and Henry James reveals that writers can use language effectively in a variety of ways. In general, however, we can expect the language in any literary work to be forceful, fresh and unhackneyed, and suitable to the purposes of the work. Thus, the gentle style of Washington Irving would be as unsuitable for *Gulliver's Travels* as the complex, ornate style of Henry James would be for *Huckleberry Finn.*

5. *Morality.*   This may seem like a strange requirement, somewhat as if I were saying, "Good stories should have a moral to them." The term "morality," however, is intended in the much broader sense of "sense of value." Applied to literature, the standard means that a work of art should say something of value. It should draw attention to human problems, say that some things are worth doing or believing in, condemn or applaud certain ways of living or certain viewpoints; in sum, it should make a statement that is more significant than the "Chocolate cake is the world's best dessert" kind of comment we talked about in an earlier chapter. We cannot, however, require that the statement the author makes be one that we agree with. We cannot, as we can with arguments, challenge a creative artist's a priori assumptions. The work is his own creation, and he is entitled to his values. Although we may not, like Voltaire, believe that man is basically foolish or selfish, and we may not agree with Dreiser that people are simply victims of circumstance, we must grant any author the right to his viewpoint. If our criticism is truly objective, we should judge only the way he expresses and illustrates that viewpoint. This critical tenet is, needless to say, difficult to observe.

If a work of literature meets most of the standards set forth here, we can judge it as "good" and support that judgment with concrete evidence. Making judgments about the relatively few works that measure up to all of these requirements or the great body that meet almost none of them is comparatively easy. A play like Eugene O'Neill's *Long Day's Journey Into Night* and a poem like Robert Frost's "After Apple Picking," immediately impress us as fine works. And it doesn't take much critical perception for most of us to realize that the run-of-the-mill "entertainments" ground out for the mystery, science fiction, and adventure story market are poorly done. The real problem comes in deciding about the many pieces of literature that fall somewhere in between, books, for example, like Ken Kesey's *One Flew Over the Cuckoo's Nest* or William Golding's *Lord of the Flies.* We feel that in many ways such books are good but also suspect that they have defects, that they are less than great. Such uncertainty, however, should not prevent you from attempting a judgment. There is, after all, no reason why you cannot make a qualified statement: "This book measures up on points 1, 3, and 4, but it lacks the qualities given in points 2 and 5." Give reasons for your judgment, and no one can ask more of you.

Two final points on both reading and writing about literature are important. First, do not confuse these two statements: "I like this book" and "This is a good book." If you say, "I like this book," you are

Personal preferences

expressing your taste, making a statement of preference. You may want to defend your preference, but you do not have to prove that the book is a good piece of writing. If, however, you assert, "This is a good book," you have an obligation to support that statement by showing how it meets the standards that are generally set forth for good literature. Nor should you be ashamed of liking books that cannot be classified as "good literature." Almost all of us enjoy some kinds of so-called escape literature: romances, mysteries, or science fiction. If you enjoy them, read them and make no apologies.

Classics and famous authors

Second, do not be intimidated by a famous name or by any literary work that has long been labeled a "classic." While it is true that works by authors whose reputations have endured for decades or centuries are more likely than not to have value, you should judge the work on its own merits. Shakespeare did write some mediocre plays and both Faulkner and Hemingway have more than one second-rate novel to their credit. The following poem is a good example of a bad work by a renowned poet.

All the breath and the bloom of the year in the bag of one bee;
All the wonder and wealth of the mine in the heart of one gem;
In the core of one pearl all the shade and the shine of the sea;
 Breath and bloom, shade and shine—wonder, wealth,
  and—how far above them—
   Truth, that is brighter than gem,
   Trust, that's purer than pearl—
  Brightest truth, purest trust in the universe—all were for me
   In the kiss of one girl.

The alliteration in the poem is overdone, the imagery hackneyed and fuzzy, the meter sing-song, and the whole effect is painfully sentimental. Yet the poet was one of the finest of his century: Robert Browning. (In his defense, it should be pointed out that the poem was written when he was seventy-seven, in the year of his death.)

Trust your own judgment

Finally, then, you should trust your own critical faculties. There is no reason why you cannot make sound judgments about literature if you read carefully and apply common-sense standards to what you read; nor is there any reason why writing persuasively about literature should be any more difficult than writing about any other topic. You have the tools that you need.

The following two papers on a well-known poem, "To His Coy Mistress" by Andrew Marvell, illustrate the advantages of using the rhetorical approach to write about literature. The papers were done in response to that familiar assignment, "Write a short critical analysis of a poem." The writer of the first paper started by asking himself these questions: What is the author's purpose? That is, what thesis or main idea does he want to express in the poem? What means does he use to achieve that purpose? Is he successful? Why or why not? The writer of the second paper, understandably confused about what constituted a "critical analysis," began with no particular purpose or approach in mind and simply wrote about the poem.

Here is the poem.

To His Coy Mistress

Had we but world enough, and time,
This coyness, lady, were no crime.
We would sit down and think which way
To walk and pass our long love's day.
Thou by the Indian Ganges' side
Should'st rubies find; I by the tide

Of Humber would complain. I would
Love you ten years before the flood:
And you should, if you please, refuse
Till the conversion of the Jews.
My vegetable love should grow
Vaster than empires, and more slow.
An hundred years should go to praise
Thine eyes, and on thy forehead gaze.
Two hundred to adore each breast;
And thirty thousand to the rest.
An age at least to every part,
And the last age should show your heart.
For, lady, you deserve this state;
Nor would I love at lower rate.
   But at my back I always hear
Time's winged chariot hurrying near;
And yonder all before us lie
Deserts of vast eternity.
Thy beauty shall no more be found;
Nor in thy marble vault shall sound
My echoing song; then worms shall try
That long preserved virginity;
And your quaint honor turn to dust;
And into ashes all my lust,
The grave's a fine and private place,
But none, I think, do there embrace.
   Now therefore, while the youthful hue
Sits on thy skin like morning dew,
And while thy willing soul transpires
At every pore with instant fires,
Now let us sport us while we may;
And now, like am'rous birds of prey
Rather at once our time devour,
Than languish in his slow-chapt pow'r.
Let us roll all our strength, and all
Our sweetness, up into one ball;
And tear our pleasure with rough strife,
Through the iron gates of life.
Thus, though we cannot make our sun
Stand still, yet we will make him run.
                 Andrew Marvell, c. 1681

Paper I

In this poem Andrew Marvell seems to be addressing himself to young ladies who think that it is romantic and amusing to tease their lovers by insisting that they pay court to them for months and flatter them with extravagant compliments in order to win their sexual favors. He wants these young women to realize that their coyness is foolish and unrealistic: while they are playing their games, time is running out. Rather than waste their youth and beauty in "playing hard to get," they should enjoy life now. In order to convince his audience, Marvell constructs a careful, concretely supported argument, which vividly illustrates his point.

Marvell's persona in the poem is a devoted but impatient lover; his persuasive purpose is frankly seduction. To achieve it, he sets up an argument from circumstance and reinforces it by appeals to his mistress's vanity and fears. The argument itself is built on an "If—but—therefore" structure: If we had unlimited time, I would be happy to court you for an eternity; but we, being only mortal, are going to age and die; therefore, let us take our pleasure while we can.

Much of the force of the argument comes from the contrast of tone and imagery in the three sections. In the first part, the persona flatters his mistress by using a lofty tone and extravagant phrases to show that his love really is high-minded: "I would/love you ten years before the flood;" "An hundred years should go to praise/Thine eyes," "Two hundred to adore each breast;/And thirty thousand to the rest." His phrases suggest that his adoration is so great it would last for an eternity.

In the second stanza, however, the persona begins his argument from circumstance: because of time, he is *forced* to forget about eternity and think about the present. He brings in images of death to make his point: "thy marble vault," "worms," "dust," "ashes," and "the grave." What lies ahead is not unending pleasure, but "deserts of vast eternity." He tries to frighten the girl by suggesting that her beauty will be gone and that that virginity which she has preserved so carefully will be destroyed by worms, not a man. He plays on her fear of being alone by suggesting that in the grave, none embrace.

In the last stanza, the persona uses images of lust and violence to contrast with the repulsive circumstances he has pictured in the previous section. He is saying, "While we are young and passionate, let us seize the day!" The phrases "instant fires," "am'rous birds of prey," and "tear our pleasure with rough strife" conflict dramatically with the lofty, leisurely tone of the first stanza. And he makes what he is suggesting here sound much more attractive than languishing by the Ganges gathering rubies.

Although we cannot know whether the persona's appeal was literally successful—or whether this particular situation really existed—the poem itself is certainly a success. The poet has taken a theme which is so common that he ran the danger of writing a hackneyed poem, and through vivid diction and contrast of tone and imagery made his message seem fresh. His skillful use of traditional rhetorical techniques clothed in poetic language is one of the chief strengths of the poem.

Paper II

Andrew Marvell's famous poem "To His Coy Mistress" tells the story of a young man who is trying to persuade his girl to go to bed with him. He starts out by saying that he would be glad to spend as much time as she liked in praising and admiring her if they had thousands of years to waste. Apparently the girl is more interested in getting compliments than she is in having the man make love to her.

In the second part of the poem the man explains why he thinks they cannot afford to waste time with his talking and admiring her. When he says that he hears Time's chariot at his back, he means that time is going by faster than they think. If they aren't careful, they'll both be old or dead and they never will have the chance to enjoy sex. He talks about the girl being in a marble vault and the worms eating on her. This is an ugly picture but he uses it to scare the girl into giving in to him.

In the last part of the poem he tries to persuade the girl that while they are still young, they ought to enjoy sex now. He says they ought to have "sport" and "pleasure" while they can and concentrate all their strength on having a good time. If they do this, the time will go by quickly.

The meaning of this poem seems to be that young men are going to get very impatient with girls who lead them along but don't want to give in to them sexually. Under those circumstances, a man is going to try to talk a girl into sex by saying there isn't much time or by insinuating that they are missing a lot of pleasure. Girls should know that they can't expect men to wait indefinitely; either they should marry them or quit going with them.

The poem is a good one because Marvell is writing about something that has been going on for a long time; men always try to talk girls into sex and girls try to put them off. Marvell does a good job of showing the man's point of view. The first stanza of the poem makes girls who tease men and play hard to get look silly and immature. The reader doesn't have much sympathy for the "coy mistress." Then the talk about death in the second part makes Marvell's argument seem reasonable. The reader tends to sympathize with the lover and think at the end that he is right. For this reason I would call the poem a successful one.

The difference in the quality of the two papers is partially the result of the first writer's using a rhetorical approach to a writing assignment. He had a sense of purpose to his writing and a plan for supporting his analysis. He not only used evidence from the poem throughout his paper, but he continually kept in mind the effect that the poet was trying to achieve with his audience and discussed the way those effects were achieved. The result is a well-organized and solid critical analysis.

The writer of the second paper, although he seems to have some appreciation of the poem, has done a poor job of analyzing it because he had no clear sense of purpose when he began. He has spent more time summarizing than analyzing or evaluating. Moreover, he has made almost no use of internal evidence to support his points and thus has missed the opportunity to discuss one of the poem's major strengths, its imagery. The result is a rather dull paper that does credit neither to the poem nor to the reader's appreciation of it.

Appendix

Sample Passages for Rhetorical Analysis

1. The Great Barbecue

Congress had rich gifts to bestow—in lands, tariffs, subsidies, favors of all sorts; and when influential citizens made their wishes known to the reigning statesmen, the sympathetic politicians were quick to turn the government into the fairy godmother the voters wanted it to be. A huge barbecue was spread to which all presumably were invited. Not quite all, to be sure; inconspicuous persons, those who were at home on the farm or at work in the mills and offices, were overlooked; a good many indeed out of the total number of the American people. But all the important persons, leading bankers and promoters and business men, received invitations. There wasn't room for everybody and these were presumed to represent the whole. It was a splendid feast. If the waiters saw to it that the choicest portions were served to favored guests, they were not unmindful of their numerous homespun constituency and they loudly proclaimed the fine democratic principle that what belongs to the people should be enjoyed by the people—not with petty bureaucratic restrictions, not as a social body, but as individuals, each free citizen using what came to hand for his own private ends, with no questions asked.

It was sound Gilded Age doctrine. To a frontier people what was more democratic than a barbecue, and to a paternalistic age what was more fitting than that the state should provide the beeves for roasting. Let all come and help themselves. As a result the feast was Gargantuan in its rough plenty. The abundance was what was to be expected of a generous people. More food, to be sure, was spoiled than was eaten, and the revelry was a bit unseemly; but it was a fine spree in the name of the people, and the invitations had been written years before by Henry Clay. But unfortunately what was intended to be jovially democratic was marred by displays of plebeian temper. Suspicious commoners with better eyes than manners discovered the favoritism of the waiters and drew attention to the difference between their own meager helpings and the heaped-up plates of more favored guests. It appeared indeed that there was gross discrimination in the service; that the farmers' pickings from the Homestead Act were scanty in comparison with the speculators' pickings from the railway land-grants. The *Credit*

Mobilier scandal and the Whisky Ring scandal and divers other scandals came near to breaking up the feast, and the genial host—who was no other than the hero of Appomattox—came in for some sharp criticism. But after the more careless ones who were caught with their fingers where they didn't belong, had been thrust from the table, the eating and drinking went on again till only the great carcasses were left. Then at last came the reckoning. When the bill was sent in to the American people the farmers discovered that they had been put off with the giblets while the capitalists were consuming the turkey. They learned that they were no match at a barbecue for more voracious guests, and as they went home unsatisfied, a sullen anger burned in their hearts that was to express itself later in fierce agrarian revolts.[1]

2. The Freeloaders

Let's call the couple J. and K. They are young, early 20's, fairly educated, unmarried but living together and Hip with an upper case H.

They live in a rent-controlled apartment in lower Manhattan, but right now are not even paying the city-mandated minimum. They are in the midst of a rent strike because the landlord wants them to pay for their own lights and heat.

Neither is working. He gets unemployment compensation, she gets welfare. Both receive money each month from parents with whom they have nothing to do.

They rise at 10. Or maybe 11. Or maybe later.

They brush with toothpaste ripped off a local supermarket counter, dry with towels copped from local hotels and dress in clothes supplied in part by the Salvation Army. He wears shoes he kept from the Army. She puts on bell-bottoms, knit blouse and wide belt shoplifted from one of the downtown department stores.

They eat a full breakfast, thanks to items purchased with federal food stamps, off plates which they walked off with from a neighborhood church party, using knives and forks, provided by the landlord to whom they refuse to pay rent.

The morning mail is closely checked. There is a state report on their application for a federal education grant. There is a letter from a large manufacturing company apologizing for a fictitious complaint about a fly in the canned goods—"One case of our product has been

[1] From *Main Currents in American Thought,* Vol. III, pp. 23–24, by Vernon L. Parrington, copyright, 1930, by Harcourt Brace Jovanovich, Inc,; renewed, 1958, by Vernon L. Parrington, Jr., Louise P. Tucker, Elizabeth P. Thomas. Reprinted by permission of the publishers.

shipped to you, please accept it along with our regrets that you were inconvenienced." There is also a note from the telephone company, along with stamps worth 75 cents which J. and K. were supposed to have lost (they didn't) trying to make a pay phone call.

The couple is overjoyed at the telephone refund, and decide to try again. They write another complaint, on stationery picked up while visiting their congressman's office, and this time they say they lost $1.50 on an attempted long distance call from a 14th Street pay booth. They use an old Christmas seal for the stamp, since they know Post Office scanners will probably not spot the fake.

They pet their dog, which they got free from the SPCA, and whose veterinary bills are paid for by public assistance, and they leave their pad for the street.

It's a routine day. J. must give the employment service a list of fictitious employment refusals to indicate he is actively seeking work. K. must go down to the welfare clinic for her new granny glasses and birth control pills.

They kiss goodby. Her lipstick is an Avon sample.

J. takes the subway, but does not pay. He arranges to have a young acquaintance drop a coin at the token attendant's feet, and while the man is distracted he jumps over the turnstiles. He picks up a paper from a garbage can, puts a slug in a candy machine and boards his transportation.

K., meanwhile, takes a bus to her destination. It's free of course. She gets on with a $5 bill and the driver winces because he is authorized only to take exact change. She winks, wiggles, pleads and he tells her to, oh, well, take a seat. She sits next to an old man whom she engages in conversation, tells him she is a runaway from Seattle who is ever so lonesome for her mom and dad and would he possibly consider lending her $1 to help buy a ticket home?

In the afternoon, J. and K. regroup at the public library, where they check out several books and read more of the day's newspapers. The newspapers carry lists of upcoming weddings, bar mitzvahs, etc., which they will crash for banquet goodies. The papers also provide them with times and places of free entertainment, such as exhibitions, recitals, lectures, etc., all over town.

For late lunch they go to an automat and eat the left-behind food of other patrons. For dinner they visit a more elegant place, enjoy a large meal, thank the waiter, give compliments to the chef and walk out without paying.

Finally, it's evening. And they have an important engagement. J.

makes a phone call using a No. I washer instead of a dime. He gets instructions which he jots down with a pencil he was given once when filling out forms for veterans' benefits. Then they hitchhike to lower Manhattan and get out adjacent to the Federal Building. They are handed posters by members of a tax-exempt, religious organization and, you guessed it, spend the rest of the night chanting in a picket line, protesting the oppressive, corrupt, capitalistic society.[2]

3. The Happy Housewife Heroine

In the early 1960's *McCall's* has been the fastest growing of the women's magazines. Its contents are a fairly accurate representation of the image of the American woman presented, and in part created, by the large-circulation magazines. Here are the complete editorial contents of a typical issue of *McCall's* (July, 1960):

1. A lead article on "increasing baldness in women," caused by too much brushing and dyeing.
2. A long poem in primer-size type about a child, called "A Boy Is A Boy."
3. A short story about how a teenager who doesn't go to college gets a man away from a bright college girl.
4. A short story about the minute sensations of a baby throwing his bottle out of the crib.
5. The first of a two-part, intimate "up-to-date" account by the Duke of Windsor on "How the Duchess and I now live and spend our time. The influence of clothes on me and vice versa."
6. A short story about a nineteen-year-old girl sent to a charm school to learn how to bat her eyelashes and lose at tennis. ("You're nineteen, and by normal American standards, I now am entitled to have you taken off my hands, legally and financially, by some beardless youth who will spirit you away to a one-and-a-half-room apartment in the Village while he learns the chicanery of selling bonds. And no beardless youth is going to do that as long as you volley to his backhand.")
7. The story of a honeymoon couple commuting between separate bedrooms after an argument over gambling at Las Vegas.
8. An article on "how to overcome an inferiority complex."
9. A story called "Wedding Day."

[2] Tom Tiede, "The Freeloaders," *Austin (Texas) American & Statesman,* March 11, 1971. Reprinted by permission of Newspaper Enterprise Association.

10. The story of a teenager's mother who learns how to dance rock-and-roll.
11. Six pages of glamorous pictures of models in maternity clothes.
12. Four glamorous pages on "reduce the way the models do."
13. An article on airline delays.
14. Patterns for home sewing.
15. Patterns with which to make "Folding Screens—Bewitching Magic."
16. An article called "An Encyclopedic Approach to Finding a Second Husband."
17. A "barbecue bonanza," dedicated "to the Great American Mister who stands, chef's cap on head, fork in hand, on terrace or back porch, in patio or backyard anywhere in the land, watching his roast turning on the spit. And to his wife, without whom (sometimes) the barbecue could never be the smashing summer success it undoubtedly is . . ."

There were also the regular front-of-the-book "service" columns on new drug and medicine developments, childcare facts, columns by Clare Luce and by Eleanor Roosevelt, and "Pots and Pans," a column of readers' letters.

The image of woman that emerges from this big, pretty magazine is young and frivolous, almost childlike; fluffy and feminine; passive; gaily content in a world of bedroom and kitchen, sex, babies, and home. The magazine surely does not leave out sex; the only passion, the only pursuit, the only goal a woman is permitted is the pursuit of a man. It is crammed full of food, clothing, cosmetics, furniture, and the physical bodies of young women, but where is the world of thought and ideas, the life of the mind and spirit? In the magazine image, women do no work except housework and work to keep their bodies beautiful and to get and keep a man.

This was the image of the American woman in the year Castro led a revolution in Cuba and men were trained to travel into outer space; the year that the African continent brought forth new nations, and a plane whose speed is greater than the speed of sound broke up a Summit Conference; the year artists picketed a great museum in protest against the hegemony of abstract art; physicists explored the concept of anti-matter; astronomers, because of new radio telescopes, had to alter their concepts of the expanding universe; biologists made a breakthrough in the fundamental chemistry of life; and Negro youth in Southern schools forced the United States, for the first time since the

Civil War, to face a moment of democratic truth. But this magazine, published for over 5,000,000 American women, almost all of whom have been through high school and nearly half to college, contained almost no mention of the world beyond the home. In the second half of the twentieth century in America, woman's world was confined to her own body and beauty, the charming of man, the bearing of babies, and the physical care and serving of husband, children, and home. And this was no anomaly of a single issue of a single women's magazine.[3]

4. Non-Medical Indices of Final Placement

Structurophilia Structurophilia is an obsessive concern with buildings—their planning, construction, maintenance and reconstruction—and an increasing unconcern with the work that is going on, is supposed to be going on, inside them. I have observed structurophilia at all hierarchal levels, but it undoubtedly achieves its finest development in politicians and university presidents. In its extreme pathological manifestations (*Gargantuan monumentalis*) it reaches a stage where the victim has a compulsion to build great tombs or memorial statues. Ancient Egyptians and modern Southern Californians appear to have suffered greatly from this malady.

Structurophilia has been referred to, by the uninformed, as the Edifice Complex. We must be precise in differentiating between this simple preoccupation with structures and the Edifice Complex which involves a number of elaborately interrelated, interconnected and complicated attitudes. The Edifice Complex tends to afflict philanthropists wishing to improve education, health services or religious instruction. They consult experts in these fields and discover so many at their respective levels of incompetence that formulation of a positive program is impossible. The only thing they agree on is to have a new building. Frequently the advising educator, doctor or minister suffers from structurophilia and therefore his recommendation to the donor is, "Give me a new building." Church committees, school trustees and foundation boards find themselves in the same *complex* situation. They see so much incompetence in the professions that they decide to invest in buildings rather than people and programs. As in other psychological complexes, this results in bizarre behavior.

. . . .

[3] Betty Friedan, *The Feminine Mystique* (New York: Dell Publishing Co., Inc., 1963), pp. 34–36. Reprinted from *The Feminine Mystique* by Betty Friedan. By permission of W. W. Norton & Company, Inc. Copyright © 1963 by Betty Friedan.

Which Is Which   Usually the structurophilia victim has a patholog-ical need to have a building or monument named in his honor, whereas the Edifice Complex afflicts those who are trying to improve the quality of some human endeavor but end up by only producing another building.[4]

5. An Apology for Idlers

Extreme *busyness,* whether at school or college, kirk [church] or mar-ket, is a symptom of deficient vitality; and a faculty for idleness implies a catholic appetite and a strong sense of personal identity. There is a sort of dead-alive, hackneyed people about, who are scarcely con-scious of living except in the exercise of some conventional occupa-tion. Bring these fellows into the country or set them aboard ship, and you will see how they pine for their desk or their study. They have no curiosity; they cannot give themselves over to random provocations; they do not take pleasure in the exercise of their faculties for its own sake; and unless Necessity lays about them with a stick, they will even stand still. It is no good speaking to such folk: they *cannot* be idle, their nature is not generous enough: and they pass those hours in a sort of coma, which are not dedicated to furious moiling in the gold-mill. When they do not require to go to office, when they are not hungry and have no mind to drink, the whole breathing world is a blank to them. If they have to wait an hour or so for a train, they fall into a stupid trance with their eyes open. To see them, you would suppose there was no-thing to look at and no one to speak with; you would imagine they were paralyzed or alienated: and yet very possibly they are hard workers in their own way, and have good eyesight for a flaw in a deed or a turn of the market. They have been to school and college, but all the time they had their eye on the medal; they have gone about in the world and mixed with clever people, but all the time they were thinking of their own affairs. As if a man's soul were not too small to begin with, they have dwarfed and narrowed theirs by a life of all work and no play; until here they are at forty, with a listless attention, a mind vacant of all material of amusement, and not one thought to rub against another, while they wait for the train. Before he was breeched, he might have clambered on the boxes; when he was twenty, he would have stared at

[4] Dr. Lawrence J. Peter and Raymond Hull, *The Peter Principle* (New York: William Morrow and Company, Inc., 1969), pp. 109–112. Reprinted with omissions by permission of William Morrow & Company, Inc., from *The Peter Principle* by Dr. Lawrence J. Peter and Raymond Hull. Copyright © 1969 by William Morrow & Company, Inc.

the girls; but now the pipe is smoked out, the snuff-box empty, and my gentle man sits bolt upright upon a bench, with lamentable eyes. This does not appeal to me as being Success in Life.[5]

6. Shoes

They are one of the most ordinary types of working shoe: the blucher design, and soft in the prow, lacking the seam across the root of the big toe: covering the ankles: looped straps at the heels: blunt, broad, and rounded at the toe: broad-heeled: made up of most simple round-nesses and squarings and flats, of dark brown raw thick leathers nailed, and sewn coarsely to one another in courses and patterns of doubled and tripled seams, and such throughout that like many other small objects they have great massiveness and repose and are, as the houses and overalls are, and the feet and legs of the women, who go barefooted so much, fine pieces of architecture.

They are softened, in the uppers, with use, and the soles are rubbed thin enough, I estimate, that the ticklish grain of the ground can be felt through at the center of the forward sole. The heels are deeply biased. Clay is worked into the substance of the uppers and a loose dust of clay lies over them. They have visibly though to the eye subtly taken the mold of the foot, and structures of the foot are printed through them in dark sweat at the ankles, and at the roots of the toes. They are worn without socks, and by experience of similar shoes I know that each man's shoe, in long enough course of wear, takes as his clothing does the form of his own flesh and bones, and would feel as uneasy to any other as if A, glancing into the mirror, were met by B's eyes, and to their owner, a natural part though enforcement of the foot, which may be used or shed at will. There is great pleasure in a sockless and sweated foot in the fitted leathers of a shoe.

The shoes are worn for work. At home, resting, men always go barefooted. This is no symptom of discomfort, though: it is, insofar as it is conscious, merely an exchange of mutually enhancing pleasures, and is at least as natural as the habituated use and laying by of hats or of "reading-glasses."

So far as I could see, shoes are never mended. They are worn out like animals to a certain ancient stage and chance of money at which a man buys a new pair; then, just as old Sunday shoes do, they become the inheritance of a wife.

[5] Robert Louis Stevenson, "An Apology for Idlers," in *Essays by Robert Louis Stevenson*, ed. William Lyon Phelps (New York: Charles Scribner's Sons, 1918), pp. 82–83.

Ricketts' shoes are boldly slashed open to accommodate as they scarcely can the years of pain in his feet. The worst of this pain is in stirrup corns, a solid stripe of stony and excruciating pearls across the ball of each foot; for two years, years ago, he rode mules all of each day. Recognizing my own tendency half-consciously to alter my walk or even to limp under certain conditions of mental insecurity, and believing Ricketts to be one of the most piteously insecure men I have ever known, I suspect, too, that nervous modifications in his walking have had much to do with destroying his feet.[6]

7. The Color Line

Prejudice of race has at some time in their history afflicted all nations. "I am more holy than thou" is the boast of races, as well as that of the Pharisee. Long after the Norman invasion and the decline of Norman power, long after the sturdy Saxon had shaken off the dust of his humiliation and was grandly asserting his great qualities in all directions, the descendants of the invaders continued to regard their Saxon brothers as made of coarser clay than themselves, and were not well pleased when one of the former subject race came between the sun and their nobility. Having seen the Saxon a menial, a hostler, and a common drudge, oppressed and dejected for centuries, it was easy to invest him with all sorts of odious peculiarities, and to deny him all manly predicates. Though eight hundred years have passed away since Norman power entered England, and the Saxon has for centuries been giving his learning, his literature, his language, and his laws to the world more successfully than any other people on the globe, men in that country still boast their Norman origin and Norman perfections. This superstition of former greatness serves to fill out the shriveled sides of a meaningless race-pride which holds over after its power has vanished. With a very different lesson from the one this paper is designed to impress, the great Daniel Webster once told the people of Massachusetts (whose prejudices in the particular instance referred to were right) that they "had conquered the sea, and had conquered the land," but that "it remained for them to conquer their prejudices." At one time we are told that the people in some of the towns of Yorkshire cherished a prejudice so strong and violent against strangers and

[6] James Agee and Walker Evans, *Let Us Now Praise Famous Men* (New York: Ballantine Books, 1966), pp. 244–245. Copyright © 1939 and 1940 by James Agee. Copyright © 1941 by James Agee and Walker Evans. Copyright © 1960 by Walker Evans. Reprinted by permission of Houghton Mifflin Company.

foreigners that one who ventured to pass through their streets would be pelted with stones.

Of all the races and varieties of men which have suffered from this feeling, the colored people of this country have endured most. They can resort to no disguises which will enable them to escape its deadly aim. They carry in front the evidence which marks them for persecution. They stand at the extreme point of difference from the Caucasian race, and their African origin can be instantly recognized, though they may be several removes from the typical African race. They may remonstrate like Shylock—"Hath not a Jew eyes? Hath not a Jew hands, organs, dimensions, senses, affections, passions; fed with the same food, hurt with the same weapons, subject to the same diseases, healed by the same means, warmed and cooled by the same summer and winter, as a Christian is?"—but such eloquence is unavailing. They are Negroes—and that is enough, in the eye of this unreasoning prejudice, to justify indignity and violence. In nearly every department of American life they are confronted by this insidious influence. It fills the air. It meets them at the workshop and factory, when they apply for work. It meets them at the church, at the hotel, at the ballot-box, and worst of all, it meets them in the jury-box. Without crime or offense against law or gospel, the colored man is the Jean Valjean of American society. He has ceased to be the slave of an individual, but has in some sense become the slave of society. He may not now be bought and sold like a beast in the market, but he is the trammeled victim of a prejudice, well calculated to repress his manly ambition, paralyze his energies, and make him a dejected and spiritless man, if not a sullen enemy to society, fit to prey upon life and property and to make trouble generally.[7]

8. Heart of Darkness

"Going up that river was like traveling back to the earliest beginnings of the world, when vegetation rioted on the earth and the big trees were kings. An empty stream, a great silence, an impenetrable forest. The air was warm, thick, heavy, sluggish. There was no joy in the brilliance of sunshine. The long stretches of the waterway ran on, deserted, into the gloom of overshadowed distances. On silvery sandbanks hippos and alligators sunned themselves side by side. The broadening waters flowed through a mob of wooded islands; you lost your way on that river as you would in a desert, and butted all day long against shoals,

[7] Frederick Douglass, "The Color Line." *The North American Review,* June, 1881.

trying to find the channel, till you thought yourself bewitched and cut off forever from everything you had known once—somewhere—far away—in another existence perhaps. There were moments when one's past came back to one, as it will sometimes when you have not a moment to spare to yourself; but it came in the shape of an unrestful and noisy dream, remembered with wonder amongst the overwhelming realities of this strange world of plants, and water, and silence. And this stillness of life did not in the least resemble a peace. It was the stillness of an implacable force brooding over an inscrutable intention. It looked at you with a vengeful aspect. I got used to it afterwards; I did not see it any more; I had no time. I had to keep guessing at the channel; I had to discern, mostly by inspiration the signs of hidden banks; I watched for sunken stones; I was learning to clap my teeth smartly before my heart flew out, when I shaved by a fluke some infernal sly old snag that would have ripped the life out of the tin-pot steamboat and drowned all the pilgrims; I had to keep a lookout for the signs of dead wood we could cut up in the night for next day's steaming. When you have to attend to things of that sort, to the mere incidents of the surface, the reality—the reality, I tell you—fades. The inner truth is hidden—luckily, luckily.''[8]

[8] Joseph Conrad, *The Heart of Darkness,* in *Youth: A Narrative and Two Other Stories* (Edinburgh: William Blackwood and Sons, 1902), pp. 104–106.

Sample Student Themes

For Chapter 2, Page 50

Audience: Several veterinary doctors

Characteristics: very select and critical, animal lovers

Persona: Been around animals all of life, experienced with animals and people

Character traits: Intellegent, confident, excited about the field, good worker

Chief points of argument: Grew up with animals, experienced with animals, have devoted my life to them

My story begins on a ranch outside the small town of Athens, Texas. My childhood days were spent there among several types of wildlife. My pets ranged from chickens, dogs, baby fawn, horses and even snakes. I grew up with them and became quite attached to them. My father's work was cattle and I became quite talented with them. Between school, the 4–H Club and my father job I learned most of the aspects of livestock work, in particular, their manners, moods, and needs.

My first actual veterinary work was with the town vet., Dr. Syler. I worked with him for 3 years during summer and vacations. During that time I became quite knowlagable on the subject. It was here that I learned of the psychology of animals and of the people that owned them.

In school my greatest interests were in sciences. My grades were respectable. All through Jr. and Sr. High I was well known in the live stock arenas. I began reading all available material on Zoology or any related fields. My studies improved greatly and I graduated top of my class.

With high school behind me I began looking ahead. My eye was on the veterinary school of Texas A&M. I gained admittence easily and quickly became engulfed by the vet program. I soon found myself doing all types of bizzare and interesting experiments with my teachers. I breezed through with honors and recieved my degree.

It was at this time when I fell in love and got married. I am now settled down and want to pursue my interest to the fullest. I feel your school can fullfill my hopes. I am very excited about this field and I am very confident that I will be one of the finest veterinarians in the world. I would have no other way.

Thank you for your time.

For Chapter 2, Page 50

Audience: members of the Lions Club of Houston

Characteristics: older men—will want to make sure they're spending their money wisely, somewhat old fashioned

Persona: I want to appear optimistic about my goal. I want to show them I am confident in myself and I am quite capable. Also I want to appeal to them that I'm an all around person, in the fact I play basketball and I am sociable, but still make good grades

Chief points of argument: (1) Courses I'm taking, (2) goals and desires, (3) grades and general attitude, (4) extra activities, (5) views on college

Dear Members of the Lions Club:

I have almost completed my freshman year at the University of Texas and have just been informed that it will be impossible to continue my studies in pre-med unless I receive a substantial scholarship. Therefore, I am writing to you for any help you can give me. First of all, you must understand that it is very difficult for me to handle both my school work and an extra job, as I will try to explain.

The courses I am enrolled in this semester are Biology, Physics, English, Chemistry, and two labs. My schedule consist mainly of science courses because of my major and its requirements. I've always enjoyed science and as a result, done well. My grade point average last semester was a 3.26 and should be about the same this semester. I spend most of my time studying, which is necessary to get into medical school. However, I do find some time for extra activities.

I played on the junior varsity basketball team at the University this year. At the first of year, I found it a challenge, because I was just trying-out and I was not on scholarship. I enjoyed every minute of it. Now that the season is over, I play golf in my spare time.

Education is very important to fulfil my goal, which is to become a doctor. Not only will education or college, help to get me into medical school, but it rounds out a person. The individual has a prime opportunity to meet people and learn more about the world and himself. School is a wonderful, fundamental experience in which I cannot miss.

Once again, I am asking for a substantial scholarship, which will enable me to continue my education. Please consider.

Sincerely,

For Chapter 2, Page 50

Audience: Admission Board of Medical Doctors

Characteristics: hard working, intelligent, dedicated

Persona: autobiographical voice

Character traits: serious, slightly emotional report

Chief points of argument: experienced, mature, dedicated, determined

Dear Sirs;

The following is my autobiographical summarization.

My basic interest in the medical profession is inherent. My father has converted himself from a farm boy into the Cheif Supervisor of laboratories at the Veterans Administration Hospital in Kerrville Texas. Through all of my school years I was raised in the atmosphere of the medical field. We lived in many different cities and attended as many different schools. The good experiences not with-standing I eventually dropped out of school in nineteen sixty-six at the age of seventeen. After a year had passed, I joined the United States Marine Corp and gained a high school diploma through the GED program. I was sent to their school for medical corpsmen and after graduation received orders for Vietnam.

It was my service in the battlefield and also in the rear areas that I gained immeasurable raw experience. While attached to the "Delta Med" hospital in Dong Ha South Vietnam, I was introduced to the complete spectrum of medical disorders. Working closley with a navy doctor I became familure with emergancy treatment of gunshot, blood loss, fracturs, punctures, infections and many more situations including some cardiac arrests and childbirth. During this time I also experienced two typhoid epidemics and the anticipated cases of fatal and nonfatal venereal diseases. Towards the latter months of my first year I was asked to remain in the combat zone. Due to the lack of experienced personell in my field I extended my tour of duty for an additional year.

During this second year in Vietnam I was envoled in working at the childrens hospital at Dong Ha. Observing remarkable cases of diseased children transformed into healthy children gave me the satisfaction that doctors must feel. Observing several other cases that ended in disability or death provided the disappointment that doctors must also feel. The emotional side of medicin is not unfamilure to me.

After my return from overseas my immediate goal was to gain entrance to college. My lack of a proper diploma proved to be an obstacle although not an insurmountable one. After completing the necessary tests I was admitted to the University of Texas at Austin under their special student program. My transcript is enclosed.

Finding myself in the uncomfortable situation of self-analysis I will conclude by stating that I have the experience, desire, maturity and capabilitys that few medical applicants possess.

Respectfully,

For Chapter 4, Page 92

Part I

This passage has the following characteristics of jargon: 1) it frequently uses euphemisms; 2) it uses abstract and difficult words instead of simple, concrete words; and 3) it uses phrases and terms not ordinarily used in discussion.

The author uses several euphemisms in this passage. In the second paragraph the phrase "high density population area" is used instead of "city" or "town." This phrase is inconcise and weakens the passage. A second example is in the third paragraph in the phrase "suffer from psychic dislocation." The author tried to use nice words to say "mental upset." In doing this he weakened the passage with an inconcise word. The author makes the same mistake in using the phrase "socioeconomically deprived families" rather than "lower-class" or "poor."

In using the word "neophyte" in the third paragraph the author weakened his writing by use of a vague and abstract term. It would have been much more effective and concise had he used the words "beginner" or "new."

In the last paragraph the author did not write as anyone would normally speak in an ordinary discussion. The word "hazarded" in the first sentence is totally incorrect. This sentence could have been left out entirely. The second sentence could have been broken down into a shorter and more exact statement because it is too wordy.

By completely relying on jargon to convey his point in this passage, the author proves that its usage is confusing to the reader and weakens his writing considerably.

Part II

High school personnel in charge of the guidance of the students who will go on into areas other than vocational study should keep in mind the differentiating characteristics of the various colleges and universities. The number of schools available makes it possible to offer maximum learning opportunities for the individual student. The most meaningful learning experiences will be encountered by students who do not attempt to further their educations in a familiar environment.

One of the factors to be considered is that colleges in large cities attract many applicants from the lower class families. There will be a concentration of intelligent and hard-working students who show minimal interest in non-productive social and political activities. Fraternities and sororities are not made available to the student. The guidance person should try to dissuade socially minded young people from attending large urban universities.

Some colleges with proportionately lower enrollments have an attraction for those young people who are apt to be advanced both politically and ethically. The new student from a middle-class background who opposes these attitudes will suffer some mental upset if he attends this kind of institution when enforcement of rules has been abandoned.

The young person who does not have an integrated personality may be susceptible to undergoing an identity crisis. He is less apt to be traumatized if he chooses a medium-sized college located in a small area that minimizes opportunity for contact with individuals of different characteristics.

For Chapter 4, Page 92

Bunch o' Bull

This passage has the following characteristics of jargon: the excessive use of abstract words and passive voice, and many euphemisms. It also contains unnecessary wordiness, weak verbs, and pretentious diction.

In the first paragraph, my complaint is excessive wordiness. An example is: "High school personnel that are charged with the guidance of that portion of the student body . . ." Those fifteen words can easily be narrowed down to: "high school counselors." When I first read it, it sounded like being a high school counselor was a real fancy job; like calling the head janitor the departmental chairman of hygiene and maintenance. It gives it an effect of being important. Not only could it be described as excessive wordiness, but also a euphemism. Another expression that caught my attention was substituting the words "institutions of higher learning" for something as simple as "colleges and universities." I feel the latter sounds more concrete and effective.

The first sentence in the second paragraph, ("The following factors are to be considered . . .") is what I would term a "neutral statement." It plays an insignificant role and if brevity and condensation are being sought, then the sentence should be omitted. I feel that the reader's mind will automatically deduce for itself that "the following factors are to be considered." The author is also guilty of not using strong enough words. He says that "colleges . . . attract a preponderance of enrollees . . ." Using the word "hundreds" or "thousands" instead of "preponderance" would seem to give it a more massive effect. He also uses genteel expressions to try to cover up "an ugly truth." I refer to the term "socioeconomically deprived families" that the author uses instead of saying "low income families" or "poor families." I agree; there must be a certain degree of politeness maintained but excessive or abusive use of it only weakens the implication that an author desires to achieve.

The author also has a tendency to use foreign words or pretentious diction. He uses the term "avant garde," which is of French derivation. The term describes someone with ideas concerning extreme change of some sort. The author could have said " . . . for those young people who are apt to have radical or liberal ideas in their political inclinations and their ethnic systems." It sounds more concrete and solid. The same goes with the word "parietal" which means "life and order within an organization" (in this case—college). "Parietal" may sound more intelligent and sophisticated but it has no effect whatsoever if the reader has no idea what the word means. I can understand that when an author uses a specific word for a specific purpose to emit or describe a particular idea, then it's only fair to both the author and the reader to use a word that accurately fits. But if I were to read a small passage such as this one, I want to be able to read and fully comprehend it in one single sitting without interruptions— looking up words all because a certain author wanted to create an intelligent and sophisticated impression.

I feel that jargon, if used correctly, *can* make some reading material readable and maybe even enjoyable. Jargon can be analyzed to reveal many things about the author—his ignorance, his preferences, prejudices and even his technique, but I cannot conceive the idea of excessive jargon being used in material that is used for the sole purpose of information. That is what is commonly called today: a bunch of bull, because it cripples the original purpose of informative material—to publish an unbiased truth.

Part II

I think I would rewrite the passage in the following manner:

High school counselors who constantly push graduating students into academic studies rather than other sources of education should keep in mind the many different kinds of schools that are available to all kinds of people with different interests in mind. Not everybody is cut out for the academic field.

They should also consider that colleges situated in a densely populated area cater mostly to the hundreds of low income families. Fraternities and sororities are not available to students in these colleges, therefore a counselor should not urge a socially active student to a college of this nature. This also works vice-versa; one who is naturally inhibited should consider a school that is reasonably well-controlled and peaceable.

In conclusion, one should choose a college that is not only academically suitable but also suitable to the individual's personality for a well-rounded, well-stabilized and comfortable education.

For Chapter 4, Page 92

Analysis

This passage has the following characteristics of jargon: wordiness, pretentious language, and abstract words.

Although this article is concerned with the factors that should be considered before a person selects a college, the idea is almost totally lost by the continual use of jargon. One of the most obvious forms is wordiness. This is illustrated in the opening sentence when the author said, "of that portion of the student body who will go into areas of study other than vocational" instead of simply stating "those students who plan to attend college." In the same sentence the phrase "of the various institutions of higher learning" was used. Again, the concise term "universities" would have been sufficient. Another example of wordiness is the sentence "The neophyte student that is antipathetic to these attitudes will, it is not too unreasonable to anticipate, suffer some psychic dislocation." The clause that is set apart in commas has no relevance to the sentence; it is merely padding. Wordiness has no useful purpose. Trying to understand the meaning of a wordy passage is as difficult as trying to decipher a hieroglyphic message.

Pretentious language is another form of jargon that is used in this article. In several instances multisyllable words were used when a simpler one would have been equally effective. For example a student was called a "scholastic." "Preponderance" was used in place of "majority." "Extremist" was replaced by the French words *avant garde.* Even the euphemism "socioeconomically deprived families" was substituted for "poor." Pretentious language only annoys the reader. He is irritated by the author's attempt to appear intelligent.

The use of abstract words is another form of jargon that devaluates the effectiveness of this article. At one point the author mentioned a "meaningful learning experience." "Meaningful" is a concept that is defined according to the values held by the individual. Also, what is beneficial or a "learning experience" to one person could be insignificant to another. The term "fully integrated personality" was also used. Again, the reader has the responsibility of deciding what to denote for the word. The substitution of abstract words for concrete words weakens this article. Instead of relaying a definite message, abstractions only convey a vague idea.

This article is poorly written, because it uses excessive wordiness, pretentious language, and abstract words. These faults not only annoy the reader, but they also distract from the over-all impact and effectiveness.

Revised Paragraph

Since the United States has numerous and diversified colleges, it is possible for the student to be selective in his choice. Before making this decision there are certain factors that the person should evaluate. One is that students from poor families usually attend colleges that are in large cities. Most often these students are primarily interested in working and studying, and they are apathetic toward the school's social functions. If a person values social activities he should not attend large urban universities. On the other hand, small colleges tend to attract students who have extreme political or ethical beliefs. Unless a person is capable of adjusting to such radical behavior, he probably would not be happy while attending a small college. For these two reasons a student who comes from a middle-class background should strongly consider attending a medium-size college in a semi-urban community.

For Chapter 5, Page 130

ISM

In a passage from "The Conscience of a Conservative," Barry Goldwater tries to persuade his readers that federally sponsored welfare is a communist plot to undermine the U. S. government and destroy the individual. Connotation and contrast are his tools in casting a foreign plot against the American ideal. Today his argument is dated, melodramatic and unsuccessful.

The suffix "ism" is the key to the passage. It sets the tone of the piece, and so should be understood. In the early 1960s the two great powers were fearful of being obliterated by the other. That fear saturated our society. The two powers were classed by "isms." Americanism; anything that was good, individualistic, profitable, etc. Communism; anything bad, atheistic, government dominated, etc. A large number of words in the national vocabulary triggered an immediate, unthinking impression of good or bad in many Americans. Goldwater makes effective use of these words and their connotations in this piece, trying to implant in the American mind the theory that welfare payments made by the federal government are dangerously un-American.

Welfare is not individualistic, not American. Its connotation is bad. The word coupled with "ism" takes on the connotation of a foreign communist ideology. Goldwater opens the piece using the word "welfarism" in the first sentence, connoting that a welfare recipient receives a foreign ideology, communism.

With the word "transforms" Goldwater foretells a rapid, irresistible conversion of all that is good in the American character, individualism, dignity, industriousness, self-reliance and spirituality into that that is deplored; dependency, animal soullessness. He charges this to the "ism" as he does the loss of the feeling of responsibility for family and community, which connotes degradation to Americans.

With a series of scare words and phrases, Goldwater broadens and deepens the damage to be done the American character by the plot. The word "mortgage" implies the individual will sell himself for a welfare check. In the word "concedes" he surrenders to the government powers of life and death, and any voice he may have had. In this passage Goldwater has the American unknowingly selling himself into abject slavery.

"Collectivist" encompasses socialist and communist. Coupling collectivist with "designs" Goldwater brands federal welfare a communist plot against the individual freedom of Americans, but he offers an escape. The plot can be shattered if the readers impress on their leaders the truth that the "material and spiritual sides of men are intertwined." The phrase is vague. Its connotations are good, its tone soft, inviting agreement or compliance. Its probable meaning is "tell your congressmen to vote against federal welfare if they want your support next election day."

In the early 1960s the passage suggested a plausible theory to frightened Americans. His efforts were successful. Today the words have been overused. "Wolf" has been cried too often. Ism has lost its scare value and the new generation doesn't know its meanings. His argument is too melodramatic and heavyhanded to succeed.

For Chapter 5, Page 130

Connotation Used in Goldwater's Theme

Goldwater is trying to persuade his reader that welfare endangers people's character as well as their independence; his main tool is the use of connotation which helps him emphasize his reasons for being against welfare. In this manner he is successful because of the bad impressions the connotative words give to the Welfare State.

Most Americans seem to have a fear of being deprived of their freedom or independence. With this in mind Goldwater uses connotative words throughout his theme that gives the impression of one being a prisoner of welfare. In addition, Goldwater feels that a man on welfare loses his feeling of responsibility towards his family and his friends. In a sense this man becomes completely dependent upon the government.

In the beginning of the theme Goldwater says that a man on welfare "mortgages himself to the federal government." The word mortgage is usually used in the giving up of personal property when one is in debt. The connotation is that a person is selling himself or maybe even selling his soul to the government in return for certain benefits. And he also goes on to say that a person on welfare is giving the "ultimate" in political power to the government. Ultimate would imply the very highest in political power leading one to believe that the government has total control over a person on welfare.

Mr. Goldwater expresses the opinion that welfare transforms a person's character. At first the person is a dignified, industrious, self-reliant spiritual being. Now I think Goldwater uses these words mainly because these words have good connotations because all people like to be thought of in this manner. But then Goldwater goes on to say that when a person goes on welfare he becomes a dependent animal creature which would connotate a bad, inhuman quality as well as a lack of independence. Furthermore, he implies that it is an animal impulse for the government to just give people welfare because it is owed to them as compared with the human instinct of charity.

Goldwater uses "collectivists' design on individual freedom" in place of the word welfare. These words connotatively give the allusion that it is a small group of people who are trying to take away people's freedom.

The passage by Goldwater is effective when putting across the viewpoint that a Welfare State will make people totally dependent upon the government. Each of his connotative words gives the idea of someone handing over their independence to the government.

For Chapter 5, Page 130

Analysis of a Political Essay

In an article from *Conscience of a Conservative*, Barry Goldwater attacks the welfare system. While he delivers a seemingly straightforward attack and an alternate proposal one may infer more from an analysis of his choice of words, than from a mere casual reading.

In an excerpt from *Conscience of a Conservative*, Barry Goldwater delivers an attack on Welfare. He does not oppose the individual programs or the way they are administered. Rather he attacks the entire concept of welfare from the government. His main complaint against "Welfarism" is the damage done to the individual's "spiritual being." He says that eliminating man's self-sufficiency can make him a "dependent animal creature." He feels that these negative results are inevitable; that "there is no avoiding the damage . . ." done to the recipient's character and pride. Mr. Goldwater proposes that welfare be made a "private concern" promoted by "institutions that have been established for this purpose." He concludes by emphasizing "that the material and spiritual sides of man are intertwined"—man cannot be proud without the responsibility for his personal needs.

Mr. Goldwater approaches the question of welfare in an original way. Rather than restating the familiar conservative view that welfare is unfair to the taxpayer, he attempts to show its negative influence on the recipient. "Mortgaging oneself" connotes a sacrifice by the individual. A mortgagee loses a measure of his independence since he has sold himself to an impersonal system—the government. "He concedes to the government the ultimate in political power"—the power to withhold the necessities of life.

In explaining the harms of reliance on others for income, the author refers to the "evils" of "Welfarism." "Evil" implies that which is morally bad, wicked, or harmful. This paints a totally negative picture of welfare. He describes the debasing of the recipients. Their "spiritual being"—a phrase that brings to mind all that is holy or good in man—is destroyed and man is left no better than a "dependent animal creature." This damage to the recipient's character is described as being unavoidable.

Mr. Goldwater then proposes that private charities replace Welfare. This would answer the moral problem of damage done to the recipient's character since "the receiver understand[s] that charity is the product of the humanitarian impulses of the giver." The author feels that the needy will thus be cared for in "a way that will preserve their freedom." However it seems that the welfare recipients are not the only beneficiaries of Mr. Goldwater's plan. Certainly there is an implied advantage for the taxpayer. If welfare is a private concern, each individual is free to give as much or as little as he wants. In any event, taxes would be reduced considerably. Whether this is his intention or not, Mr. Goldwater's plan can attract the support of many who may not be overly concerned with the damage done to the character of welfare recipients, but who *do* like the economic aspects of his proposal.

The reader observes a logical sequence to the author's thoughts. Mr. Goldwater pinpoints the problem as he sees it, demonstrates the need for change, and proposes a plan to answer that need. His reasoning seeks to appeal to a broad base—welfare recipients and taxpayers alike. And finally he seeks to elevate the issue to a philosophical level, moving from a specific attack on the welfare system to an attack on the designs of collectivists as a whole. To one unfamiliar with the specifics of the welfare system, Mr. Goldwater's arguments seem very persuasive.

For Chapter 6, Page 176

The Mouse

Thesis sentence: A drug addict is poor and unkempt. Drug addiction is dangerous.

A cornerstone was missing from under the house so walking across the room was like descending a gently sloping hill. The yellowed linoleum which covered the floor was torn in many places along the beaten trail to the back door. A broken light bulb hung in a socket at the end of a wire which fell through a hole in the ceiling. The dim light enhanced the dinginess of the room. Dark brown water spots covered the sagging sheet rock ceiling. In one corner there was a torn cot with a dirty, rumpled sheet on it. Above the cot hung a dust-covered statuette of Christ on the cross. On the floor, beside the cot, lay several lewd magazines.

A large wooden table was in the center of the room. Four paper plates and a vase of plastic flowers were on it. The paper plates contained left over food from previous meals. The dust on the flowers blocked out all but a faint red and blue coloring on the plastic petals.

A couple of orange crates were propped up next to the sink. A small, cheap radio and an old, double-edge razor were on a soiled towel which had been spread across the top of the crates. A bar of soap which was lying in the basin of the sink had been half-eaten away by water dripping from the faucet.

A beer can was sitting on the window sill. The wind was slowly shifting the tattered curtains in and out of a broken window pane. The dust-covered window made the brightness of midday look like the gloominess of dusk.

In another corner of the room there was a syringe with a needle attached to it. Next to it lay a young man with glassy eyes staring blankly at the ceiling. About two feet from the young man, next to a hole in the wall, a small mouse had eaten the cheese from a mouse trap. It was also staring blankly at the ceiling.

For Chapter 6, Page 176

Thesis sentence: A description of a room that will make a comment on the occupant is describing first the surroundings of the room, how it is decorated and how clean or dirty it is kept; all of which I have combined in a short story about a lady who goes to pick up her new maid.

The day came when I could finally go pick up my new maid. Being exhausted from last night's party, I asked James to bring the Rolls around and take me. We hurried through the iron gates, down 5th Avenue until we reached the west side of town. Shortly we arrived in front of a ghetto housing project, deep in the Lincoln Courts.

I proceeded down the empty hall looking for room seven. I came to a door which was cracked open slightly, which had rusted hinges which squeaked as I push open the door and walked in. For a moment, I thought I had walked into a garage. The room looked as if a herd of elephants had stampeded through non-stop. It was dimly lit with a naked light bulb which swayed back and forwards as the wind rushed in the door. Expecting any minute for Tarzan to swing through on a vine and grab me, I decided to sit down. Stumbling over an empty beer can and a pair of "unmentionables," I heard a rat scramble across the wooden floor. As I sat down in the chair whose bottom seemed to be quite hard. Wondering why the chair was so low and hard I suddenly realized that the bottom was touching the floor. Trying to stand up I accidently put my hand in a pile of ashes and dirt which apparently missed the ash tray. Which I later saw next to the unmade bed which smelled from being wet and dried without seeing the out of doors. Unable to hold my breath any longer, I went back to the living room wondering if anyone would ever come. As I sat on the old tattered couch a cloud of dust rose from the cushions as if I had dropped a bomb. I jumped up not realizing I was caught by a spring which stuck out of the couch and ripped my clothes. As I rushed for the door, I was grabbed by an unseen vail of spider webs. I burst into the hallway taking spider, his home and family with me. Leaving behind the ruins and my new maid. Even though I had not seen her she was not the woman for me.

Two weeks later I discovered I had gone to the wrong room. My maid's room was actually nicer than her neighbors which only goes to show you can't judge a maid by her house, especially if you're in the wrong house.

Tips on Reading Expository Prose

Many of the difficulties that a student encounters in a freshman composition course are directly connected to reading. He finds himself responsible for understanding, analyzing, and writing about a new kind of material—essays and books that focus on ideas rather than on information. Mastering such material requires more than routine reading; it requires careful, active reading, reading that is purposeful and methodical.

The first step is to ask yourself what you expect to get out of your reading. The answer should include at least these points:

1. To discover and to be able to state in one or two sentences the author's main idea. What is the thesis or primary generalization upon which the essay or book is based?

2. To understand why the author thinks as he does. What is the reasoning that underlies his beliefs? What kinds of arguments does he advance to support his position?

3. To decide whether the author's approach is primarily rational, primarily emotional, or whether it is a balance of the two. If it is rational, is his reasoning sound? If it is emotional, what specific emotions are appealed to?

4. To evaluate how well the author presents and supports his idea. What are the reasons for his success or failure?

Next, before you begin on the text itself, take the time to examine whatever nontextual material accompanies the article. You should look for the following information:

1. The name of the author. Is he living? If not, when did he live? What is his nationality? What qualifications does he have to write on his topic? What else has he written? Information of this kind may be in a footnote, in the preface, in a special bibliographical section of the book, or at the beginning or end of an article.

2. Date and place of publication. This is important if you are to put the writing in its historical context.

3. Title. Does it seem to have special significance? Does it give you a clue to the content of the essay?

4. Titles of subdivisions or sections. Can you tell from these how the essay is going to progress?

Begin reading the text itself with the assumption that in order to understand it you will have to read it at least twice, probably three times if the material is difficult. Although the first reading should be more than just a skimming, it can be done comparatively quickly. Read the introduction carefully to get an idea of the author's purpose; then read through the rest of the essay without stopping to underline or annotate. As you read, note key words that seem to recur frequently; they will give a clue to the author's main idea. Try to determine the tone and style of the essay. Is it humorous, serious, sarcastic, objective, or what? Is the writing simple or complex, casual or formal? Pay special attention to italicized words or phrases, noting if possible why they have been stressed. Carefully read the concluding paragraph or section, because it is here that the author will probably pull together and reinforce his main points. If on this first reading you encounter words that you don't know, stop and look them up. This step is an especially important one when you are reading expository material, for although you may be able to skip over unfamiliar words when you are reading fiction and still grasp the meaning, when you read an essay the very word that you fail to look up may be essential to understanding the essay.

After reading the whole essay over once, you should have a reasonably good grasp of the author's main idea, but you are probably not prepared either to write on the essay or to discuss it intelligently. In order to do that you need to reread the material slowly and actively with a pencil or highlighter in your hand. I prefer the pencil because I can use it to make notes as I go along; I also use a six-inch plastic ruler as a pacer and an aid to underlining.

Begin your second reading with the conscious intention of stopping at frequent intervals in order to absorb the material and make notes on what you have read. You should time your pauses according to the difficulty of the material. If it is clearly written and deals with relatively simple ideas, you may be able to read several paragraphs or even a whole section at once; if, however, the ideas are complex or totally unfamiliar and the writing rather abstract, you will probably need to stop after each paragraph. As you are reading, ask yourself these questions. What is the main assertion in this section? What are the key words? Which sentences in the material are primary and which sentences are secondary in the sense that they restate, expand, illustrate, or support the main idea? In all expository writing, much of the material is illustrative or explanatory, and it is essential that you learn to distinguish between the main statements and elaborations on them.

Fortunately, authors often give you useful clues that help you to spot important sentences or passages. Watch for signal words and phrases such as "It is essential," "An important point," "The primary reason," "Significantly"; watch for definitions and for words that announce conclusions: "consequently," "therefore," "as a result," "thus," and "we must conclude"; also look for words signaling order: "first," "second," and "finally."

When you have finished a unit of the reading, stop and force yourself to summarize what you have just read. If you cannot do it or are confused about the author's meaning, go back and reread; then try again. As tedious as this method may seem, this *immediate recall,* as it is labeled by educators, is probably the most important step in your reading. Experiments have shown that most forgetting takes place immediately after one learns something; thus, in the long run you will save yourself time and retain far more of what you read if you reinforce your learning by stopping to summarize as you go along. Moreover, as a writer develops a thesis he builds on and refers back to concepts he has set forth early in an essay. If you have not grasped those concepts, you will have to go back and reread in order to understand the whole. So make it a rule to understand every paragraph and section as you read.

When you are sure you understand a unit of the material, *and only then,* stop to underline or mark and take notes. If you stop to underline before you have fully grasped the key points in a section, you may find that you have emphasized the wrong things, and the work will have to be done again. Waiting to underline until you are sure what is important will ensure your marking your book in a way that will be instantly useful to you when you want to review for a paper or exam. Underline thoughtfully but sparingly, marking only crucial passages. If you find that you are underlining half the sentences on a page, you are probably not reading as carefully as you should. Occasionally, of course, an entire paragraph or passage contains essential material. In that case, draw a line down the margin and star the section.

Writing notes and capsule summaries in the margins of your book is another major aid to comprehension and review. Sometimes a note may be just a reminder about the contents of a section: for example, if you are reading an essay on existentialism, you might jot down "despair," "anguish," and "forlornness" in the margins beside the sections dealing with those concepts. Such notes would help you remember the author's main points. More extensive notes that sum up content are an even greater help for both immediate retention and future review. For instance, you might expand your note on existentialism by writing "anguish: uncertainty and distress about decisions and their consequences." Or you might sum up key ideas in an essay by S. I. Hayakawa with notes like these: "hasty judgments block thinking"; "need to be aware of basis of our inferences." *Studying* a book or essay almost necessarily involves making these kinds of marginal notes. Ask your teacher to show you his teaching copy of the text you are using, and you will find a book that is underlined and annotated. From long experience he has learned that the quickest and surest way to comprehend an essay thoroughly is to read it slowly, actively, and with a pencil in his hand.

When you have finished this step-by-step reading of an essay, you should then go back and view the material as a whole. Think about what you have read and reflect on it. What have you learned? Was it worth reading? Why do you think so? Do you agree or disagree with the author? Why? Finally, ask yourself the questions that you started out with. By now you should be able to answer them clearly and make a thoughtful, supported criticism of what you have read.

The initial reaction of a student who has never done this kind of reading is nearly always, "But it's so slow! I'll never get through all I have to read if I go at it this way." Well, it is slow; there is no denying that. It is also, however, remarkably efficient. When you have prepared a reading assignment in this way, you have learned it thoroughly. You are ready for class discussion, a quiz or exam, or writing a paper. If you need to review the material for a major examination, you can do so quickly by rereading underlined portions and marginal notes. In the long run the process takes less time and produces far better results than the kind of passive reading and rereading that many students depend on.

SAMPLE PASSAGES OF ANNOTATED READING

purpose: to state rule of way society should deal with individual

The (object of this essay) is to assert one very simple principle, as entitled to govern absolutely the dealings of society with the individual in the way of compulsion and control, whether the means used be physical force in the form of legal penalties, or the moral

assertion: only reason soc. can interfere with liberty is self-protection

coercion of public opinion. That principle is, that the sole end for which mankind are warranted, individually or collectively, in interfering with the liberty of action of any of their number, is self-protection. That the only purpose for which power can be rightfully

expansion

exercised over any member of a civilized community, against his *can't interfere for his own good*

will, is to prevent harm to others. His own good, either physical or moral, is not a sufficient warrant. He cannot rightfully be compelled to do or forbear because it will be better for him to do so, because it will make him happier, because, in the opinions of others, to do so would be wise, or even right. These are good reasons for remonstrating with him, or reasoning with him, or persuading him, or entreating him, but not compelling him, or visiting him with any evil in case he do otherwise. To justify that, the conduct from which it is desired to deter him, must be calculated to produce evil to some one else. The only part of the conduct of any one, for which he is amenable to society, is that which concerns others. In the part which merely concerns himself, his independence is, of right, absolute. Over himself, over his own body and mind, the individual is sovereign.

only conduct soc. should control is what hurts others

It is, perhaps, hardly necessary to say that this doctrine is meant to apply only to human beings in the maturity of their faculties. We are not speaking of children, or of young persons below the age which the law may fix as that of manhood or womanhood. Those who are still in a state to require being taken care of by others, must be protected against their own actions as well as against external injury. For the same reason, we may leave out of consideration those backward states of society in which the race itself may be considered as in its nonage. The early difficulties in the way of spontaneous progress are so great, that there is seldom any choice of means for overcoming them; and a ruler full of the spirit of improvement is warranted in the use of any expedients that will attain an end, perhaps otherwise unattainable. Despotism is a legitimate mode of government in dealing with barbarians, provided the end be their improvement, and the means justified by actually effecting that end. Liberty, as a principle, has no application to any state of things anterior to the time when mankind have become capable of being improved by free and equal discussion. Until then, there is nothing for them but implicit obedience to an Akbar or a Charlemagne, if they are so fortunate as to find one. But as soon as mankind have attained the capacity of being guided to their own improvement by conviction or persuasion (a period long since reached in all nations with whom we need here concern ourselves), compulsion, either in the direct form or in that of pains and penalties for noncompliance, is no longer admissible as a means to their own good, and justifiable only for the security of others.[1]

rule applies only to mature people not children

not savages or the uncivilized

despotism ok for barbarians

when people are rational and civilized

compulsion not legit. except to protect others

[1] John Stuart Mill, *On Liberty* (Indianapolis: The Bobbs–Merrill Co., Inc., 1956), pp. 17–18.

2 ways to cure trouble caused by faction:
(1) remove causes
(2) control effects

There are two methods of curing the mischiefs of faction: the one, by removing its causes; the other, by controlling its effects.

2 ways to remove causes:
(1) destroy liberty
(2) make everyone the same

There are again two methods of removing the causes of faction: the one, by destroying the liberty which is essential to its existence; the other, by giving to every citizen the same opinions, the same passions, and the same interests.

getting rid of liberty: worse than faction

It could never be more truly said than of the first remedy, that it is worse than the disease. Liberty is to faction what air is to fire, an ailment without which it instantly expires. But it could not be less folly to abolish liberty, which is essential to political life, because it nourishes faction, than it would be to wish the annihilation of air, which is essential to animal life, because it imparts to fire its destructive agency.

trying to make everyone same impractical

The second expedient is as impracticable as the first would be unwise. As long as the reason of man continues fallible, and he is at liberty to exercise it, different opinions will be formed. As long as the connection subsists between his reason and his self-love, his opinions and his passions will have a reciprocal influence on each other; and the former will be objects to which the latter will attach themselves. The diversity in the faculties of men, from which the rights of property originate, is not less an insuperable obstacle to a uniformity of interests. The protection of these faculties is the first object of government. From the protection of different and unequal faculties of acquiring property, the possession of different degrees and kinds of property immediately results; and from the influence of these on the sentiments and views of the respective proprietors, ensues a division of the society into different interests and parties.

natural for me to have dif. opinions

dif. abilities cause dif. interests

★ gov't's first job is to protect differences protecting dif. in ability causes unequal property distribution

∴ division of society things causing faction based in human nature

The latent causes of faction are thus sown in the nature of man; and we see them everywhere brought into different degrees of activity, according to the different circumstances of civil society. A zeal for different opinions concerning religion, concerning government, and many other points, as well of speculation as of practice; an attachment to different leaders ambitiously contending for preeminence and power; or to persons of other descriptions whose fortunes have been interesting to the human passions, have, in turn, divided mankind into parties, inflamed them with mutual animosity, and rendered them much more disposed to vex and oppress each other than to co-operate for their common good. So strong is this propensity of mankind to fall into mutual animosities, that where no substantial occasion presents itself, the

(1) dif. opinions on religion & government

(2) attachment to dif. leaders

men so inclined to take sides they'll do it for trivial reasons

⋕ but main cause: unequal distribution of property

most frivolous and fanciful distinctions have been sufficient to kindle their unfriendly passions and excite their most violent conflicts. But the most common and durable source of factions has been the various and unequal distribution of property. Those who hold and those who are without property have ever formed distinct interests in society. Those who are creditors, and those who are debtors, fall under a like discrimination. A landed interest, a manufacturing interest, a mercantile interest, a moneyed interest, with many lesser interests, grow up of necessity in civilized nations, and divide them into different classes, actuated by different sentiments and views.

⋕ regulate faction from property dif. is main task for modern laws

The regulation of these various and interfering interests forms the principal task of modern legislation, and involves the spirit of party and faction in the necessary and ordinary operations of the government.[2]

Booker T. Wash. represents old Negro attitude of adjustment & submission

Mr. Washington represents in Negro thought the old attitude of adjustment and submission; but adjustment at such a peculiar time as to make his programme unique. This is an age of unusual economic development, and Mr. Washington's programme naturally takes an economic cast, becoming a gospel of Work and Money to such an extent as apparently almost completely to over-shadow the higher aims of life. Moreover, this is an age when the more advanced races are coming in closer contact with the less developed races, and the race-feeling is therefore intensified; and

program stresses work & ⋕ ignores higher aims of life

program goes along with idea Negro inferior

Mr. Washington's programme practically accepts the alleged inferiority of the Negro races. Again, in our own land, the reaction from the sentiment of war time has given impetus to race-prejudice against Negroes, and Mr. Washington withdraws many

withdraws demands of Negroes as men & Am. citizens

of the high demands of Negroes as men and American citizens. In other periods of intensified prejudice all the Negro's tendency to self-assertion has been called forth; at this period a policy of submission is advocated. In the history of nearly all other races and

other minority groups: self-respect worth more than property

peoples the doctrine preached at such crises has been that manly self-respect is worth more than lands and houses, and that a people who voluntarily surrender such respect, or cease striving for it, are not worth civilizing.

In answer to this, it has been claimed that the Negro can sur-

[2] James Madison, "Federalist Paper No. 10," in *The Federalist Papers,* ed. Roy P. Fairfield (Garden City, N. Y.: Doubleday Co., Inc., 1961), pp. 17–18. From THE FEDERALIST PAPERS edited by Roy P. Fairfield, copyright © 1961, 1966 by Roy P. Fairfield. Reprinted by permission of Doubleday & Company, Inc.

Wash. claims Negro must submit to survive — asks blacks to give up 3 things

(1) political power
(2) civil rights
(3) education
instead should try for:
(1) indus. training;
(2) money; (3) conciliation of So.

vive only through submission. Mr. <u>Washington</u> distinctly <u>asks that</u>
<u>black people give up</u>, at least for the present, <u>three things</u>,—
    First, <u>political power</u>,
    Second, <u>insistence on civil rights</u>,
    Third, <u>higher education of Negro youth</u>,—and <u>concentrate all</u>
<u>their energies on industrial education</u>, the <u>accumulation of wealth</u>,
and the <u>conciliation of the South</u>. This policy has been coura-
geously and insistently advocated for over fifteen years, and has
been triumphant for perhaps ten years. <u>As a result</u> of this tender of
the palm-branch, <u>what has been the return</u>? In these years there
have occurred:
    (1.) The disfranchisement of the Negro.
    (2.) The legal creation of a distinct status of civil inferiority for
the Negro.
    (3.) The steady withdrawal of aid from institutions for the higher
training of the Negro.

result of policy

(1) Negro can't vote
(2) Negro's a second class citizen
(3) less help f a Negro colleges

    These movements are not, to be sure, direct results of Mr.
Washington's teachings; but his propaganda has, without a
shadow of doubt, <u>helped their speedier accomplishment</u>. The
question then comes: <u>Is it possible, and probable, that nine mil-</u>
<u>lions of men can make effective progress in economic lines if they</u>
<u>are deprived of political rights, made a servile caste, and allowed</u>
<u>only the most meagre chance for developing their exceptional</u>
<u>men</u>? If history and reason give any distinct answer to these ques-
tions, it is an emphatic <u>No</u>. And Mr. Washington thus faces the
<u>triple paradox</u> of his career:

Ques.: can Negroes make progress if they accept the 3 things?

Ans.: No

paradox of Wash's work

(1) wants to make blacks property holders, but blacks can't defend rights without vote

    (1.) He is striving nobly to make Negro artisans business men
and property-owners; but it is utterly impossible, under modern
competitive methods, for workingmen and property-owners to defend their rights and exist without the right of suffrage.

(2) insists on self-respect but submission undermines it

    (2.) He insists on thrift and self-respect, but at the same time
counsels a silent submission to civic inferiority such as is bound to
sap the manhood of any race in the long run.

(3) wants grade schools & voc. schools but no teachers if no Negro colleges

    (3.) He advocates common-school and industrial training, and
depreciates institutions of higher learning; but neither the Negro
common-schools, nor Tuskegee itself, could remain open a day
were it not for teachers trained in Negro colleges, or trained by
their graduates.[3]

---

[3] William E. Du Bois, *The Souls of Black Folk* (Chicago: A. C. McClurg & Co., 1903), pp. 50–52.

A Glossary of Usage

accept—except
Accept means "receive" or "agree to."
Except as a preposition means "excluding"; as a verb it means "omit" or "make an exception."
Examples:
> They *accept* the conditions of the treaty.
> Everyone came *except* John.
> The registrar *excepts* handicapped students from the schedule.

access—excess
Access means "admission to" or "approach."
Excess means "too much" or "more than is necessary."
Examples:
> He has *access* to the building.
> The accident happened on the *access* road.
> He smokes to *excess.*
> There will be an *excess* profits tax.

affect—effect
Affect is a verb meaning "change" or "influence."
Effect may be a verb meaning "bring about," but in most writing is used as a noun meaning "result."
Examples:
> Changes in the weather *affect* his mood.
> The black lights produced a startling *effect.*

aggravate
In formal usage *aggravate* means "to make worse" or "intensify." Informally it is used as a synonym for "annoy" or "exasperate."
Formal:
> His insolence *aggravated* an already difficult situation.
Informal:
> George's habits *aggravate* me.

all right—alright
All right is the preferable spelling for this phrase indicating agreement. Many dictionaries now give alright as acceptable, but your audience

might not agree. It is best to remember that *all right* takes the same form as "all wrong."

Example:

Mary is *all right* now.

allusion—illusion

The similarity in sound between these two words sometimes confuses students. *Allusion* means "reference"; *illusion* means "misconception" or "misleading image."

Examples:

The author's *allusion* to Prometheus was confusing.

He is under the *illusion* that she loves him.

already—all ready

Already means "prior to a certain time"; *all ready* means "prepared."

Examples:

John was *already* in bed.

The train had *already* left.

The car is *all ready* to go.

A lot—alot

A lot is a colloquialism that is acceptable in informal writing, but it must be written as two words. "Much," "many," or another modifier expressing quantity is preferable in more formal writing.

Formal:

He had many friends.

Informal:

She went to a lot of trouble to arrange the party.

among—between

See *between*.

amount—number

Amount generally refers to a bulk quantity or to a mass; *number* refers to several units. *Number* as a subject takes a singular verb.

Examples:

The *number* is rising steadily.

He has a large *number* of friends.

He has a large *amount* of money.

as—like

See *like—as.*

as—that

The use of *as* as a substitute for *that* in introducing a clause is too colloquial for most writing.

Colloquial:

> I don't know *as* I will go.

Acceptable:

> I don't know *that* I will go.

bad—badly

Bad is an adjective that modifies nouns or acts as a complement to linking verbs. *Badly* is an adverb used to modify verbs or adjectives. People who are trying too hard to speak elegantly frequently make the mistake of completing a linking verb such as "feels" or "looks" with badly.

Correct:

> Jim feels *bad* about the accident.
> George looks *bad* since his illness.
> The team played *badly* tonight.

Incorrect:

> Joan looks *badly* without makeup.
> I feel *badly* about not going.

between—among

Purists use *between* when referring to two persons or objects, *among* when referring to more than two. The distinction is a comparatively minor one.

Examples:

> The quarrel was *between* Joe and me.
> The money was distributed *among* the members of the team.

can—may

Traditional grammarians specify that *can* should be used only to indicate capability, and *may* to indicate permission. The distinction is rapidly disappearing, and in all but the most formal writing the terms may be used interchangeably.

Examples:

> John *can* lift a 150 pound weight.
> You *may* take the book home with you.

center around—center on

Center around is an illogical expression.
Center on is preferable.

Illogical:
   The talk *centered around* the war.
Preferable:
   The talk *centered on* the war.

cite—site—sight

Students frequently confuse these three words. *Cite* is a verb meaning "refer to," *site* is a noun meaning "location" or "place," and *sight* as a noun means "view" or "spectacle."

Examples:
   He will *cite* two other occasions on which the play had been used.
   Fred showed them the *site* of the new building.
   The children had never seen such a wonderful *sight.*

collective noun

A collective noun refers to a group of individuals or things considered as a single entity, for example, *team, platoon, congregation, jury.* It may take a singular or plural verb according to the context of the sentence.

Examples:
   The *team* is going to win.
   The *jury* were divided in their opinion.

complement—compliment

Complement as a verb means "complete" or "fit with"; as a noun it means a "word or phrase that completes."
Compliment as a verb means "speak favorably of"; as a noun it means "favorable remark."

Examples:
   That dress *complements* her dark hair.
   Linking verbs must be followed by a *complement.*
   He *complimented* them on their foresight.
   Jack is always ready with a *compliment.*

could of

An incorrect form of "could have."

Correct:
   We *could have* taken the bus.
Incorrect:
   We *could of* taken the bus.

data, media, criteria, phenomena

These are plural forms of the singular nouns *datum, medium, criterion,* and *phenomenon* and take plural verb forms. Except in formal usage, however, a singular verb is acceptable with *data.*

Acceptable:

The *data are* inaccurate.
The *data is* reliable.

Correct:

The mass *media are* influential in our culture.
His *criteria are* clearly stated.
These *phenomena indicate* the presence of oxygen.

different from—different than

The preferred usage is "different *from,*" but the distinction is a fine one. Most dictionaries give either form as acceptable.

double negative

Regardless of its acceptance in other languages, the construction is considered substandard in English. "Hardly" and "scarcely" are negative words and should not be used with other negatives.

Unacceptable:

He *didn't* do *nothing* wrong.
Jane *can't hardly* pass English.

Correct:

He *did nothing* wrong.
Jane *can hardly* pass English.

due to

Although widely used, this phrase is usually avoided by careful writers. "Because of" is preferable.

Acceptable:

Due to icy roads, he could not come.

Preferable:

He was unable to come *because of* icy roads.

effect

See *affect—effect.*

etc.

Etc. is a contraction of the Latin phrase *et cetera,* meaning "and other things." Although it is acceptable in informal speech, too often it is a lazy substitute for writing out a full list. Because many teachers find the expression unacceptable, students would do well to avoid it.

except

See *accept—except.*

fact

Use *fact* only to refer to that which can be tested and verified. "The fact that" is an overworked and often inaccurate phrase that should be avoided whenever possible. When you do use it, be sure that it refers to something that is indisputably true, not a matter of opinion.

Incorrect:
> The *fact* that Communism is a failure was mentioned again and again.

Acceptable:
> The *fact* that Germany was defeated at Stalingrad changed the course of the war.

Preferable:
> Germany's defeat at Stalingrad changed the course of the war.

first—firstly; second—secondly

The -ly form for numerals is awkward and unnecessary. The straight form is preferable.

Awkward:
> *Firstly,* I should say thank you to my colleagues.

Preferable:
> *First,* I should thank my colleagues.

fewer—less

Fewer should be used when one is referring to individual units, *less* when one is referring to a smaller amount of a substance or quality. The distinction is a comparatively minor one.

Examples:
> They had *fewer* applicants this year.
> He had *less* money than he realized.
> A Ford costs *less* than a Buick.

formally—formerly

Formally means "in a proper manner"; *formerly* means "at a previous time."

Examples:
> We have not been *formally* introduced.
> He *formerly* played football for Alabama.

infer—imply

Although one major dictionary suggests that these words may be used interchangeably, the practice is not generally accepted. *Infer* means "conclude from the evidence" and *imply* means "suggest" or "hint." In college writing you should observe the distinction.

Examples:

> He *inferred* from conversation that Jones was a Democrat.
> The article *implied* that the students were responsible.

irregardless

An incorrect form of "regardless"; not acceptable in standard English.

its—it's

Confusion of these two forms causes one of the most common student writing errors. *Its* (in spite of its not having an apostrophe) is a possessive pronoun; *it's* is a contraction of "it is."

Examples:

> The company increased *its* profits.
> *It's* time that something was done.

lay—lie

Lay is a transitive verb that must take an object; it means "place" or "put." Its principal parts are *lay, laid, laid.*
Lie is an intransitive verb that means "recline"; its principal parts are *lie, lay, lain.*

Correct:

> The dog *lay* peacefully on the floor.
> She *laid* the pattern on the material.

Incorrect:

> I *lay* the book on the table.
> He *laid* on the ground for an hour.

like—as

The confusion of these words causes great distress to purists. In formal English *like* should be used only as a preposition, not as a conjunction to introduce a clause. *As, as if,* or *as though* should be used before clauses. The distinction is disappearing, but your teacher may want you to observe it.

Informal:

> It looks *like* there will be trouble.

Formal:

> It looks *as if* there will be trouble.

Correct:

> He looks *like* an athlete.
>
> Mary talks *like* her mother.

loose—lose

Confusion between these terms causes one of students' common spelling errors. *Loose,* although it can be used as a verb to mean "release" or "make loose," is most often an adjective meaning "unconfined." *Lose* is a verb only.

Examples:

> The bindings were too *loose.*
>
> John may *lose* his scholarship.

media

Media is a plural noun and takes a plural verb; see "data."

myself

Myself should not be used as a substitute for *I* or *me.* Its proper uses are 1) as a reflexive pronoun and 2) as an intensive pronoun.

Correct:

> I built it *myself.*
>
> I cut *myself* badly.

Incorrect:

> Mary and *myself* are going to do it.
>
> He gave instructions to Jim and *myself.*

only

An adverb or adjective meaning "solely" or "exclusively." It should always come next to the word it modifies.

Correct:

> He has *only* two more years of college.
>
> John comes *only* in the mornings.

Incorrect:

> He *only* has two more years of college.
>
> John *only* comes in the mornings.

one

An impersonal pronoun used more often in formal than informal writing. In strictly formal writing it must be used consistently and not mixed with "his" or "hers."

Formal:

> *One* has the feeling that *one* is helpless.

Informal:

> *One* has the feeling that *he* is helpless.

prepositions

There is nothing inherently incorrect about putting a preposition at the end of a sentence if the context seems to call for it. "These were the only figures he had to work *with*" is a perfectly good sentence. So is "There is the man you need to speak *to.*"

principal—principle

These two quite different words are often confused. *Principal* may be a noun or an adjective. As a noun it means "chief administrative officer of a school," "leading character," or "sum of money." As an adjective it means "first" or "main."

Examples:

> Jones is the *principal* of the high school.
> Fonteyn was the *principal* in Swan Lake.
> He invested the *principal.*
> Clark is the *principal* suspect in the case.

Principle is a noun only; it means "a rule" or "theory."

Examples:

> We must act according to our *principles.*
> The *principle* of economy should come first.

reason is because—reason is that

The reason is because is an awkward and redundant construction. *The reason is that* is preferable.

Awkward:

> The *reason* John didn't come was *because* his car wouldn't start.

Preferable:

> The *reason* John didn't come was *that* his car wouldn't start.

shall—will

Trying to make a distinction between these forms is no longer realistic or useful. They may be used interchangeably in both formal and informal writing.

should of

An incorrect form of "should have."

Correct:

> We *should have* gone yesterday.

Incorrect:

> We *should of* gone yesterday.

supposed to—used to
See "used to."

sure—certainly
Sure should be used to express certainty or assurance.

Example:

I am *sure* that his report is accurate.

Sure should not be used in formal or informal writing to replace "certainly."

Colloquial:

Alabama *sure* has a great team.

Informal:

Alabama *certainly* has a great team.

their—there—they're
Students sometimes fail to distinguish between these homonyms.

Their is a possessive pronoun.

Tom and Jane will drive *their* own car.

There is a demonstrative pronoun.

There is the man we saw yesterday.

Tell me when we get *there.*

They're is a contraction of "they are."

They're scheduled to arrive at noon.

to—too—two
This is another set of homonyms that are often confused.

To is a preposition.

We are going *to* Chicago tomorrow.

Too means "also" or "in addition."

Jane will be there *too.*

Two is a numeral.

There are *two* mistakes on that page.

unique
Unique, like perfect, describes a condition that is absolute. Modifiers should not be used with it.

Correct:

Her problem is *unique.*

Incorrect:

Her problem is *rather unique.*

This dress is *more unique.*

used to—supposed to

Because the final "d" of these verbs disappears when they are pronounced, students sometimes forget to write the complete form.

Correct:

He is *used to* starting on time.
We *used to* get there early.
This is *supposed to* be an open meeting.

Incorrect:

We *use to* get there early.
John is *suppose to* serve as president.

where—that

The colloquial construction "I saw where" or "I read where" should not be used in writing, formal or informal.

Colloquial:

I heard *where* the chairman died.

Acceptable:

I heard *that* the chairman died.
I read *that* the building had burned.

who—whom

Who is the nominative pronoun and should be used when the noun it is replacing would be acting as the subject of a sentence or clause.

Example:

This is the man *who* came with Joe.

Whom is the objective form and should be used when the noun it replaces would be an object.

Example:

There is the man *whom* we saw Friday.

In practice, *who* is generally acceptable in informal writing except when it occurs directly after a preposition.

Acceptable:

There is the man *who* I need to talk to.
Jones is the man to *whom* I will write.

will—shall

See *shall—will.*

wise

Avoid attaching *-wise* to a word as a suffix.

Jargon:

> *Moneywise* he is having troubles.
> *Gradewise* Joan is doing well.

Correct:

> He is having money troubles.
> Joan gets good grades.

would of—would have

Would of is an incorrect form of "would have."

Correct:

> We *would have* come if we had known.

Incorrect:

> We *would of* come if we had known.

Would have should not be used to replace "had."

Correct:

> If I *had* known, I would have told you.

Incorrect:

> If I *would have* known, I would have told you.

A Brief Handbook of Grammar

MECHANICS

Capitalization

The conventions of capitalization are so familiar to most of us that we put capitals in the right places without even thinking about what we are doing. Assuming, then, that most students need little help with capitalization, in this section I will review the principal rules quickly, concentrating on the few instances that may cause problems.

1. Capitalize all proper nouns and the words that are derived from them.

    George is a native of *Chicago.*
    France is a member of the *United Nations.*
    The *Mississippi* flows into the *Gulf of Mexico* at *New Orleans.*
    His command of *English* is poor.
    New Mexico and *Arizona* were the last states to join the union.
    The *United States* entered *World War II* in 1941.
    My *German* class is boring.

2. Capitalize the first word of each sentence.

3. Capitalize words referring to God or other deities: *Christ,* the *Virgin Mary, Buddha,* and *Him* and *He* (when referring to God).

4. Capitalize proper names, the days of the week, the months, and holidays.

5. Capitalize titles when they are used with a name.

    Admiral Zumwalt, Governor Smith, Chief Justice Hughes, Professor Baird, Dr. Watkins, Senator Strong, the President (when referring to the current president of the United States).

6. Capitalize the names of organizations, but not a common noun that designates a type of organization.

    The American Red Cross, the United States Senate, the University of Georgia, the Better Business Bureau, the National Association for the Advancement of Colored People, United States Steel.

But,

A university, a corporation, the federal government, a fraternity, the state hospital.

7. Capitalize the most important words (usually that means all words except prepositions and articles) in the titles of books, plays, poems, magazines, short stories, chapters, and subdivisions of chapters.

The Return of the Native
Death of a Salesman
"To His Coy Mistress"
Saturday Review

Commas

We use commas for two reasons. First, they help to clarify writing by preventing possible ambiguities or misinterpretations; second, they make writing easier to read by marking natural pauses and separations. Ideally, a writer would not worry about the rules that govern the proper use of the comma but would simply insert them as he felt they were needed for clarity or proper emphasis. In practice, however, it is useful to know the chief rules and to get in the habit of observing them almost mechanically.

1. Use commas to set off items in a series. Most authorities specify that one should insert a comma after each element in the series except the last; however, omitting the comma after the word that comes before the conjunction is permissible.

   Standard: The early explorers were searching for gold, spices, and precious gems.
   Acceptable: The early explorers were searching for gold, spices and precious gems.

   Further examples:
   The recipe called for cream, cheese, onions, and marjoram.
   Jack was willing to go to Memphis, Houston, New Orleans, or Atlanta but not to a northern city.
   The campaign was tailored to appeal to middle-aged people, workers, and retired people.
   The semester had been exhausting, frustrating, and generally depressing.

2. Use commas to set off subordinate clauses that come at the beginning of a sentence. This usage is conventional but not mandatory.

   If that pipeline is not repaired, the city will soon run out of fuel.
   Whenever a university sets excessively high standards, it will gain
       professors but lose students.
   Until we have settled that issue, there can be no peace.
   As we drove over the river, we saw that it was flooded.

   If the subordinate clause comes after the main clause, a comma is not necessary.

   We will be there if the plane gets in on time.
   I cannot come until I have finished my work.

3. Use a comma to indicate a pause in a sentence that might be misinterpreted if it were read without interruption.

   John stationed himself by the door Joe had entered, and waited. (If
       the comma is omitted, one gets the impression that it was Joe
       who waited.)
   If grumpy, Henry forgets his manners. (If the comma is omitted, the
       sentence may be read as an introductory clause or a sentence
       fragment.)
   To the insecure, female education may pose a great threat. (If the
       comma is omitted, "insecure" may be mistaken for the modifier
       of female.)
   Badly wounded, Charles slumped to the ground. (Without the
       comma, the sentence is awkward.)

4. Use a comma to separate two independent clauses that are joined by a conjunction. In some cases a comma is not absolutely necessary to clarify the meaning, but it is just as well to form the habit of using it to avoid possible ambiguity.

   He was an ambitious man, but he was not a scrupulous one.
   I hope he is in class today, for his report is the one that interests
       me.
   He will either honor the contract, or we will file suit.
   The defense lawyer withdrew his objections, and agreement was
       quickly reached.

5. Use a comma to set off interrupting, nonrestrictive phrases in a sentence. A nonrestrictive phrase is one that gives information supplementary, rather than essential, to the main idea of the sentence; a restrictive phrase is one that cannot be omitted without

seriously altering that main idea. The following examples should help to clarify this distinction, not always an easy one to make.

Restrictive clause: Anyone *who has been convicted of a felony* may not serve on a jury.

Nonrestrictive clause: A convicted felon, *no matter how good his record,* may not serve on a jury.

Restrictive clause: Students *who have been on scholastic probation for two semesters* will not be allowed to re-register.

Nonrestrictive clause: Students, *who compose one-third of the voting age population in this precinct,* will not be allowed to vote in city elections.

Restrictive clause: The document *that is the foundation of liberty in this country* is the Constitution.

Nonrestrictive clause: There are millions of Americans who know almost nothing about the Constitution, *the document that is the foundation of liberty in this country.*

Notice that in each of the sentences with restrictive clauses, the italicized portion could not be eliminated without drastically altering the meaning of the sentence. Therefore, those portions are not interrupters and should not be set off in commas. The nonrestrictive clauses, on the other hand, could be omitted; therefore, they should be set off by commas.

6. Use commas to set off other kinds of interrupting elements in a sentence: appositives, words or phrases of connection or transition, and terms of address.

Appositives (words or phrases that give us additional information about a term):

Her uncle, *the chairman of the committee,* gave her that information.

Blacklock, *an ex-policeman,* has been elected sheriff.

Tokyo, *the largest city in the world,* has unbelievable traffic problems.

Connectives or words and phrases of transition:

Needless to say, you cannot expect a college to show a profit.

At the second meeting, *however,* they decided the scheme was impractical.

For example, Russia was once our ally, but is now an opponent.

Japan, *on the contrary,* turned from an opponent to a friend.

Terms of address:

Madame Chairman, I would like to submit my report.
May I say, *your honor,* that this has been a difficult decision.

7. Use commas to mark the separation between words or phrases that indicate a contrast.

It is not money we need, but time.
They bring not peace, but a sword.
Tact, not anger, will get you what you want.
Jane is the one you should be scolding, not Sally.

8. Use commas to set off direct quotations in a dialogue.

"Nevertheless," he said, "I intend to do it."
Brian asked her, "What do you think?"
She replied, "Exactly what I thought yesterday."

9. Use commas to mark divisions in dates, addresses, and titles.

Pearl Harbor was bombed on December 7, 1941.
Monday, September 13, is his birthday.
Dr. John T. Clark, chairman
John Brownley, D.D.S.
Williams is a native of Dallas, Texas.
Joseph Miller, M.D., met Geraldine White, R.N., in Memphis, Tennessee, on April 10, 1965.

10. Connecting two sentences or two independent clauses with a comma rather than separating them or joining them with a conjunction is known as a *comma fault,* a *comma splice,* or a *comma blunder.* You should be particularly careful to avoid making this error for two reasons. First, it indicates that you are not fully aware of the meaning of the sentences or clauses you are writing or of the relationship you want to establish between them; second, joining independent elements in this manner may cause a misinterpretation.

For example, notice the problems in these sentences:

We should go tomorrow, we will have more time then. (The cause and effect relationship intended here is concealed because the writer has not joined the independent clauses with "because" or "for.")

The hotel is ugly and old fashioned, it is the fashionable place to stay. (The reader cannot tell if the writer means that the hotel is fashionable because it is ugly and old fashioned or in spite of its being so.)

Congress is going to lose this battle with the President, they will win the next one if they are better prepared. (The idea of contrast is lost here because the sentences have been joined with a comma instead of "but.")

Another reason you should be careful to avoid using a comma splice is that, along with the sentence fragment, it is considered by many English teachers to be a particularly serious grammatical error. There is no point in provoking possibly severe penalties when the error is easily avoided.

Exceptions to the rule: Joining short parallel independent clauses with commas is permissible.

He came, he saw, he conquered.

They married, they had a child, they divorced.

11. Do not overuse commas. Students sometimes get so concerned about correct punctuation that they use more commas than they need to make their meaning clear. The result is choppy sentences that move more slowly than they should. Often you will find that omitting a few of the commas that are dictated by tradition rather than by the need for clarity will improve such sentences.

    Overpunctuated: Last night, when the meeting was over, Randall, tired and, therefore, irritable, made a serious, although not fatal, error.

    Acceptable: Last night when the meeting was over, Randall, tired and therefore irritable, made a serious although not fatal error.

    Overpunctuated: Of course, the solution is not the best one possible, but, under the circumstances, we can live with it.

    Acceptable: Of course the solution is not the best one possible, but under the circumstances we can live with it.

The Semicolon

Learning to use semicolons properly can solve many of your punctuation and transition problems.

1. Use a semicolon to connect clauses that are independent but very closely related.

Jarvis is not at his best when he lectures; he communicates better in seminar classes.

The issue is not who is right and who is wrong; it is who can make his views prevail.

Yesterday we were confronted with the waste of our natural resources; today we are confronted with pollution as well.

Any of these sentences could be separated by a period, but the two ideas expressed in each are so closely related that a semicolon makes for tighter construction.

2. Use a semicolon to precede a transition word that connects independent clauses.

Hawkins will probably be our next district attorney; moreover, he will make a good one.

My opinion will not make any difference; nevertheless, I feel that I must express my views.

The statute of limitations on that crime expired a year ago; as a result, Miller cannot be tried.

3. Use a semicolon to separate a series of clauses or phrases that have internal commas.

Those who participated in the meeting were Gerald Young, the man who had been present at the first test of the plane; Peter Whipple, the pilot who had flown it on the first mission; Robert Mills, the financier who had underwritten the project; and Mrs. Herbert Conn, the wife of the man who had designed the plane.

4. Use the semicolon to separate a series of closely related parallel clauses linked together into a long sentence.

All Christians believe that blessed are the poor and humble, and those who are ill-used by the world; that it is easier for a camel to pass through the eye of a needle than for a rich man to enter the kingdom of heaven; that they should judge not, lest they be judged; that they should swear not at all; that they should love their neighbors as themselves; that if one take their cloak, they should give him their coat also; that they should take no thought for the morrow; that if they would be perfect, they should sell all they have and give it to the poor.

This sentence from John Stuart Mill's *On Liberty* is a model of organization because he has taken advantage of the semicolon to tie several separate ideas together as economically as possible. A student might not want to attempt anything so elaborate, but the technique can be used on a less ambitious scale. For instance:

There are several advantages to the plan: if we lose our director, we can easily find another one; if one of the participants drops out, we will still have enough members to work with; if we should fail, we will not have a great deal of money invested.

The Colon

The uses of the colon are few, but they are important.

1. Use the colon to introduce a list or a series of examples.

    The conditions that we must observe are these: put quotation marks around all quoted matter, give the name of the magazine or book from which it was taken, give the name of the author in full, and specify the date on which it was first published.

    These colleges participated in the conference: the University of Ohio, the University of Dallas, Wayne State University, Westminster College, Harvard University, Rice University, and Our Lady of the Lake College.

2. Use a colon to indicate that an amplification or explanation of your first statement will follow.

    Johnson will give his consent on one condition: all royalties from the article must be contributed to charity.

    The expedition faced almost insuperable problems: there were no maps of the territory, the Indian tribes in that region were hostile, and the Eastern banks refused to advance any money to buy supplies.

3. The colon is one method of introducing a quotation.

    The opening words of the Declaration of Independence give the justification for the document: "When in the course of human events, it becomes necessary for one people to dissolve the political bands which have connected them with another, and to assume among the powers of the earth, the separate and equal station to which the laws of Nature and of Nature's God entitle them, a decent respect to the opinions of mankind requires that they should declare the causes which impel them to the separation."

    Kennedy's inaugural address closed with this statement: "With a good conscience our only sure reward, with history the final judge of our deeds, let us go forth to lead the land we love, asking His blessing and His help, but knowing that here on earth God's work must truly be our own.''

Dashes and Dots

Make sparing use of dashes as punctuation because it is all too easy to slip into the habit of relying on a dash instead of stopping to think what kind of punctuation would best meet your needs. Probably you should limit them to two functions.

1. Use dashes to set off parenthetical material when you want to emphasize the contrast between that material and the rest of the sentence.

    To lose one's temper because of a slighting remark—and certainly there are times when it is difficult not to do so—is a self-defeating indulgence.

    In spite of the delays and interruptions—and God knows we had plenty of them—we managed to finish the project on time.

2. Use a dash to indicate any sudden change in the structure or direction of a sentence.

    As a stern Calvinist, Jordan believed in predestination, original sin, the election of saints—and his own infallibility.

    Michael had everything she admired in a man: humor, ability, elegant manners, rugged good looks—and a great deal of money.

    If you look at the issue from the Communists' point of view—but then we are not capable of doing that.

    Dots, the symbol of an ellipsis or omission, have only one major function in writing, but it is an important one. You should use three separated dots (. . .) to indicate that you have omitted something from a quotation. If what remains forms a complete sentence, add a fourth dot (. . . .) to stand for the period of that sentence. It is essential that you use this symbol to indicate any omissions; otherwise you may mislead your audience by giving the impression that you are quoting in full. Here are two examples of its use:

Unless anyone who approves of punishment for the promulgation of opinions flatters himself that he is a wiser and better man than Marcus Aurelius . . . let him abstain from that joint assumption of infallibility of himself and the multitude, which the great Antoninus made with so unfortunate a result.

—John Stuart Mill

I believe that no people ever groaned under the heavy yoke of slavery but when they deserved it. This may be called a severe censure upon by far the greatest part of the nations of the world who are involved in the miseries of servitude. But however they may be thought by some to deserve commiseration, the censure is just. . . . The truth is, all might be free, if they valued freedom and defended it as they should.

—Samuel Adams

Quotation Marks

1. Quotation marks are used around all quoted material that is within the text of any writing.

   Eldridge Cleaver says, "There is in James Baldwin's work the most grueling, agonizing, total hatred of blacks . . . that one can find in the writings of any black American writer of note in our time."

   If, however, a quotation runs to more than three lines, it may be indented and single spaced in the text and the quotation marks omitted. There are numerous examples of that form in this text. If you are giving a quotation within another run-in quotation, single quotation marks should go around the inside quotation.

   James remarked, "My father's favorite slogan was 'There's a sucker born every minute.' "

2. Occasionally you may want to use quotation marks to set off a word that you are using humorously or ironically. Use this device sparingly because too often it gives the impression you are apologizing for your diction. If you think a word is unsuitable, get rid of it rather than put it in quotation marks.

   Acceptable: Their "benefactors" absconded with the last of their savings.

   The language of the petition was, you might say, "down-to-earth."
   Apologetic: My roommate is a real "nut."

3. Use quotation marks to identify a word or term to which you wish to call special attention.

   "Hopefully" is a word often used incorrectly.
   In this context the word "discipline" refers to a special field of study.

4. Use quotation marks around the titles of articles, short stories, short poems, essays, and sometimes chapter headings.

"The Fall of the House of Usher"
"To His Coy Mistress"
"The Double Standard of Aging"

5. Commas and periods always are placed inside quotation marks. Semicolons and colons are placed outside quotation marks. Question marks and exclamation points may be placed inside or outside the quotation marks, depending on the context. If they belong to the quoted portion, they go inside; if they belong to the sentence as a whole, they go outside.

He made frequent use of the terms "hip," "square," and "cool it."
"If I come," he said, "it will be after lunch."
Marx always thought of himself as a "man of reason"; nevertheless, his philosophy is not always a rational one.
She said, "He is absolutely insane!"
Is this an instance of "checks and balances"?

The Apostrophe

1. The apostrophe is followed by an *s* to form the possessive of single nouns.

the cook's apron
a bride's book
our doctor's daughter
that child's toy

2. An apostrophe is placed after the *s* to form the possessive of plural nouns ending in *s* or of most names ending in *s*.

the boys' meeting
those students' books
Charles' graduation
the Jones' house

3. The apostrophe followed by an *s* is used to form the possessive of compound or group nouns or irregular plural forms.

the team's record
his sister-in-law's car
the women's luncheon
children's clothing

Notice that possessive pronouns are complete as they stand and do not take an apostrophe. *His, hers, their, its, our, my, mine, yours,* and so on.

4. An apostrophe is used to signal the omitted letter or letters in a contraction.

They're going to be late.
We're not interested in opera.
We shouldn't be here.
Jim just can't cope with exams.

5. An apostrophe is used to form the plural of individual letters or numbers.

He consistently mispronounces his *s*'s.
Jerry confuses his 6's and his 9's.

The Hyphen

Except for the stipulation that a hyphen is used to divide a word at the end of a line, there are few absolute rules for the use of the hyphen. There are some useful conventions.

1. Use a hyphen to divide a word that comes at the end of a line or to show the division of a word into syllables. There are correct and incorrect ways to divide words; when in doubt, check a dictionary for the correct form.

2. Use a hyphen in most common compounds:

mother-in-law
ten-year-old
button-down collar
sergeant-at-arms
self-help books
lieutenant-governor

3. Use a hyphen to connect the elements of a compound modifier.

a go-to-hell attitude
a self-styled liberal
a hang-dog look
down-at-the-heel appearance
a run-of-the-mill movie
a play-by-play description

4. Use a hyphen between the prefix *ex* and a noun and after a prefix that comes before a proper noun.

ex-football player
ex-husband

a pro-Japanese article
anti-Russian feelings
pro-Texan attitude
super-American

Italics

In writing or typing, an underlined word is considered to be italicized; in print, the italicized words appear in a special kind of print. There are four principal uses for italics.

1. Use italics to indicate the names of books, magazines or newspapers, movies or plays, long poems or musical compositions, and, in most cases, the names of ships, or special airplanes.

   Camus' *The Stranger*
   Williams' *The Glass Menagerie*
   Milton's *Paradise Lost*
   The New York Times
   Air Force One
   U.S.S. *Enterprise*
   The Barber of Seville
   Playboy

2. Use italics for foreign words and phrases that are not widely used in English.

   au courant
   deus ex machina
   machismo
   hubris
   bête noire

3. You may use italics instead of quotation marks to call special attention to a word.

   One variety of jargon is called *cant.*
   The concept of *due process* is of particular significance here.

4. Use italics to emphasize a word.

   His remarks cannot be called simply dissent; they must be called *treason.*
   Justice, not legality, is the issue before us.

   Be careful not to overuse this technique of italicizing for emphasis. A passage that is loaded with underlined words gives the reader the feeling that he is being shouted at.

PROBLEMS IN SENTENCE STRUCTURE

Fragments

The conventions of writing expository prose demand that, with only rare exceptions, you express yourself in complete sentences; that is, groups of words that contain subjects and verbs and that express a complete thought. There are at least three reasons for observing this rule. A practical one is that most composition teachers consider a fragment a serious grammatical error, an indication that the student is either extremely careless or does not understand how the language works. Another reason you should avoid writing in fragments is that they violate traditional sentence patterns, and therefore they interrupt the continuity of your writing and interfere with communication. A third reason for avoiding them is that a fragment is the kind of error that attracts the reader's attention and, all too often, his disapproval. Although an occasional well-chosen fragment may serve a good purpose in narrative and descriptive writing, the student writer will usually do better to express his ideas in complete sentences. It is not wise to imitate the style of the ad writers who sprinkle their copy with needless fragments as a way of catching the reader's attention.

The kinds of fragments that appear most often in student writing are usually written unintentionally, the result of the student's forgetting certain principles of grammar. Those principles are: first, a verbal, that is an infinitive, a participle, or a gerund, cannot function as the verb of a sentence; second, a dependent or subordinate clause cannot stand by itself as a sentence; third, phrases or clauses should not be separated from the rest of the sentence by a period.

The kind of verbals that are most often confused with verbs are the present participle and the infinitive. The present participle is the -ing form of the verb: *going, being, running, playing,* and so forth. The infinitive is the "to" form of the verb: *to run, to see, to understand, to write,* and so forth. Here are some examples from student papers that illustrate the kind of errors that result from confusing these verbals with true verb forms.

1. "The author makes suburbia seem inviting. *One reason being the advantages children get from living there.*" (Here the writer is confusing "being" with "is." The problem may be that she hesitates to say "reason is the advantages," but she is uncertain how to rephrase it. The result of her confusion is a sentence fragment.)
2. "Young people need to be on their own. *To show their parents that they are reliable.*" (Apparently the student wanted to avoid repeating

"Young people need," but the result is that the second sentence has no subject. He could have solved the problem by connecting the parts with "and.")

3. "The authorities did not approve of their acts. *These acts being considered detrimental to society.*" (The second clause is a modifier that the student apparently added as an afterthought. The clause is actually redundant and should either be omitted or incorporated into the main part of the sentence.)

4. "Both writers believe in freedom. *Mill saying that man cannot grow without freedom and Huxley saying that man is no better than an animal if he does not have freedom.*" (The student probably lost track of his main verbs in this long pseudosentence. He could solve the problem by substituting a comma for the period after the first "freedom" or by simply substituting "says" for "saying" after both "Mill" and "Huxley.")

Remembering one simple rule will eliminate most of these -ing sentence fragments: An -ing verb form can *never* act as the main verb of a sentence unless it is accompanied by an auxiliary verb.

Another kind of fragment occurs when a writer uses a dependent or subordinate clause as a sentence. This error seems to result from the writer's failure to recognize that certain words or constructions signal certain kinds of clauses. The commonest are these:

If, although, while, even, when, in spite of, since, and *because* signal the beginning of a dependent clause.

That, thus, therefore, so, as, for (and sometimes *because* and *since*) signal the beginning of a subordinate clause.

The relative pronouns *who, whoever, which, where,* and *that* signal the beginning of a subordinate clause.

In most cases, an unpunctuated group gof words that is introduced by one of these terms is not a complete sentence because it expresses only part of the author's full meaning. Here are some examples from student papers that illustrate these kinds of sentence fragments.

1. Kazin felt as if he were going to school more to satisfy his parents than himself. *Since he was their first child to be an American.* (Kazin's reason for feeling as he does is expressed in the clause following "since"; therefore, that clause should not be written as a separate sentence.)

2. Sartre believes that an individual's own character shapes his destiny. *While Sullivan believes that external forces are more important.* (The idea of contrast is essential to the relationship of these two clauses; therefore they should have been connected with a comma.

The second part might also have been written: "Sullivan, on the other hand, believes that external forces are more important.")

3. *If the legislature thought the standards of the University were going down.* ("If" always implies "then." The reader is waiting for the "then" part of the statement but never gets it.)

4. Trying to walk across the room, I accidentally fell over an ash tray. *Which had been left in the middle of the floor along with other miscellaneous objects.* ("Which" and everything that follows it modify "ash tray" and should not be detached from it.)

The third common kind of sentence fragment seems to result from students' failure to realize that clauses and phrases are groups of words functioning as single words, and are not sentences in themselves.

1. In his conclusion the author stresses another issue. *A point that everyone today is concerned about—individuality.* (The fragment is only an appositive phrase elaborating on the word "issue" and does not express a complete idea.)

2. When both the husband and wife are working together to keep their household going, each one feels needed. *He in a major way and she in a minor way.* (The fragment has no verb and cannot function as a sentence.)

3. "Free souls" best describes these street vendors. *Ordinary people with a unique life style who should be allowed to follow their own inclinations.* (Again, the entire fragment is a modifying phrase, not an independent idea.)

4. Examples of the kind of thing Mill is talking about happen every day. *Not only here but elsewhere in the world.* (The fragment here is an adverbial phrase that modifies "happen" and contains neither a verb nor a complete idea.)

The practiced writer who is striving for a certain effect may sometimes use a fragmentary phrase effectively. For example, he might write,

Some people claim that all rhetoric seeks to deceive. *Not necessarily.*

or

Waste, inefficiency, and corruption. These are the evils that plague our cities.

Few teachers object to fragments such as these, which are obviously deliberate and which draw special attention to a major point. But unless you are confident that you can make a sentence fragment an asset rather than a defect, you would do better to avoid them altogether.

Run-on and Fused Sentences

Although the parts of sentences should not be separated into frag-ments, neither should several independent clauses be tacked together by conjunctions to form a long rambling run-on sentence that contains several separate ideas.

Run-on: We came around the corner and saw that a crowd had gathered and there was obviously some kind of trouble and the police were trying to stop it.

Acceptable: As we came around the corner, we saw a crowd gathered. Apparently there was some kind of trouble that the police were trying to stop.

Run-on: The person who wants to persuade his audience must remember who they are and he has to think about what kind of argu-ments they will respond to for if he does not they will not listen to him and he will have wasted his time.

Acceptable: The person who wants to persuade his audience must remember who they are and what kind of arguments they will respond to. If he does not, he will have wasted his time because they will not listen to him.

Run-on: The student radicals at any college are only a small frac-tion of the whole and authorities get too upset about them and they overreact and then the situation gets worse, but the officials should just let the radicals talk and then everyone would realize how ridiculous they are.

Acceptable: College authorities allow themselves to get too upset about student radicals, who really constitute only a small fraction of the whole. By overreacting the authorities make the situation worse. If they would just let the radicals talk, everyone would soon realize how ridiculous the radicals are.

Comma Splice

See "Comma Fault" and "Comma Splice" under *Mechanics.*

Faulty Parallelism

The elements of a sentence that are alike in function should also be alike in form. For example, if you were writing about the respon-sibilities of a jury, you might do it like this:

The jury's job is to listen to the evidence, to consider it fairly and impartially, and to render a verdict that is just to both parties.

Or if you wanted to combine several ideas in one sentence you might do it like this:

The United States' ten-year involvement in the Vietnam war caused dissension in this country, aggravated inflation, and diverted resources from our domestic programs.

Sentences in which the structure is not parallel may be understandable, but often they are awkward, difficult to read, and not as unified or smooth as they might be. Notice these examples of faulty parallelism from student themes.

Original: The author's comparison of frozen meat to leather reminds one of toughness, dryness, unchewable, and not very tasty.

Revision: The author's comparison of frozen meat to leather suggests that the meat is tough, dry, unchewable, and not very tasty.

Original: After going through many frustrations and problems and then you find happiness, you will enjoy it more.

Revision: Going through many frustrations and problems and then finding happiness makes the happiness more enjoyable.

Original: The word "humanitarian" suggests the best qualities of mankind: tenderness, merciful, and considerate.

Revision: The word "humanitarian" suggests the best qualities of mankind: tenderness, mercy, and consideration.

Original: The teachers were making him compete against others instead of to teach him anything.

Revision: The teachers were making him compete against others instead of trying to teach him anything.

Original: The main assets of a state university are economical, convenience, and the atmosphere is friendly.

Revision: The main assets of a state university are economy, convenience, and friendly atmosphere.

Dangling Modifiers

A dangling modifier is a modifying phrase or clause that either has nothing to modify or, because of the way it is placed in the sentence, modifies a term other than the one for which it was intended. A dangling modifier is at best confusing, at worst ludicrous. Traditional English sentence patterns lead the reader to believe that the thing to be modified will come after the modifier. When it does not, the reader is annoyed, perplexed, or perhaps amused. In any case, the effect is not what the writer intended.

Having read "Science Has Spoiled My Supper," a TV dinner just does not appeal to me. (The reader is momentarily confused because he knows the TV dinner hasn't done the reading.)

Viewed from the top floor, I found the panorama exciting. (The reader expects to learn what is being viewed from the top floor; obviously "I" isn't viewing himself from the top floor.)

Lacking common sense, motorcycle riding is dangerous. (The reader expects to find out who is lacking common sense, but he is never told.)

Most sentences containing dangling modifiers are more awkward than they are obscure; with a little effort the reader can usually decipher their intended meaning. Nevertheless the student who writes such sentences reveals that he does not have a clear idea of the relationship between the parts of his sentence. Here are some more examples that illustrate the point.

Original: When hiring employees, their appearance and attitude is an employer's main concern.

Revision: When hiring employees, an employer must be concerned about their attitude and appearance.

Original: While in the process of growing up, parents give their children more freedom as they grow older.

Revision: As children grow older, parents usually give them more freedom. (The original is redundant as well as badly constructed.)

Original: By forcing a student to dress according to a code, his creativity is stifled and discouraged.

Revision: By forcing students to dress according to a code, school authorities stifle and discourage their creativity.

Notice that in two out of three of these sentences, part of the problem is that the subject of the main clause is an abstraction rather than a person or thing. If the writer had used a concrete subject, he would probably have realized that the modifier did not fit. Excessive use of the passive voice in the main clause also seems to produce dangling modifiers.

Original: After having argued all morning, a decision was reached.

Revision: After having argued all morning, they reached a decision.

Original: By learning about genetics, many children with birth defects could be avoided.

Revision: By learning about genetics, many people could avoid having children with birth defects.

Original: When given all the relevant information, problems of this kind can be solved.

Revision: When given all the relevant information, people can solve this kind of problem.

Probably the best way to avoid writing dangling modifiers is to think out your entire sentence before you begin to write it. If you know precisely what you are going to say, you are not apt to change directions in the middle of the sentence.

Faulty Predication

A subject and a verb are necessary parts of any sentence. The relationship between them and any element that may follow, such as an object or a complement, is called the "predication" of the sentence. When a writer constructs a sentence that sets up an illogical or unrealistic relationship among the parts of the sentence, the resulting error is called "faulty predication." These errors almost always stem from the writer's doing one of two things: first, completing the verb "to be" with an illogical complement; or, second, combining a subject and verb that cannot reasonably go together.

A quick review of the conventions governing the patterns of subject/linking verb/complement sentences may help you to understand the problem of illogical complements. The chief linking verb that concerns us here is "to be" in all its forms; am, are, is; was, were; shall be, will be; have been, has been; had been; shall have been, will have been. When one of these forms is the main verb in a sentence, the word or phrase that completes it can be one of only two things: a noun or noun phrase, or an adjective or adjective phrase. The reason for this restriction is that the verb "to be" says something *about* the subject; it either equates it with something else or precedes a description of it. For this reason, the word that follows the linking verb must be one that fits with it logically. You are setting up a kind of equation, and for that equation to make sense the second part of it must make a reasonable statement about the first part.

Here are some student examples that illustrate errors in predication with the verb "to be."

Original: The idea is unfavorable to the American society. (An idea cannot logically have the quality of being favorable or unfavorable.)

Revision: The idea is distasteful to the American society.

Original: When the Negro came to our country it was in the form of slavery. (Negro cannot logically be a form of slavery.)

Revision: When the Negro came to our country, he came as a slave.

Original: A weather factor to be considered is school starting early. (School starting early cannot reasonably be equated with a weather factor.)

Revision: Because school starts early, the weather will be warm in the first months of the semester.

Original: Man is not infallibility. (Infallibility is an abstract characteristic and cannot be equated with man.)

Revision: Man is not infallible.

Original: An example of early conditioning is when small children are taught to hate flowers and books. (This sentence illustrates the commonest predication error; a noun cannot equal "when.")

Revision: An example of early conditioning is teaching small children to hate flowers and books.

Original: Subversive propaganda is when someone tries to turn people against their country. (Again, a noun cannot equal "when.")

Revision: Subversive propaganda is literature designed to turn people against their country.

You can avoid this "is-when" pitfall by simply making it a rule never to use that particular word combination.

The second kind of predication error results from writers' combining subjects and verbs that cannot logically go together.

Original: Both novels want the reader to be aware of the dangers of too much security. (A novel is an inanimate object that cannot want anything.)

Revision: Both novelists want the reader to be aware of the dangers of too much security.

Original: Some of America's problems can be dealt with rapidly and with a degree of certainty, but others evade this feeling of certainty. ("Problems" is an abstract term that cannot combine with the verb "evade.")

Revision: Some of America's problems can be dealt with rapidly and with some certainty; others cannot.

Original: Larger cars respect the Volkswagen because of the way it can get through congested traffic. (Again, a car is an inanimate object that cannot respect something else.)

Revision: The drivers of large cars respect Volkswagen drivers because of the way they can get through congested traffic.

Original: The wishes of the majority approved the Articles of Confederation, but then changed their minds after it was adopted. (The writer seems to have forgotten that his subject is "wishes" and that wishes do not have minds to change.)

Revision: Most people approved the Articles of Confederation but changed their minds after it was adopted.

VERBS

The Terminology of Verbs

Agreement   The rule that there must be agreement between the subject and verb of a sentence means that the form of the verb must show the same number and person as the subject. Plural subjects take plural verb forms; singular subjects take singular verb forms. A first person subject must take a first person verb, a second person subject must take a second person verb, and so on.

I am angry with the crowd.
He is angry with the crowd.
They are angry with the crowd.

Auxiliary verbs   Auxiliary verbs are verbs that are used with other verbs to show tense, voice, or mood. The chief ones are *be, can, have, do, may, might, should, will,* and *would.*

The compliment *was* returned.
I *should* have enough money by tomorrow.
This *has* been a terrible ordeal for her.
Jim *is* planning on a big crop.

Linking verb   A linking verb is one that acts as a connector between the subject and the predicate nominative or predicate adjective that completes the sentence or clause. The verb *to be* is the commonest linking verb; other verbs that often function as linking verbs are *feel, seem, appear, look, become,* and *remain.* If you can substitute a form of *to be* for the verb in a sentence and retain the approximate meaning of the original, the verb is acting as a linking verb.

This room *seems* dark. = This room *is* dark.
James *looks* sick. = James *is* sick.

Mood Mood is a term used to describe the manner in which a verb is being used. There are three grammatical moods: indicative, subjunctive, and imperative. The indicative mood is used in sentences stating facts or propositions in either declarative or interrogative forms; the subjunctive mood is used in sentences expressing doubt, wishfulness, or a statement that is contrary to fact; the imperative mood is used in sentences expressing commands.

Number The terms "singular" and "plural" designate the number of a verb.

Regular/irregular verbs Regular verbs are inflected in the standard manner by adding *-ed* to the present form to form the past and the past participle forms. *Look* and *kill* are typical regular verbs. Irregular verbs are inflected by changing the root of the verb. Typical examples are *eat, ate, eaten; see, saw, seen; go, went, gone.* A list of the most common irregular verbs and their principal parts is given further on in this section.

Tense Tense refers to the time designated by a verb: present, past, or future.

Transitive/intransitive verbs A transitive verb is one that takes a direct object. An intransitive verb is one that does not take a direct object.

> *Transitive:* The dog always *lays* his bone on the porch.
> *Intransitive:* The dogs *lie* peacefully on the porch.

Verbals Verbals are words that are constructed from verbs but act in other capacities. The three forms are gerunds, participles, and infinitives.

Gerunds, which are formed by adding *-ing* to the present tense, act chiefly as nouns.

> *Swimming* is his favorite sport.
> It is easy to postpone your *studying.*

Participles may be in the past or progressive form of the verb and may be active or passive. In most cases they act as modifiers.

> *Having considered* the matter carefully, Joe spoke.
> *Seen* from this angle, the building is handsome.

The infinitive is the *to* form of a verb: *to be, to see, to eat.* It usually functions as a noun but can also serve as an adjective or adverb.

Harry is eager *to leave* for medical school.
To know her is *to love* her.
To see the other man's point of view is not easy.

Voice, active and passive When the verb of a sentence is in the active voice, the subject is doing the acting; when it is in the passive voice, the subject is being acted upon.

Active: Jealousy *consumed* the audience as they watched.
Passive: As the audience watched, it *was consumed* by jealousy.

Problems with Verbs

1. *Disagreement between subject and verb in number and person.* Although almost every college student knows that the subject and verb of a sentence must agree in number and person, agreement errors seem to be a persistent problem with some writers. The following rules cover those constructions that cause most of the difficulties.

   a. If two or more subjects in a sentence are connected by *and,* the verb should be plural.

      Incorrect: Overthrowing the present government and replacing it with a people's democracy *is* two of his major objectives.
      Correct: Overthrowing the present government and replacing it with a people's democracy *are* two of his major objectives.
      Incorrect: Sylvia, Grace, and I *was* going to town.
      Correct: Sylvia, Grace, and I *were* going to town.

   There is an exception. If the two subjects connected by *and* are considered a unit, a singular verb should be used.
      Correct: "Law and order" *is* a popular slogan.
      Gin and tonic *is* considered a sophisticated drink.

   b. If two or more subjects in a sentence are joined by *or, nor,* or *but,* the verb should be singular.

      Incorrect: Either Stanley or Roger *are* to be nominated.
      Correct: Either Stanley or Roger *is* to be nominated.

      Incorrect: Not prudence, but courage *are* needed here.
      Correct: Not prudence, but courage *is* needed here.

   c. When a modifying phrase comes between the subject and the verb, the verb should agree with the subject of the sentence.

Incorrect: A person in one of these occupations *have* to be pleasant and friendly.

Correct: A person in one of these occupations *has* to be pleasant and friendly.

Incorrect: Words such as "stuffy," "bleak," and "dreary" *connotes* unpleasantness.

Correct: Words such as "stuffy," "bleak," and "dreary" connote unpleasantness.

Incorrect: Other high quality colleges in Texas, such as Rice, Baylor, Texas Christian, and Southern Methodist, *costs* thousands of dollars more in tuition.

Correct: Other high quality colleges in Texas, such as Rice, Baylor, Texas Christian, and Southern Methodist, *cost* thousands of dollars more in tuition.

d. When a sentence begins with *there* or *here* followed by a linking verb, the verb should agree with the subject that follows the verb.

Incorrect: There *is* many things about this program that concern us.

Correct: There *are* many things about this program that concern us.

Incorrect: *Is* there a lot of children in your neighborhood?
Correct: *Are* there a lot of children in your neighborhood?

Incorrect: Here *is* the rules of the game.
Correct: Here *are* the rules of the game.

e. Pronouns that refer to individual units take a singular verb; the commonest of these pronouns are *each, every, everyone, nobody, somebody, everybody, anybody, one, either,* and *neither*.

Incorrect: Everyone of them *are* guilty.
Correct: Everyone of them *is* guilty.

Incorrect: Neither of them *admit* the error.
Correct: Neither of them *admits* the error.

f. The pronouns *any* and *none* may take either singular or plural verbs.

None of the boys *was* responsible for the theft.
None of the boys *were* responsible for the theft.
Any of the answers *is* acceptable.
Are any of the answers acceptable?

g. In a sentence of the subject/verb/complement pattern the verb agrees with the subject rather than the complement.

Incorrect: One characteristic of jargon *are* euphemisms.
Correct: One characteristic of jargon *is* euphemisms.

Incorrect: Too many absences *was* the chief problem.
Correct: Too many absences *were* the chief problem.

h. Collective nouns may take a singular or plural subject, depending on the context in which they are used. If the noun refers to a unit, a singular verb should be used; if the context suggests several individuals considered separately, a plural verb should be used.

The congregation *wants* a new minister.
The congregation *were* divided on the issue.
The team *has* a wonderful record.
The winning team *divide* the gate receipts among the members.

i. Some nouns that appear to be plural in form are, in practice, singular and should take singular verbs. Some of the more common nouns of this kind are *linguistics, ethics, mathematics, physics, news, economics,* and *electronics.*

The news tonight *is* depressing.
Ethics *is* the study of the good life.

2. *The use of nonstandard forms for the past tense or past participle of irregular verbs.* The only practical way to avoid using nonstandard verb forms is to memorize the principal parts of the most common irregular verbs so well that their use becomes automatic; for less common ones such as *abide, strive,* or *tread,* check the dictionary if you are in doubt. If the verb is regular, the dictionary will give only the present form; if it is irregular, all three forms will be given. Be particularly careful to avoid substituting the past form of a verb for a past participle form when the two are different. The following examples are incorrect:

I *have* already *ate.*
Jack *had ran* out of money.

Principal Parts of the Common Irregular Verbs

Present	Past	Past Participle
awake	awoke, awaked	awoke, awaked
be	was	been
bite	bit	bitten

Present	Past	Past Participle
blow	blew	blown
break	broke	broken
bring	brought	brought
buy	bought	bought
catch	caught	caught
choose	chose	chosen
come	came	come
cost	cost	cost
cut	cut	cut
do	did	done
dive	dove, dived	dived
drag	dragged	dragged
drink	drank	drunk
drive	drove	driven
eat	ate	eaten
fall	fell	fallen
freeze	froze	frozen
give	gave	given
grind	ground	ground
grow	grew	grown
hang (execute)	hanged	hanged
hang (suspend)	hung	hung
hurt	hurt	hurt
keep	kept	kept
know	knew	known
lay	laid	laid
leave	left	left
lead	led	led
let	let	let
lie	lay	lain
lose	lost	lost
ride	rode	ridden
ring	rang	rung
rise	rose	risen
see	saw	seen
shake	shook	shaken
shrink	shrank	shrunk
sing	sang	sung
speak	spoke	spoken
steal	stole	stolen
swim	swam	swum

Present	Past	Past Participle
swear	swore	sworn
swing	swung	swung
take	took	taken
write	wrote	written

3. *Inconsistency of verb tenses.* Keep the tenses of verbs in a paper or theme consistent, switching from past to present only if the logic of your writing requires it.

   a. Make the tense of a subordinate clause logically consistent with that of the main clause.

     Consistent: After they heard the main speaker, they were ready to leave.

     Inconsistent: After they heard the main speaker, they are ready to leave.

     Consistent: As the crowd gathers, Jim becomes more and more excited.

     Inconsistent: As the crowd gathers, Jim became more and more excited.

   b. Do not switch back and forth from past to present tense when you are writing straight expository prose.

     Inconsistent: The author's examples *are* [present] not randomly chosen. He *told* [past] of conversations with several officers, but he *does not* [present] mention any conversations with enlisted men. This kind of sampling technique *invalidated* [past] his reasoning.

     Consistent: In 1973 the gasoline consumers of this country faced a bitter choice. They had to decide whether they were going to pay exorbitant prices for their gasoline, or whether they were going to accept rationing.

If, however, the logic of your exposition demands that you speak of certain events in the past, you may mix your tenses without being inconsistent.

     We now know that Hitler was more than a tyrant; he was a master psychologist as well.

It is customary to use the present tense in writing of documents or works of literature, regardless of when they were written.

> In the *Republic* Plato asserts that all art is inherently inferior because it is, by definition, an imitation.

> The Constitution of the United States sharply restricts the power of the individual states.

> In his novel *Herzog* Saul Bellow writes with contempt of people he calls "reality teachers."

4. *Misuse of the subjunctive mood of verbs.* When the context of a sentence calls for it, use the subjunctive mood of a verb. By contemporary standards of usage, the subjunctive mood is necessary in only a few instances.

  a. Use the subjunctive mood to express a wish or to make a statement that is contrary to fact.

> *Colloquial:* If I *was* you, I would refuse to go.
> *Preferable:* If I *were* you, I would refuse to go.

> *Colloquial:* We wish that it *was* possible to compromise.
> *Preferable:* We wish that it *were* possible to compromise.

  b. Use the subjunctive mood in *that*-clauses which follow verbs indicating requests, orders, or suggestions.

> I suggest that he *be given* another chance.
> Stiles moved that the committee *adjourn.*
> The judge ordered that the prisoner *be executed* on May 1.

PRONOUNS

The Terminology of Pronouns

Agreement The rule stating that pronouns must agree with their antecedents means that a pronoun must be of the same gender, number, and person as the noun for which it stands.

Case Pronouns have three categories of syntactic relationship, or cases: subjective, objective, and possessive.
Subjective pronouns function as subjects and as subjective complements; they are *I, you, he, she, it; we, you, they,* and *who.*
Objective pronouns function as objects; they are *me, you, him, her; us, you, them,* and *whom.*

Possessive pronouns show possession: they are *my (mine), your (yours), his, her (hers), its; our (ours), your (yours), their (theirs),* and *whose.*

Demonstrative pronouns   Demonstrative pronouns indicate or point out; they have the special function of specifying relative position. The singular demonstrative pronouns are *this* and *that;* the plural forms are *these* and *those.*

Indefinite pronouns   Indefinite pronouns have no gender or case. They include *any, anyone, anybody, anything, all, another, both, each, either, everybody, everyone, everything, nobody, none, no one, one, other, several, some, somebody, someone, something.*

Interrogative pronouns   Interrogative pronouns are used to state direct questions. They are *who, whom, which, what.* The *whoever, whatever,* and *whichever* forms are sometimes used in interrogative phrases.

Reciprocal pronouns   Two pronoun phrases indicate action between or among individuals or groups and thus are called reciprocal pronouns. They are *each other* and *one another.*

Reflexive pronouns   Reflexive pronouns are created by adding *-self* to personal pronoun forms. They are *myself, yourself, himself, herself, itself; ourselves, yourselves, themselves.* Avoid the nonstandard forms *hisself* and *theirselves.*

Reference   The rule stating pronoun reference cannot be faulty means that a pronoun must take the place of an identifiable unit, a word or clause, in the same sentence or in a previous sentence.

Relative pronouns   Relative pronouns introduce phrases or clauses. They are *that, what, which, who, whom,* and *whose.* The *-ever* forms of interrogative pronouns also act as relative pronouns.

Problems with Pronouns

1. Probably the commonest pronoun errors result from writers' not observing the convention that a pronoun must agree with its antecedent in person, number, and gender. While that convention is violated frequently in informal speech, it is well to observe it in all but the most informal writing. The rules governing pronoun usage in those constructions that cause the most difficulty are as follows:

a. Pronouns that refer to plural subjects, whether they are plural in form or two subjects connected with *and,* must be plural.

Incorrect: To me, *every* person is an individual and *they* should be treated as one. (*Every* is singular, but the pronoun *they* is plural.)

Correct: To me, *every* person is an individual and *he* should be treated as one.

Incorrect: The author explains how children are taught to have feelings that are not *his.* (*His* refers to children; thus it should be replaced by the plural form.)

Correct: The author explains how children are taught to have feelings that are not *theirs.*

Incorrect: Students should attend a college or university that best meets *his* needs and where there are other students like *him.* (*Students* is plural, but *his* and *him* are singular.)

Correct: Students should attend a college or university that best meets *their* needs and where there are other students like *them.*

b. The indefinite pronouns *anybody, anyone, everyone, everybody, each, nobody, no one, either,* and *neither* are singular in form and should be followed by singular pronouns. Constructions in which these pronouns are followed by a prepositional phrase with a plural word are particularly troublesome.

Incorrect: *Everyone* feels that *their* rights have been violated.

Correct: *Everyone* feels that *his* rights have been violated.

Incorrect: *Neither* of the suspects was told of *their* rights.

Correct: *Neither* of the suspects was told of *his* rights.

Incorrect: *Anybody* who invested in that stock lost *their* money.

Correct: *Anybody* who invested in that stock lost *his* money.

c. The indefinite pronouns *both, all,* and sometimes *none* are plural in form and should be followed by plural pronouns.

Incorrect: *Both* of the boys *is* guilty.

Correct: *Both* of the boys *are* guilty.

None of the contestants had *their* entries returned.

Not *all* of the soldiers have received *their* orders.

d. The pronouns that follow collective nouns may be either singular or plural in form, depending on the context of the sentence. If the collective noun seems to refer to a unit, use the singular pronoun; if it seems to refer to several individuals, use the plural pronoun.

The *committee* went beyond the instructions that were given *it*.
The *committee* complained that the work took an excessive amount of *their* time. (Notice that inserting "members" after committee would remove any possible confusion.)
That *team* always rose to any challenge that was given to *it*.
The *teams'* uniforms were given to *them* yesterday.

e. Use the relative pronoun *who* when the antecedent is a person; use the relative pronoun *which* or *that* if the antecedent is an animal or thing. The use of *that* to refer to people is now generally accepted, but *who* remains preferable.

> *Incorrect:*   Those are the sailors *which* were decorated.
> *Acceptable:*   Those are the sailors *that* were decorated.
> *Preferable:*   Those are the sailors *who* were decorated.

There is an exception. Because there is no possessive form of the pronoun *which,* the possessive form *whose* may sometimes be used to avoid awkward constructions.

> *Awkward:*   The Bureaus of Agriculture and Labor were among those the appropriations *of which* were cut.
> *Preferable:*   The Bureaus of Agriculture and Labor were among those *whose* appropriations were cut.

2. Another common error in pronoun usage results from the writer's failing to distinguish between the subjective and objective forms of pronouns when they are used in phrases or as the objects of prepositions or transitive verbs. To choose the correct form you must determine how the pronoun is functioning in the phrase or sentence. If it is functioning as a subject or as a predicate nominative, use the subjective form of the pronoun; if it is functioning as an object or in apposition with an object, use the objective form. Mastering the following guidelines should help to clarify the problem.

a. Use the subjective form for a pronoun that is the subject of a sentence.

> *Incorrect:*   The Cooks and *us* are going to the ballet next week.
> *Correct:*   The Cooks and *we* are going to the ballet next week.

Incorrect: Jeffrey and *him* were given special recognition.
Correct: Jeffrey and *he* were given special recognition.

Note that the problem here is caused by the plural subject. Almost no one would write "Us are going to the ballet." Therefore, to test your construction, phrase the sentence as it would be phrased if the pronoun were the only subject.

b. Use the subjective form for a pronoun that is acting as the subject of a clause.

> I feel that *he* will be our next president.
> We will be notified when *she* receives the award.

A perennial problem in this kind of construction is the who/whom confusion. The rule is that you should use *who* when the pronoun is acting as a subject, *whom* when it is acting as the object of a preposition or verb. The best way to determine which pronoun you should use is to recast the sentence or question using another kind of relative pronoun. For example,

> There is the man (who, whom) we met yesterday.

Ask yourself, "Would I say 'I met he'?" Since the answer is obviously, "No, I would say 'I met him.' " you should use the objective form, *whom.* Imagine you wanted to express the thought: This is the man (who, whom) will run for president next year. You should ask yourself, "Would I say 'He will run for president' or 'Him will run for president'?" Since you would choose the former construction, you should use the subjective form, *who.*

> *Incorrect:* May is the girl *whom* entered the convent last spring.
> *Correct:* May is the girl *who* entered the convent last spring.

Jenkins is the man *who* they claim is the brains behind the organization. (Notice that the intervening phrase "they claim" does not affect the case of the pronoun.)

c. Use the subjective form of the pronoun when it is in apposition with the subject of a sentence.

> *Incorrect:* The subcommittee—Joe, Bob, and *me*—submitted a report yesterday.
> *Correct:* The subcommittee—Joe, Bob, and *I*—submittted a report yesterday.

d. Use the subjective form of the pronoun if it is the complement of a linking verb.

Incorrect: The principal knew instantly that the culprits were Jim and *me.*

Correct: The principal knew instantly that the culprits were Jim and *I.*

Incorrect: Delegates to the convention are Harold, Clarence, and *me.*

Correct: Delegates to the convention are Harold, Clarence, and *I.*

e. Use the objective form of a pronoun that functions as the object or indirect object of a verb.

Incorrect: The judge appointed Walton and *I* to the board.
Correct: The judge appointed Walton and *me* to the board.

Incorrect: Marshall will send a copy to Kenneth and *I.*
Correct: Marshall will send a copy to Kenneth and *me.*

f. Use the objective form of a pronoun when it is the object of a preposition.

Incorrect: The prize was divided between *he* and Carlos.
Correct: The prize was divided between *him* and Carlos.

Incorrect: That is the man *who* I wish to speak to.
Correct: That is the man to *whom* I wish to speak.

Incorrect: Wilson is the person *who* Jones chose as his successor.

Correct: Wilson is the person *whom* Jones chose as his successor.

g. Use the objective form of a pronoun when it is in apposition with an object.

Incorrect: He selected three people, Johnson, Clark, and *I,* to prepare the report.

Correct: He selected three people, Johnson, Clark, and *me,* to prepare the report.

h. Use the objective form of a pronoun when it acts as the subject or object of an infinitive phrase.

Correct: Creighton is to notify *him* at once.
Lewis was surprised to see *him* at the opera.

i. Use the possessive form of a pronoun when it precedes and modifies a gerund.
Justin is angry about *his* having lied.
Our going to the exhibit proved to be a mistake.

3. Yet a third common error in the use of pronouns is faulty pronoun reference. By definition, a pronoun must refer to something, usually a preceding noun or a noun clause, although sometimes the reference may be to an idea that has been expressed in a previous sentence. Unless the reader can immediately identify the referent of the pronoun, the sentence is faulty and should be revised. Pronoun references that produce awkward or confusing sentences should also be revised.

Original: Congress obviously regarded the supersonic plane as impractical, *which* stopped its development. (*Which* has no clear referent other than the general idea of the main clause.)

Revision: The judgment of members of Congress that the supersonic plane was impractical stopped its development.

Original: Existentialists believe that a man is totally responsible for everything that happens to him, *which* I cannot accept. (The sentence is awkward and potentially confusing. The writer may mean that he cannot accept the statement that existentialists believe what they do or that he cannot accept their belief.)

Revision: Existentialists believe that a man is totally responsible for everything that happens to him; this is an idea *which* I cannot accept.

Or,

I cannot accept the existentialist belief that a man is totally responsible for everything that happens to him.

Original: The author's references to teen-age drug addicts and juvenile delinquents are particularly effective because *this* happens every day. (There is no clear referent for *this.* The writer cannot logically say that addicts or delinquents "happen.")

Revision: The author's references to teen-age drug addicts and juvenile delinquents are particularly effective because one hears of such individuals every day.

Original: Biologists may soon know how to control heredity, but *it* is an idea whose time has not yet come. (The sentence is awkward and possibly confusing. Does the writer mean that heredity is an idea?)

Revision: Biologists may soon know how to control heredity; however, the public is not ready to accept this kind of control.

ADJECTIVES AND ADVERBS

Adjectives may modify only nouns and pronouns; adverbs, however, may modify adjectives, verbs, prepositions and conjunctions, and other adverbs. Although there are a few words that function as both adverbs and adjectives—*fast, slow, better, worse, early,* and *late* are the commonest—most adverbs are formed by adding *-ly* to the adjective form: *quick, quickly; clear, clearly; exact, exactly.* Adjectives are compared by adding *-er* or *-est* to the base word when the word is short and by putting *more* or *most* in front of the word if it is comparatively long: *shorter, shortest; meaner, meanest;* but, *more* miserable, *most* miserable and *more* precise, *most* precise. Except for a very few words—fast, well, early, late, soon, and slow—the comparative forms of adverbs require inserting more or most before the word: *more* clearly, *most* clearly and *more* swiftly, *most* swiftly. A very few rules govern the correct use of adverbs and adjectives.

1. Adjectives should not be used to modify verbs.

    Incorrect: The Coxes were *real* upset about the accident.
    Correct: The Coxes were *really* upset about the accident.

    Incorrect: The legislators passed the law as *quick* as possible.
    Correct: The legislators passed the law as *quickly* as possible.

2. Adjectives should not be used to modify adverbs or other adjectives.

    Incorrect: The story was *reasonable* accurate.
    Correct: The story was *reasonably* accurate.

    Incorrect: The officer spoke to us *real* sharply.
    Correct: The officer spoke to us *very* sharply.

3. If a modifier follows the verb but refers to the subject of the sentence, use the adjective form.

    The corners must be kept *clean.*
    That measurement was thought *accurate* at the time.

4. When the main verb is a linking verb or one that describes sensory actions, an adjective rather than an adverb should complete it. Verbs in this category are *is, feel, look, appear, sound, taste, become, seem,* and *smell.*

    Incorrect: That color *looks* well on her.
    Correct: That color looks *good* on her.

    Incorrect: Keith's voice sounds *weakly* this morning.
    Correct: Keith's voice sounds *weak* this morning.

Index